About the Author

Dr Christine Page MBBS, MRCGP, DCH, DRCOG, MFHom is a medical doctor who has been acclaimed as 'one of the greatest living Mystics'. The author of groundbreaking books including *Spiritual Alchemy*, she is known on both sides of the Atlantic for her teachings and the pioneering ways in which she combines modern science with ancient wisdom. Visit her website at www.christinepage.com

DR CHRISTINE PAGE
MBBS, MRCGP, DCH, DRCOG, MFHom

■ Frontiers of Health ■

How to Heal the Whole Person

RIDER

LONDON • SYDNEY • AUCKLAND • JOHANNESBURG

3 5 7 9 10 8 6 4 2

First published in the United Kingdom in 1992
by The C. W. Daniel Company Limited.
Revised 1994, reprinted 1996, revised 2000, reprinted 2002.
This edition published in 2005 by Rider,
an imprint of Ebury Press, Random House,
20 Vauxhall Bridge Road, London SW1V 2SA
www.randomhouse.co.uk

Random House Australia (Pty) Limited
20 Alfred Street, Milsons Point, Sydney,
New South Wales 2061, Australia

Random House New Zealand Limited
18 Poland Road, Glenfield,
Auckland 10, New Zealand

Random House South Africa (Pty) Limited
Isle of Houghton, Corner of Boundary Road & Carse O'Gowrie,
Houghton 2198, South Africa

The Random House Group Limited Reg. No. 954009

Designed and produced in association with
Book Production Consultants plc, Cambridge.
Typeset by Cambridge Phototypesetting Services.
Printed and bound in Great Britain by
CPI Antony Rowe, Chippenham, Wiltshire

Papers used by Rider are natural, recyclable products
made from wood grown in sustainable forests.

A CIP catalogue record for this book
is available from the British Library

ISBN 9781844131075

This book gives non-specific, general advice and should not be relied on as a substitute
for proper medical consultation. The author and publisher cannot accept responsibility
for illness arising out of the failure to seek medical advice from a doctor.

DEDICATION
I would like to thank my mother,
Pat Jarvis and the many patients
who were my teachers

Contents

Introduction

One of the questions I am often asked is: "When did you first become interested in spiritual matters?"

My answer is that I do not remember a time when I was not aware of the spiritual world.

My mother was involved in spiritual healing and I recall listening to her as she talked about "fringe medicine" and recounted esoteric teachings. For me she was reinforcing views that were already part of my own inner truth.

Little did I imagine how important this early introduction to the links between the mind, the body and the spirit would be in my later life and especially in my chosen career.

My earliest childhood memory is when I was about 14 months old. I remember watching as one of my favourite dolls fell between two wooden chairs and smashed into tiny pieces. I was devastated; I watched with horror as the pieces were unceremoniously resigned to the dustbin. I could not believe that it was not possible to make this life, however imaginary, whole again and that so little was done in pursuit of this goal.

That incident appears to have triggered an inner desire to do all in my power to help people towards health and wholeness. In fact, the words health and healing come from the Germanic word "wholeness" or to make whole. I soon realised that such healing had to start with the helper, myself.

When it came to the time to make a decision concerning a career, I chose one of the health professions with the hope that here I would be in a position to help people along their path in life, hopefully with a caring but objective approach.

So when I entered the doors of my medical school some 18 years ago I was full of hope that here was the fulfilment of a dream. On my first day, with eight fellow students, I stood around a table upon which lay my first dead body ready to learn all I could about a human being.

It soon dawned that there was only one problem, this body was missing an essential item … life itself.

I therefore eagerly awaited my graduation onto the wards. Here we, as medical students, were licensed to poke and prod any poor unsuspecting patient in order to expand our knowledge of the disease state. Any verbal interruption from the patient was often seen as an unwelcome intrusion.

"Just answer my questions, please." There was little time for discussions of social and emotional problems.

I recognise from my own career that, when working in a hospital, it is often difficult to remember that all patients have another life outside and that, first and foremost, they are people.

As I listened to my patients talk it became clear that many of them had stressful lives including marriage breakdowns, problems with the children, job losses, sick relatives, etc. and that despite my medical training I was inadequately prepared to deal with such problems.

Diseases of the body and the mind were definitely seen as separate entities, with the latter referred to the psychology or psychiatry departments of the hospital. Any connections which were made came under the title of psychosomatic illness (psyche- mind, soma- body).

However, it was often the case that this term was used as a diagnosis when extensive tests had failed to reveal a cause for the patient's illness. The patient left the doctor's surgery with the belief that their symptoms were "all in their mind" which created further stress and a feeling of hopelessness.

It became obvious that this was a major flaw in the healing package offered by the medical profession, one which thankfully is now being addressed in modern medical training.

During this time I was having my own problems. The experience of being in close proximity to the suffering of others caused havoc with my sensitivity. I was overwhelmed by the physical and emotional pain of my patients and felt that I was not in a position to offer aid due to lack of knowledge.

As a result, on several occasions, I slid gracefully to the ground in a dead faint at the sight of blood and pain. The solution at that time was to bury my feelings behind a frenzy of activity whenever I felt vaguely inadequate.

The donning of a white coat added extra protection to a sensitive soul. Within it I became anonymous and appeared detached, unemotional and professional. Or so I believed.

In retrospect I see that all I achieved was to bury my feelings and I believe that for many doctors this approach causes a great deal of harm and should be looked upon as one of the commonest causes of our high suicide and alcoholism rates.

It took some time to realise how important it was to value myself for just "being there" and that although my medical expertise was important, it was unconditional compassion which enhanced the healing process.

During my studies I became more and more aware that, despite a similar diagnosis, different patients reacted in different ways to the disease and to the chosen treatment.

There was no such thing as a "sure bet" as to whether a patient would leave the hospital fully cured or would die without any advance warning.

I was trained to talk in terms of statistical prognosis. "Eighty per cent of people die with a certain disease within two years."

Nobody ever told me what happened to the other 20%.

What made them live? Why were they different?

I concluded that not all disease could be attributed to the germ. There have been numerous studies which have shown that despite the existence of a virus or bacteria within a close community, or where on several occasions these were administered in error to a group of individuals, only a small proportion of those involved developed symptoms of disease.

In the nineteenth century Claude Bernard, a great medical researcher, wrote: "Illnesses hover constantly about us, their seeds blown by the wind, but they do not set into the terrain unless the terrain is ready to receive them."

Pasteur, the father of microbiology, is reputed to have said on his deathbed: "Bernard is right. The germ is nothing; the terrain is all."

The terrain equates to the environment and this must include both our inner and outer worlds.

Further evidence revealed that non-identical twins brought up in the same environment showed wide variations in their personality and in the diseases which they acquired throughout their lives. Similarly, not all smokers died of heart or lung disease, not all drinkers had liver damage and the same stress factors did not affect all people in the same way.

The variations within disease patterns must come from within and, with this in mind, I focused my attention on the other factors involved in the holistic paradigm ... the mind and the spirit.

In the 70s, it became fashionable to talk about stress. It was seen as a widespread problem affecting people of all ages and in all walks of life and became an acceptable answer in the search for the cause of many chronic diseases.

But although stress could be identified as a problem, it appeared more difficult to eradicate despite attempts to relax, meditate, etc.

I concluded that it was not the stress which was the problem but the strain which we felt when it was applied.

Stress is a fundamental requirement for life. In the dictionary it is defined as "... an impelling force applied to a form or structure". The word impelling not only signifies forward movement but also the **degree of** importance placed upon such an action. Without this we would vegetate, fail to grow and die of lack of primary nourishment.

Strain is defined as "... to be stretched tight beyond the legitimate range". Strain is registered when we move beyond our optimal range of existence, forced on by emotional pressures such as fear and guilt. I believe that such influences are the primary cause of many diseases.

The effects of strain are commonly seen in the physical body as in the case when an extremely heavy load is lifted from the ground resulting in a slipped disc. When we take on too much work in the office the strain may manifest in the form of irritability or weeping, or manifest in the physical body as a headache.

Whatever the signs or symptoms whether physical or mental, the answer is the same; reduce the amount of stretch to within the normal range and the signs of dis-stress will disappear.

The only problem here is that it appears there is no "normal range" for the whole human race or even for members of the same family or same age group.

Appley and Trumbull, who were stress researchers in 1967, concluded that reaction to stress varies considerably from individual to individual and from response to response.

The individual may in fact react to the same stressor in a different manner at different presentations.

In my quest for understanding the connection between the mind and the body, I came across the studies carried out by Greer, et al (1979), who recognised four categories of coping mechanisms adopted by patients with breast cancer. Most patients exhibit more than one of these mechanisms during their illness, but there is usually one which is prominent. These are:

A) STOIC ACCEPTANCE; here there is a realistic appreciation of the facts of the illness which is shown by a calm, fatalistic and a rather passive attitude towards the disease.

This is the commonest attitude adopted and connects closely with personality traits which are often found in those who develop cancer.

B) HELPLESSNESS/HOPELESSNESS; despair about the illness and no motivation to adapt.

This is the closest to a state of depression and is commonly seen at the beginning of any grieving process.

C) FIGHTING SPIRIT; here the patient is determined to fight their illness and to recover from it.

These individuals have probably always been fighters and have a desire to be in control of any situation especially their own treatment. They will read all the books, seek second opinions and organise support groups.

D) DENIAL; the failure to absorb the knowledge concerning the diagnosis and its implications.

There is an apparent amnesia covering any aspects of the disease especially those connected with the diagnosis and therefore a failure to ask appropriate questions when time is given for such an exchange.

In the case of denial, an observer who personally prefers the honest approach will see the patient's refusal to talk about his or her cancer as a challenge. They will take it upon themselves to encourage the patient to talk about their fears and concerns in order to prevent the suppression of emotions they believe may lead to further disabling problems.

As I learnt to my cost, such an approach has little regard for the wishes of the patient and is purely satisfying the ego of the observer.

Having been presented with the truth clearly and simply, the patient has every right to choose not to talk about the subject which manifests as a denial.

I remember my own naivety when faced with a patient who was dying of lung cancer. When I entered the house, I was met by the wife, who hurried me past the patient and into the kitchen where I was told in great detail about her husband's cancer and the present problems.

We then went back into the bedroom where the husband lay and started to talk about the weather and the minor problems of the illness.

After another similar visit, I asked the wife whether her husband was aware of the diagnosis and if he realised he was extremely ill. She said that she was not sure because they never talked about his ill health.

Being a good conscientious doctor, I felt that the truth should be brought into the open and went back into the bedroom.

"Do you know what is wrong with you?" I asked.

"Yes, I have cancer" he replied.

"Do you know how ill you are?" I continued.

"Yes, I know I am dying."

"Have you talked to your wife about this?" I asked.

"No, I do not want to worry her" he replied.

As I left the house his wife said with a sigh:

"So he knows, and there is no use in pretending anymore."

Seeing her face I realised I had betrayed their trust in me and acted against the wishes of the couple in my misplaced desire to help.

The next day the patient's condition deteriorated and he went into hospital.

He did manage to come home for a brief period before he died and I felt that it was appropriate that I was called to see him in his dying moments, and that I could be there to comfort his wife in the days that followed.

My wish to bring everything into the open had destroyed the delicate fabric of denial which had been built up between these two people as a coping mechanism. As with many experiences within my working life, I felt very humbled, but grateful to learn such an important lesson from my patients.

Coping mechanisms are used not only in cases of cancer but within any situation when there is change in the flow of life. Doctors use these mechanisms every day to deal with the stresses which they encounter, especially those which affect them deeply.

Lessons concerned with the emotional aspects of dying, death and grieving were not part of my medical training. At the age of 23 years and without formal tuition, I was expected to know how to tell someone that they or their relative were dying. I questioned this omission from the syllabus and came to the conclusion that the reason why it was not taught was because many people, including those in the medical professions, have not come to terms with their own mortality.

I had first-hand experience at an early age of watching someone I loved die, and dealing with the subsequent grief. Fortunately, most people do not have to face this situation until they are much older. And yet they are asked to give advice and support in such matters when their training is so inadequate. I feel strongly that this is another area which should no longer be relegated to the realms of religion but be encompassed in medical training. I would like to believe that this indeed has happened and that the modern houseman is more equipped to deal with such important issues.

There is no right or wrong way to deal with a problem and all those within the caring professions should recognise that they are not there to judge but rather to give guidance and support where appropriate.

Unfortunately, it is not always so easy to be non-judgemental due to the practitioner's own human frailties. This is compounded by the position of authority given by society to those in the caring professions.

The opinion of the doctor, and the way in which it is presented, is seen to influence greatly the patient's disease process as shown by studies on the placebo effect.

Positive reinforcement, the placebo, given by the doctor whilst prescribing a treatment is estimated to relieve symptoms in 30% of patients. This has been verified in research studies where the reinforcement was given alongside a sugar tablet which secretly replaced the real drug.

Deepak Chopra in his book Quantum Healing (1989) talks about the "Nocebo" effect which is the negative placebo response. This is a situation where patients are given negative information which leads to a deterioration of their condition.

"You won't last the year" or "You'll probably develop side effects of nausea and vomiting with this drug".

Bernie Siegel, in "Love, Medicine and Miracles", tells the story of two men who by mistake were given the wrong diagnosis. The one who had cancer, and statistically should have died, left the hospital: the other, with a minor problem, left the ward in a coffin.

The response of the nocebo effect on the disease state has not been analysed statistically but I would be surprised if it did not equal that of the placebo response.

I have no doubt as to the influence of the mind in the creation and continuation of the disease process and that it does not always need to be negative. For example, it has been observed on oncology wards that when patients are given positive but honest advice concerning the side effects of the drugs, fewer problems actually manifest.

I remember an old woman who "had turned her head to the wall and decided to die". She refused food and drink and was slowly fading. As is common practice in cases of near death, her nephew as next of kin was contacted.

Without any signs of emotion or concern, he calmly asked what time he should visit to collect her belongings and the death certificate. The nurse appalled by his callousness went to inform the aunt that she had spoken to the nephew, omitting certain sections of the conversation.

The aunt hearing what she wanted to hear, ie. that someone in her family cared, immediately turned and asked for something to drink. Consequently, when the nephew arrived to pick up the death certificate, he found his aunt sitting up in bed full of life and vigour.

Matters of life and death are not in the hands of doctors and health practitioners but in the hands of some far greater power. That which is consciously perceived is but the tip of the iceberg. Anybody who attempts to estimate the quantity or quality of life belonging to another person is attempting to play God and is bound to fail along the way.

Amazing things happen when people are ill. They develop strengths which up to that point had been well and truly hidden.

One of the criticisms levelled at me when I speak to groups of doctors is that it is wrong to give false hope and that patients should face up to their morbidity and mortality.

I do not think that we are talking about hope, false or otherwise, but about honesty and truth. We are being asked to give advice on the basis of our years of experience and learning but in the end the decision is that of the patient.

As a newly qualified doctor I believed that I had the answer to all medical problems. As I grew older and wiser I learnt to say "I do not know" adding, where appropriate, "but I know someone who can help".

As doctors I think we believe we are responsible not only for the patient but also for the presence or absence of disease. Such a belief is not limited to the medical profession but can be found within all those who care for the health of others.

My experience is that patients do not ask us to be responsible for their disease, but to care for them in whatever way we decide has the maximum chance of giving peace from suffering which, ultimately, may be to allow the soul to rest.

My training taught me that life was sacrosanct and that death was failure. I believe that while we still view the body and the mind as the totality of the human being we will always fail, for the only certainty of life is that we will all die some day. Life is terminal.

The spirit must be included in any discussion or teaching concerning man and can no longer be relegated to the religious sections of our community.

The failure to address the issues concerning the whole person became more and more apparent in my own work within general practice where I became aware that 80% of my patients had chronic diseases for which I prescribed medicines which, although relieving the symptoms, did not necessarily alter the underlying disease state.

We appeared to be no closer to understanding the riddle of disease than we were 100 years ago despite modern technology. We still did not know why some people died young while others lived to a ripe old age or why some people contracted illness while others remained apparently healthy.

In the search for answers, my attention once again moved to fringe or rather complementary medicine as it was now known.

I saw that in most of these therapies there was an underlying belief in the connection between the mind, the body and the spirit and that many methods such as reflexology, acupuncture and homoeopathy worked with the principle of an energy or life force flowing through the body which in disease had become blocked creating disharmony within the physical form.

To release the block and allow the recreation of harmony was the main aim of most practitioners who worked within these healing arts.

At last I felt I was connecting with my own inner truth that unless we treat the whole person we cannot hope to achieve a cure.

But, despite my involvement in both orthodox and complementary medicine, I still felt that I had little understanding of the meaning of life and how illness fitted into this process. I believed that nothing happened by chance or without a purpose on some level and that illness was no exception.

The significance of disease varies according to the culture in which it is found. In many cultures it is seen as a weakness and equates to failure.

Several of my male patients confess that they would rather die than face the humiliation of admitting that they were ill. Many of them achieve their ambition long before retirement age!

The early doctors understood the importance of the holistic approach. Hippocrates (420BC), the father of modern medicine was trained as a priest healer. These healers were followers of Aesculapius, the Greek god of healing, whose symbol, the single snake around a rod, is still used by many medical institutions. The priest healers believed that total healing must include the mind, the body and the spirit.

In his later life, Hippocrates transferred his allegiance from a holistic view to one which was more reductionist. He stated that he believed the cause of an illness existed purely within the soil of the disease, ie. the physical body. Slowly, this theme was adopted by all those who cared for the sick, and disease was divided into that dealt with by the doctor, that by the priest and that by the psychiatrist.

However, it is interesting to note that until recently every doctor had to take the Hippocratic oath (circa 420BC) which starts:

"I swear by Apollo the physician, by Aesculapius ... etc ..."

As my studies continued, I searched my medical books for reference to the spirit. When none was found, I transferred my attentions to the esoteric teachings which I had met as a child.

I was enthralled by the wisdom within the Alice Bailey books and attended workshops and lectures. Much that I heard struck a chord deep inside and I began to expand my understanding as to the purpose of life on earth.

I believe that we all originate from the one Source which has many names: the Light, God or the Creator. This Source gives birth to many individual lights or souls and each one of us possesses such a soul.

The purpose of our life upon this earth is to develop self-consciousness which means to know and accept ourselves as spiritual beings. As this awareness increases we work towards wholeness and such wholeness brings the ultimate goal, unity with the Creator.

The soul's path on earth provides many experiences which can lead to such growth. In this world of duality we learn to accept and love both our so called negative aspects and our positive aspects for they are all part of the whole.

In order that the soul can work within the earth, it takes on three items of "clothing": the emotions, the logical mind and the physical body. These three together constitute the personality or ego.

The soul or Self is still firmly linked with the Source of life via the spirit. Through this connection we are aware of ourselves not only as a personality but also as part of the Universal pattern of life.

The soul is not an alien force which is trying to influence us beyond our will but can be seen as a loving parent showing the way to an often fearful child. The soul needs the personality and they need to work together as friends.

One aspect of this life which to some is seen as a gift and to others as a hindrance … is the presence of free will.

Free will equates with choice; choice to accept the experience and choice to learn the lesson which it offers.

For many free will brings fear of failure and of making a mistake. In truth, there is no such thing as a mistake; nothing is wasted. The most negative events offer some learning for the soul even if it is only not to follow that path again.

Others become lost in the experience and fail to see that it is not the details of the situation which matter but the opportunity for change which is offered.

And what does the soul want from life?

As I travel the world giving workshops and seeing patients on a one-to-one basis, I am amazed to find that despite the wide variation of cultures, religions and levels of wealth there is always a common theme: "I want to be myself".

The Self that they talk about contains seven spiritual aspects:

■ Self-knowledge
■ Self-responsibility
■ Self-expression
■ Self-love
■ Self-worth
■ Self-respect
■ Self-awareness

Total Self-consciousness encapsulates all these aspects and is a harmonic existence created through unification of the many parts which constitute spiritual man.

For many of us the personality holds sway over the control of our daily life. As the influence shifts from the personality to the soul, this is registered as disharmony by the mind, for it is now receiving the two different vibrations, one being transmitted from the level of the soul and one from the level of the personality.

If the vibration of the soul is simply allowed to replace that of the personality then the shift occurs with minimal disruption to the life of the individual.

However, if there is resistance to change, then initially this disharmony is felt within the mind leading to symptoms of strain, frustration, anger, depression etc. If, despite these messages, no action is taken to change the vibration, then the disharmony can manifest as physical disease.

Such a manifestation not only increases the awareness of the individual to the fact that there is disharmony present (seeing is believing) but also in many cases acts as the vehicle for the change to take place. I believe that this is the process which is occurring in at least 80% of mental and physical disease seen today, which include trauma.

This book is designed to go within; to attempt to make a link between the ancient esoteric knowledge and modern man. Following my years of medical practice I am convinced that to relegate signs and symptoms purely to the means of naming a disease is to ignore a vital clue given to us by the soul itself.

I believe that if we can decode the message of the disease, we can come to a greater understanding as to the area of soul growth being developed at that time.

In this way, we in the caring professions would then be able to support the patient in a more constructive manner and the patient would be able to contribute actively to their healing process.

To have a conscious understanding of the process of soul growth is not essential for life, but I am sure that it makes the journey much easier.

I fully accept the valuable contribution of modern medicine to health care especially in acute situations. One of my prime tasks is to teach complementary practitioners to know when to refer to orthodox medicine in accordance with the threat posed by the condition to the life force of the patient.

However, true care must include the activities of the mind and the soul. The physical body is purely a vehicle for the soul and the spirit. Treating one aspect in isolation from the others will lead to an incomplete cure although on a physical level the patient may appear healed.

Healing can never restore anybody to their original form.

Disease by its very essence must bring about change in the individual and this point is often misunderstood and even avoided both by the patient and by their practitioner.

My patients often say: "Just make me feel better physically and then I can cope with the emotional problems."

But this is completely the wrong way round. Yes, by relieving the pain and other acute symptoms, the patient is able to have the strength to move forward. But in many cases, until the emotional issues are resolved, disharmony will remain even though the signs of disease can be suppressed by modern drugs.

Once true harmony has been achieved it can never be destroyed. It may be mislaid from time to time but, like riding a bicycle, we never forget the technique once it is learnt.

For true health and wholeness, time is irrelevant. Many people are in such a hurry to restore health that they miss golden opportunities for soul growth. Because of this, the lesson is repeated unnecessarily, until the deeper message of disease is understood.

Others give up and accept their illness not in a positive fashion but with resignation. They "suffer" from a disease ... the word amplifying their feelings.

Both groups have entered a cul-de-sac where there appears to be no way out. I ask that the reader may consider my ideas as a possible means of breaking the deadlock.

In the end it is not relevant what disease is present, what type of personality you are, what astrological sign you were born under or what type of constitution is present.

What is relevant is how you deal with the situations which come towards you and to use these experiences to enrich and expand soul consciousness.

The material for the book comes from experiences within my own life especially those involved with disease and healing. The names and certain features of the individuals described in the following chapters have been altered to maintain confidentiality. The essence of the story is the same.

Much of the esoteric knowledge comes from the teachings of Alice Bailey who received the information from a Tibetan Master. But in the end it is not the knowledge which is important, but the application of this knowledge to life.

Knowledge is powerless without wisdom and love. If the words which you read strike a chord somewhere and provide understanding to an inner problem then I am well pleased.

If they don't ... then that's fine too.

Since writing the first edition of this book nine years ago much has changed both in my life and in our understanding of health and illness. Medical advances have reduced the incidence of some diseases whilst others have become more prevalent, affecting a younger population and, unfortunately in the case of cancer, often becoming more rampant.

In the psychospiritual field, there has been a tremendous surge of interest in subjects related to chakras and energy fields enhanced by the input from many fine speakers and writers around the world. The public are no longer bewildered by esoteric terms and are searching for a deeper meaning to their life, eager to take on greater responsibility for their health.

This new edition is more comprehensive and explicit in terms of both the chakras and illnesses, based on my own experience and increasing wisdom over the intervening years. I offer new insights into the function of each chakra which seem very appropriate to this moment in the history of mankind. I want to thank and honour all those who have shared their journey with me and given me the opportunity to tell their story.

Dr Christine Page
October 1999

1 Chapter

The Origin of the Soul

In order to understand the mind, body, spirit connection, I feel that it is necessary to attempt to provide an esoteric explanation behind the origin of spiritual man.

In the world of science the theory of the "Big Bang" is offered as a credible explanation behind the creation of the Universe.

As a parallel in esoteric terms, we learn about an Energy or Divine Life which is the source of all that is visible and invisible within the Universe. Everything in existence is an expression of this One Life.

When this Divine Energy Source takes form, two poles of expression are created which result in the duality of life which is exhibited throughout the universe.

These two aspects of duality are usually described as:

a) Spirit or the Father.
b) Matter or the Mother.

Born out of the union between the Father and the Mother is the Son or the Soul.

In view of the fact that the Soul represents the unity between Spirit and Matter it can also been seen that ultimately the Soul is a reflection of the initial Life Energy.

> Out of the One comes the Two.
> Out of Two comes the Three.
> Together they represent the One.

The essence of the Father and Mother express different aspects of Divine Intelligence.

The essence of the Father or Spirit is seen in terms of positivity, masculinity, dominance, outward movement, logic and assertiveness. It expresses the Will to create and with this to grow.

The essence of the Mother or Matter is seen in terms of negativity, femininity, receptiveness, inward movement, sensitivity and nurturing. It expresses the Wisdom to bring together all that is required to nurture the seed of the Creator leading to new birth and the continuation of life.

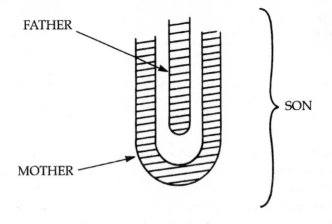

FATHER

MOTHER

SON

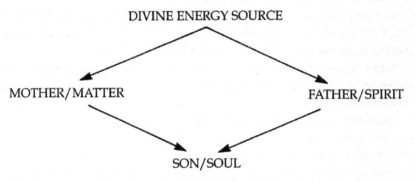

DIVINE ENERGY SOURCE

MOTHER/MATTER

FATHER/SPIRIT

SON/SOUL

Their union is brought about by the power of attraction or love which manifests as the essence of the Son or Soul.

Love unites all, leading to the extinction of separation.

The energy of the Will is an electrical force whereas that of Love is a magnetic force. Together they create electromagnetic energy which is symbolised by the sun which brings life to all form.

In human terms, we see the father as the provider of the seed and of the materials required in order that the baby should grow.

The mother provides the receptive qualities of the womb and with her wisdom uses the materials provided by the father to gain optimal benefit for the baby.

Both have equal importance in the creation of this child (the Soul) which is an expression of the power of their love.

■ The Path of the Soul

Every living object is created through the interaction between the spirit and matter. Therefore every living object has a soul, from an atom to a planet. In many cases the soul is collective, ie. the same soul for a group of objects.

In man, the soul is individualised, creating diversity within an apparently common form.

In the human body, this uniqueness is expressed within the pattern of fingerprints and in the genetic information stored within the chromosomes.

Both spirit and matter contain an innate level of "intelligence" passed down from the original Divine Intelligence. Through their union, the soul is produced which can be seen as the level of consciousness or awareness that is achieved when these two aspects of intelligence meet. (Conscious from the Latin -scire: to know.)

Such consciousness will depend upon the degree of interaction that takes place between these two aspects and the nature of the form that is expressed.

The various life forms which inhabit the Earth are expressing different stages in the development of this consciousness, ie. that of a cell will differ

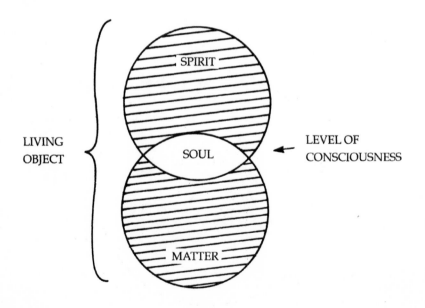

from that of a plant while some individuals are more spiritually aware than others.

The purpose of life is to increase the level of consciousness through the interaction between spirit and matter until ultimately there is no separation between these two aspects of polarity and the consciousness of the soul and the source become one.

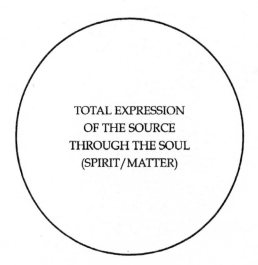

An analogy

If the spirit were a lighted candle and matter was a piece of ice, it would initially be difficult to see the flame through the ice.

If the ice is brought closer to the flame, it starts to melt and now the light of the flame can be seen more clearly through the water, ie. the water is transmitting the light of the candle.

If the heat of the flame continues to be concentrated upon the water, evaporation will occur until the water is no longer visible and is now fully transmitting the light of the candle.

In conclusion, heat increases the vibrational rate of the molecules of the water, changing it from a solid form, ice, into something far freer and lighter. At the same time it allows easier transmission of the light through the medium of steam.

In a similar manner, harmony is achieved between spirit and matter and is seen to be mutually beneficial to both.

■ The Path of Man

Man's journey is to become self-aware or self-conscious ... to know himself.

This does not happen overnight but is an evolving process.

He has the capability to see himself as a separate entity from his physical body, his emotions and from his thoughts, ie. separate from his personality which is the collective name for these three aspects of man.

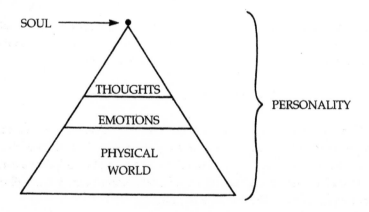

ie.

Man is not his physical world ..
his house, his car, his job.
Man is not his emotions ... his
anger, his sadness, his fears.
Man is not his thoughts ... his
analysis, his knowledge.
Man is not his personality.

This recognition can only come from an objective viewpoint which is identified as the position of the soul of the individual.

As this awareness grows, there is an increase in the conscious appreciation of the spiritual world and man's small but important role in the greater plan.

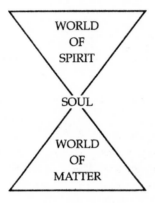

However, the very awareness of the separation between the soul and the personality has created two further poles of existence which need to be united before man can be called a truly spiritual being.

Harmony is created through unity.

Therefore, once the individual has reached a level of awareness that recognises the soul as separate from the personality, the energy of the soul, which is linked to that of spirit, must then be brought back down through the thoughts, the emotions and the physical body so that the will of the soul and the personality can become one.

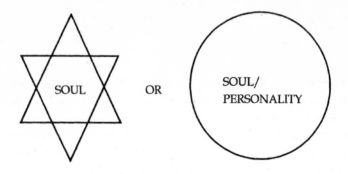

SOUL   OR   SOUL/PERSONALITY

Only then, in esoteric terms, when the soul is fully incarnate in the physical form, can the serpent who dwells at the base of the spine rise up. This is also known as the raising of the Kundalini. Such an action cannot be forced but is a natural result of attaining the necessary steps in the evolution of consciousness.

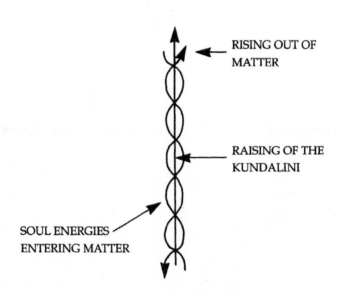

RISING OUT OF MATTER

RAISING OF THE KUNDALINI

SOUL ENERGIES ENTERING MATTER

The Essence of Duality

The creation of the two poles of existence, spirit and matter, and their unification through the formation of the son or the soul, is the basis of all life situations.

To experience, to recognise and to accept both poles brings an awareness that there is no separation but only different expressions of a common principle. All are part of the Greater Creative Energy.

An analogy

If I view a tepee from the front it appears as a structure with two sides and a central support.

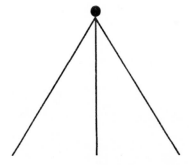

When viewed from above, I see a circle around a common point.

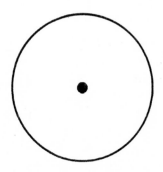

■ The Chinese Teachings

The concept of duality is also seen in Chinese philosophy where two opposing but complementary forces called **yin and yang** are described. They express the way in which things function in relation to each other and are used to explain the continual and natural process of change.

Neither can exist without the other; there are no absolutes. We cannot know night unless we know day; we talk about inspiration because we recognise expiration.

Both contain the potential for transformation into the opposite force.

Yin is described as cold, rest, passivity, darkness, responsive, inward and decreasing.

Yang is described as heat, movement, activity, brightness, stimulation, outward and increasing.

The concept of yin and yang is depicted in the Chinese Taoist symbol shown below.

YANG   YIN

The dividing line shows that the two aspects are always merging. The small contrasting circles show the potential for transformation.

The twists in the movement of a snake or the turns in a spiral also reflect this concept of balance achieved through the unification of two poles of existence.

Chinese philosophy shows that it is impossible to stay in one aspect and ignore the other.

The same concept is revealed within esoteric teachings which speak about the **Universal Law of Balance and Equilibrium**. This states that if

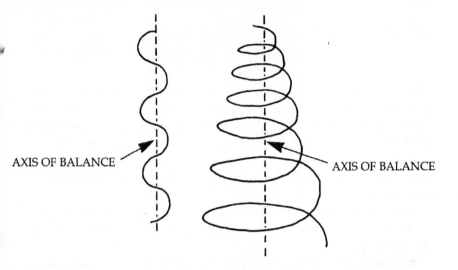

AXIS OF BALANCE

AXIS OF BALANCE

one aspect of polarity is expressed in an extreme state then its complementary aspect must subsequently be expressed to re-balance the situation.

Much of disease is an attempt to correct an imbalance through the medium of the physical form. It is an inevitability for, according to the above law, harmony needs to be re-established.

Therefore any apparent breakdown on the part of the physical or mental body should be seen as the action of a friend rather than that of an enemy.

Breakdown is to break out.

Disease is not a punishment or a sign of weakness but a natural process in the recreation of equilibrium.

For example:

A businessman who continues to burn the candle at both ends with an excess intake of alcohol, spices and coffee may manifest an illness which will curb his excesses, such as an ulcer or something that will slow him down, a heart attack. To the businessman they may be viewed as an inconvenience ... to spiritual man they are seen as his salvation.

Ignore the need for change and more permanent ways are presented in order to redress the imbalance.

Many states of ill-health are brought about by a failure to let go of old thoughts, attitudes, emotions and possessions which leads to an extreme expression of one aspect.

Fear and guilt are the commonest reasons given for the need to hold onto the past or to fail to move forward into the future. To release these old friends requires faith and this can only come when we are in touch with our own inner being.

However, blind faith, such as in a religious or political movement, can also lead to crystallisation of thought and an inability to progress.

The ability to let go and to move forward, taking only those things which are still relevant to the present day is one of the greatest healing forces within the universe.

Disease is often seen as a crisis in one's life and yet the word "crisis" comes from the Greek word "*krisis*", a decision. This is a turning point; the decision to be made is to turn from one aspect of polarity which is being expressed in an extreme manner and to face, experience and accept the other.

Sometimes the need for balance and equilibrium is seen on a wider scale and will be reflected in the appearance of "crisis" within the lives of a number of people at the same time.

The method by which the earth deals with such a crisis is seen in terms of natural disasters such as erupting volcanoes, typhoons and earthquakes where excess energy is released in order to redress the balance.

The physical body maintains a harmonic environment (homoeostasis) by detecting imbalances at an early stage and, by fine tuning, correcting them without the problem being brought into conscious awareness.

However, when the influence of the mind overrules these adjustments, then the imbalance can reach crisis point and disease is inevitable in order to recreate harmony.

Once both poles of existence have been accepted then their influence upon our learning becomes negligible. It could be said that through unity their collective note is in harmony with the individual's soul.

For example, in health, we do not have to concern ourselves that the contraction of the muscles of the heart will not be followed by relaxation or that inspiration will not follow expiration.

This state of acceptance can also be called "habituation" and allows the brain to release that which is accepted and known and to concentrate only on the more important facets of life.

Growth of Consciousness

The consciousness of the individual develops through constant movement between two poles of existence. These are initially found within each aspect of the personality: the physical, the emotional and the mental.

Through experiencing and observing the different levels of duality and accepting their existence, the individual soon comes to realise that they are not separate entities but a continuum around a common aspect of life.

The separation of the soul from each mode of existence is not achieved without some degree of suffering, pain and grief. For many, these extreme states act as a springboard for action.

A deep depression is known as "the dark night of the soul". Here there is often a state of numbness or the individual exhibits automatic actions. But it is at this time that the light of the soul can be seen. For in a lighted room, the flame of a candle is easily missed. But in a dark room the candle throws out tremendous light.

Extremes are tiring and hopefully through understanding it will become unnecessary to stay in one extreme aspect whilst attempting to avoid the other.

This is particularly appropriate in the case of the emotions where the suppression of one emotion allows it to build inside until its release is explosive and un-contained. Inevitably this then leads to further fear of this emotion and further suppression.

I commonly see this in men who have chosen to suppress their anger in an attempt to appear in control. All that happens is that their rage builds until it explodes into action thus creating further problems.

The psychologist, Jung, called the unexpressed pole of duality the "shadow side" and explained that in continually running from this aspect

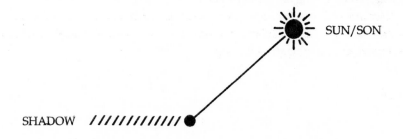

SUN/SON

SHADOW ///////////

we are only creating a greater shadow. He advised that we should face it as a friend.

Symbolically there is no shadow when we stand directly under the sun. It is only when we place distance between ourselves and the sun (the soul) that the shadow appears.

Through moving our awareness from the influence of the personality and the outer world to that of the soul, we realise that although we feel pain and sadness, they are passing phases.

The alternative is to remain ever bound to the collective mind of the physical, emotional and mental worlds and never achieve self consciousness and peace.

An analogy

A deep-sea diver dons a heavy, old-fashioned diving suit and is lowered to the bottom of the sea. His only connection with the surface is through his lifeline attached to his chest.

On the ocean bed he is no longer able to see or hear clearly and his movements are hampered by the weight of the suit.

As his life on the ocean bed continues, his memory of life on land starts to fade and his senses become primed only for life in water.

He wanders around the bottom of the sea bumping into others and asking them if they know the way. Full of their own importance they suggest that he follows them and off they both go, neither clear about directions but neither wanting to acknowledge the fact.

At a certain point, the lifeline becomes taut and our diver is forced to stop and retrace his steps. There he stands looking from left to right, dazed and frightened.

Then with extreme effort he slowly turns and raises his eyes upwards. He can make out a very dim light.

With slow but steady movements he gradually makes his way to the surface, often falling back, but now aware of a force on the other end of the line which is slowly pulling him towards the surface.

He no longer needs the directions of others for he now has his own light to follow, the light of the soul and ultimately of the Divine Source of all Light.

The soul is there to show us the way and to offer support but cannot force us to follow the light. It is within our free will to identify with the different aspects of the personality or to seek a more fulfilling, though not always easy, path.

■ The Path

The Physical World

An individual identifies with the material or physical world. He is his richness and his poverty, his sickness and his health, his darkness and his lightness.
And yet within these experiences he becomes aware that he is neither and he is both.

For example:
A rich man perceives himself as never having enough and therefore feels poor.
A pauper sees himself as rich if he finds a small scrap of bread.

Ultimately it depends on the level of perception.

As with the concept of yin and yang, words such as richness and poorness are only relative expressions of a situation rather than absolutes.
They are ever changing according to the position of the observer and the further from the site of action, the easier it is to see that these two extremes are two sides of the same coin or more appropriately different positions on a circle.

An analogy
Two little boys are standing in the playground.
"I've seen an elephant" says the first. "It has large ears and a long trunk which can swing down and pick you up from the ground."
"That's not an elephant" says the second little boy. "I saw one last month and it had large thick legs and a tail which when it was swung could knock you off your feet."
"You are wrong" shouts the first little boy. "You don't know what you are talking about."
"And you wouldn't know an elephant if it walked over you" retorts the second.

At that moment an older and wiser boy comes towards the two quarrelling children. "I have sat on top of an elephant. At the front is a long trunk and large ears. At the back is a long tail and thick legs. You are therefore both correct; the back and the front make up the whole animal which is most clearly seen from a high vantage point."

In spiritual man this vantage point is the soul.

Through man's ability to view life objectively rather than identifying with matter itself there is a natural expansion of consciousness.

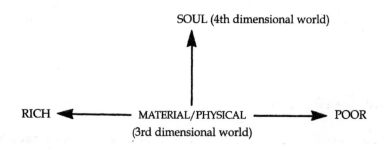

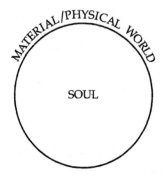

The awareness of unity through diversity parallels the principle of the creation of the soul through the union between spirit and matter.

Here the **Universal Law of Correspondence** is seen to be enacted for this states that all that happens within the spiritual realms will also occur upon the earth plane.

"As above, so below".

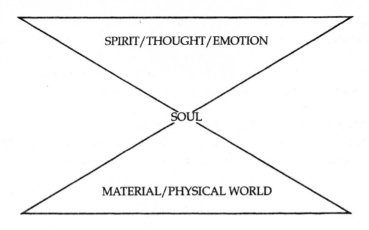

SPIRIT/THOUGHT/EMOTION

SOUL

MATERIAL/PHYSICAL WORLD

The Emotional World

As man moves along his path his identification shifts from the material world to the emotional world. He becomes his emotions. (It is never quite as clear-cut.)

He is his anger, his depression, his anxiety, his happiness, his fear, his guilt, his joy, his sorrow.

He experiences poles of emotional existence often within the same time period.

For example:

> An angry man at work may never show his anger at home because of a fear of upsetting others.

> A permanently smiling face hiding a deep depression.

> Someone who never complains bearing considerable resentment.

Once again it slowly dawns from a vantage point outside the experience that such extremes are unbalanced, tiring and prevent growth. All

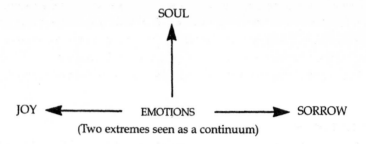

JOY ◄——————— EMOTIONS ——————► SORROW
(Two extremes seen as a continuum)

emotions are only an expression of a thoughtform which must in effect lead to action.

We cannot be one or other emotion; they are an expression of the total being and within this there can be no separation.

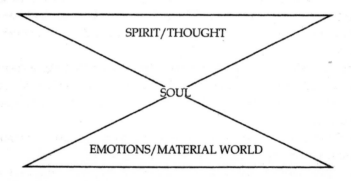

SPIRIT/THOUGHT

SOUL

EMOTIONS/MATERIAL WORLD

Man is not his emotions.

The World of Thoughts

Man then identifies with his thoughts, his belief systems, the rules and regulations which govern his life.

"I think therefore I am." (Descartes, French philosopher.)

Thoughtforms further encompass the illusion of life created by the material and emotional worlds ... we become our thoughts.

In this way our actions become reactions based on belief systems laid down following a previous life situation. In most cases there is a strong emotional attachment which is binding the "actor" to the experience and not allowing him\her to become the observer or "audience".

That is, our emotions create the thoughtform rather than the soul.

For example:

When Anne was six years old, her father left home to live with another woman. She could not understand why this had happened as she thought that her father loved her.

She came to the conclusion, in a childlike manner, that it must have been something that she did which caused him to leave.

Holding this belief inside, she carried on through life until she started to go out with boys. One relationship after another ended. In most cases the boys said that her love was suffocating and that any suggestions to ease back were met with claims that they did not love her.

She had a desperate need to please her partner for in her mind this meant that he would not desert her. Her need to be loved and her belief that this could only come from another person caused great heartache and distress.

One day whilst talking to a friend she realised that the pattern was repeating itself time and time again. She came to see that her own lack of self-love was attracting towards her those who would confirm her own inner beliefs.

As she learnt to take care of her needs and to understand the pattern of her parents' marriage, she became more self-assured.

Last year she started a new relationship but this time as a much stronger and wiser person.

Thoughtforms and belief systems are laid down in our formative years and are represented by the "shoulds and should nots" and the "do's and do nots" of life.

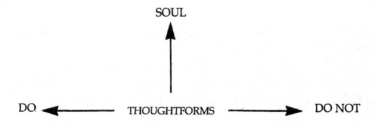

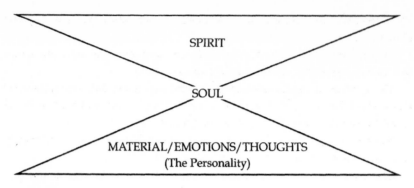

SPIRIT

SOUL

MATERIAL/EMOTIONS/THOUGHTS
(The Personality)

Throughout life we swing between rebelling and conforming to these rules until we find a balance which represents those beliefs that are still appropriate and valuable to this present age.

Such balance is found by following the Universal Laws of Life and by testing the rules to see whether or not they are still appropriate, accepting the consequences of our actions as part of the learning experience.

Only by using the intuition can we truly know which thoughts originate from the soul and which belong to our personality.

Once man knows himself as a personality and as a soul, the latter becomes the mediator for access to the spiritual planes. The next stage is for the soul to bring its energies down through the personality until the light of the soul shines out of its vehicle.

"First find yourself along the path; then lose yourself and the path is won (one)."

To achieve this, the awareness of the soul is once again tested as it passes down through the mental, emotional and physical planes.

The duality is presented again but this time, with the soul in command, the individual can see those planes for what they are and is therefore less moved by the diversity.

■ The Universal Laws

Esoteric teaching states that there are a number of Laws which govern the Universe.

A) THE LAW OF CORRESPONDENCE has already been discussed with the concept that all that occurs on a spiritual plane will also occur on the earth plane.

B) THE LAW OF RE-INCARNATION states that we do not live only one life but many.

This allows the individual to experience life in all its aspects and hence to enhance the growth of the consciousness.

The concept of re-incarnation was present in the Bible until 553AD when the Church Council of Constantinople decreed that such a belief should be excluded from religious instruction.

Following this ruling, Western man came to believe that there is only one life with the possibility of an afterlife.

Eastern philosophy, however, maintained the teachings and these thoughts are once again entering the spiritual centres in the West.

The many lives should be seen as expressing the different aspects of the self in an attempt to understand the whole.

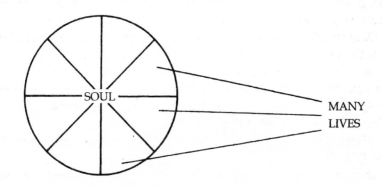

I believe that before entering the earth plane we choose the lessons that we wish to learn in this life.

This means that we choose our parents and our family and subsequent acquaintances and friends.

Our "blood" family are our greatest teachers and despite any anger or hatred towards them, they are difficult to forget. With friends it is far easier to remove yourself from their presence.

Our true spiritual family does not necessarily live under the same roof … you recognise them on first sight and like what you see. They give guidance and support at times of need and then may pass out of your life.

Whether you believe in one life or many is not entirely relevant. What is relevant is the ability to live in the present time and in the presence of your soul.

There are three other Universal Laws which govern our ability to bring towards us that which is needed for our growth.

C) THE LAW OF OPPORTUNITY. This states that the opportunities for learning and growth will always be available as will the tools necessary for the task.

D) THE LAW OF ATTRACTION. This states that we will attract towards us all that we require. It does not however always promise that this is what we want!

E) THE LAW OF KARMA. This law states that all we put out must eventually return.

... "As you sow so will you reap."

Just as the tide goes out, it will eventually come in; we breathe in and then out; contraction of a spring will be followed by relaxation.

Karma is not punishment for wrong doing. It is there to help us to understand both poles of existence and to choose to become neither.

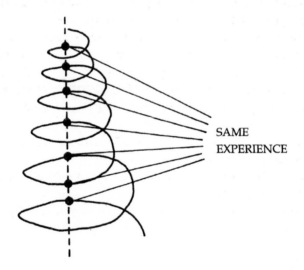

SAME
EXPERIENCE

If we choose or fail to take advantage of the opportunity before us then in view of the fact that life is a spiral, the same experience will be offered again in a different guise. However there is no guarantee that it will be easier next time!

However, in many cases each time we attempt to "climb over the wall" we lay down another layer of earth which creates a ramp for our final departure from a position of inactivity.

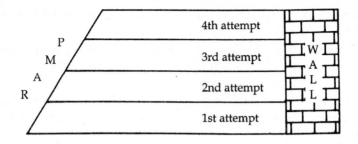

So to recap:

1) In the beginning was the Divine Energy Source.

2) In taking form, this Energy divided into two poles: Spirit and Matter.

3) The union between these two poles created the Soul.

4) The Soul expresses the degree of consciousness released through the union.

5) The purpose of life is to increase the level of consciousness which occurs through the interaction between spirit and matter.

6) The purpose of man is to develop self-consciousness, ie. to see himself as separate from his personality and then to lose this separation as the energies of the soul and personality merge to form spiritual man.

7) This increase in consciousness is achieved by experiencing and accepting various aspects of duality and recognising first their differences and then their sameness.

8) In this way man can start to see himself as both spirit and matter and then to see that they are from the same source.

9) One of man's greatest areas of friction to these ideas is in the field of the emotions or the desires.

10) Disease within the physical body is often the means by which the balance is redressed.

Exercise 1

1) Choose six things that you like about yourself, eg. your nose, your laugh, your caring nature, your ability to listen, your sensitivity and your ability to mix well with other people.

2) Choose six things that you do not like about yourself (much easier!) eg. your hips, your intolerance, your irritability, your moodiness and desire to be left alone, your love of chocolate and your bad skin.

3) Now affirm to yourself in a mirror or to another person your good points: "I like my ..." or "I like the fact that I am ..."

4) Now affirm to yourself or another that the negative points are part of your total being: "I accept my ..." and if possible "I love my ..."

5) Now look at the two lists and see if there are areas of contradiction:

"I am caring ... but intolerant."

"I like mixing with people ... but I want to be left alone."

"I love chocolate ... but I hate my bad skin."

These examples show areas of conflict around a common theme. To hate the negative points is missing the point. Their existence represents an area of imbalance.

In the above example, an over-caring nature can mean inadequate time spent in receiving and too much time spent in giving leading to an expression of the imbalance through irritability, comfort feeding and moodiness.

The clue is to detect the common theme.

In this case, poor love for self, except through the identity of the listener and the carer, leads to disharmony.

By finding time for self and becoming aware of the areas where there is neglect such as with the diet ... the so called "negative" aspects dissolve whilst those that are "positive" are harmonised.

Exercise 2

1) Choose two people with whom you feel some disharmony.

2) List those things which annoy, irritate or create fear.

3) According to the Law of Attraction, you have attracted these people towards you for your own learning. They are reflecting some aspect of yourself which is still in the shadows.

This concept is often difficult to accept but remember not to look at the deed but rather concentrate on the underlying aspect which is out of balance.

For example:

Your husband refuses to push himself forward at work always allowing others to walk over him. You see him as weak and become frustrated with never having enough money and never being able to go away on a decent holiday.

However, when it is suggested that you perhaps would like to find work, you find one excuse after another. Both of you have a feeling that "you are not good enough" and probably believe that you will fail in any attempt which is made.

Both lacked encouragement from parents and had been told "You'll never make anything of your life."

By seeing yourself in your husband you start to see that your frustration is directed inwardly. It can only be relieved if you banish all excuses and take on some creative activity which is in your reach of success.

In this way your confidence is enhanced and you give your husband a break from your nagging so that he may proceed with his own growth.

2 Chapter

The Subtle Energy Bodies

Man is more than just his physical body.

He has a soul and the soul is the product of the interaction between spirit and matter. These in turn are a product of the Divine Energy Source.

He also has a personality which involves the logical mind, the emotions and the physical body.

These various parts of man are described in esoteric terms as "bodies" and when the physical body is excluded, they are called "subtle bodies" because the latter cannot be seen with the physical eye.

Therefore man consists of not just one body but seven.

An analogy
When white light passes through a prism, the light is split into the seven distinct colours of the rainbow.

When these colours are once again passed through a prism, the seven become one; the white light:

WHITE LIGHT

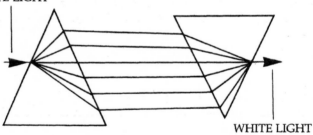

WHITE LIGHT

The "bodies" are interconnecting fields of energy each vibrating at different rates and are named from the highest rate down, in the diagram opposite.

The bodies are not found in layers but intermingle. Together they form the "aura" as seen by a clairvoyant.

It is often difficult to conceive that we are more than flesh and blood when brought up in a world in which seeing is believing.

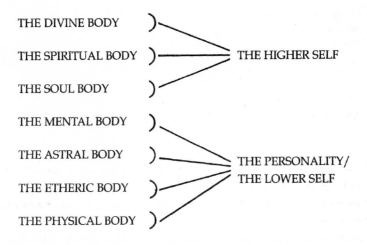

THE DIVINE BODY)
THE SPIRITUAL BODY) ———— THE HIGHER SELF
THE SOUL BODY)

THE MENTAL BODY)
THE ASTRAL BODY) ———— THE PERSONALITY/
THE ETHERIC BODY) THE LOWER SELF
THE PHYSICAL BODY)

The following analogy may help to elucidate the matter:

An analogy

If I gave you a piece of ice and asked you to put your hand through it, you may say that this is impossible.

Applying gentle heat leads to the melting of the ice and the production of water. Now your hand can pass freely through the icy water.

If I then said that I can make the water disappear, you may once again question the validity of my statement. However, with further heat the water turns to steam and then disappears into the air.

By increasing the vibration of the molecules, seeing is not always believing.

■ The Energy Bodies of Man

The energy of the higher bodies, the Divine, the spiritual and soul bodies are derived from a small part of the energy which constitutes the Divine Energy Source, the spirit and the soul, respectively.

Few individuals are in touch with the energy of their spiritual and Divine bodies. Such people are usually found among the Holy men of the ancient cultures.

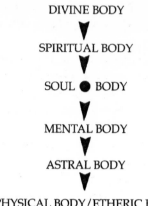

DIVINE BODY

▼

SPIRITUAL BODY

▼

SOUL ● BODY

▼

MENTAL BODY

▼

ASTRAL BODY

▼

PHYSICAL BODY/ETHERIC BODY

Together the Divine, the spiritual and the higher aspects of the soul body constitute the "**higher self**". It expresses itself though the "**higher**

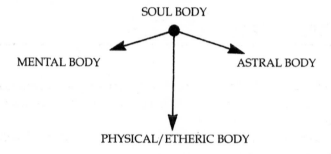

SOUL BODY

MENTAL BODY   ASTRAL BODY

PHYSICAL/ETHERIC BODY

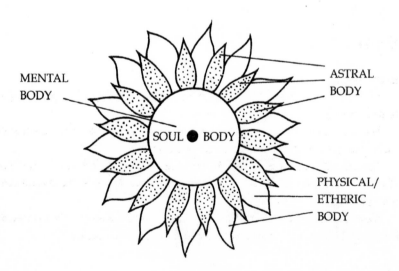

MENTAL
BODY

ASTRAL
BODY

SOUL ● BODY

PHYSICAL/
ETHERIC
BODY

mind" and is seen to be above daily concerns. It endows the individual with unconditional loving and a non-judgemental overview of life on all levels.

By reaching into the higher mind, it is far easier to see things more objectively and therefore to be able to place them in perspective.

The "**lower self**", the personality or "**the ego**" expresses itself through the "**lower mind**" and consists of the astral, mental, etheric and physical bodies.

The lower aspects of the soul body are the mediators between the higher self and the lower self.

In man, the soul chooses the personality which it believes will enable it to take full advantage of the learning situations which are presented in each life.

The various bodies are then brought together by the cohesive force of the soul which is an expression of the power of love.

The Lower Bodies

These bodies of energy are formed through the original union between spirit and matter. In this way it is seen that they too will encompass their own level of consciousness.

Their development can be seen to parallel the concept of evolution where one stage manifests into the next.

Evolution

In the beginning there was **no-thing**.

There was however the container for all life ... **the ether** (the original female energy).

Through the action of the electromagnetic force of the sun (the original male energy) the **mineral kingdom** was formed.

This kingdom is represented by crystals and rocks and also by the basic chemical elements which are used in the construction of man and all other life systems.

Next came the **plant kingdom**. Plants grow through the interaction between the sun, minerals and the water within the earth.

Following the plants came the **animal kingdom** which feeds upon the plant and mineral kingdoms in order to enhance their species.

Then came **man**; man is an omnivore; his survival is based upon the existence of the other three kingdoms.

To complete this picture of evolution, man should be seen as a small part of the total hierarchy whose combined energies or intelligence manifest as the **Divine Energy Source**.

The energy released from the food of each group is used to enhance the inhabitants of the higher kingdoms.

Man is therefore the collective energy of the mineral, plant and animal kingdoms.

When this is related back to the formation of the personality, it is seen that the "intelligence" of each kingdom is used in the creation of the lower bodies:

a) **The physical body is from the mineral kingdom**
b) **The etheric body is from the plant kingdom**
c) **The astral body is from the animal kingdom**
d) **The mental body is from the human kingdom**
   and is the seat of the will of man's soul

However, nothing is static in this world and the goal of each kingdom is to attain a higher level of consciousness.

Therefore it is seen that not only are minerals capable of storing and transmitting energy but, through the modern use of crystals in healing as well as in the field of technology, they can also act as transformers of energy which is the function of the etheric body.

The plant kingdom traps and transforms energy from the sun. But in recent years researchers have shown that plants are sensitive to their surroundings and may move away from painful or harmful stimuli.

This sensitivity and the ability to respond to the environment is the function of the astral body.

The animal kingdom is associated with instincts related to survival and procreation but in more highly evolved animals, such as domestic animals, there is an ability to exhibit some degree of individual thought.

In turn man, with his logical mind, which gives him the power of analysis, is aspiring to recognise and accept his soul as a wise and loving being.

■ The Level of Intelligence and Disease

As man expands his consciousness by experiencing the various "bodies" of his existence, he will identify with the intelligence of each kingdom which will consequently influence his mode of action at that time.

The Mental Body

As yet, imbalances from the mental body are few, since most of the apparent "mental diseases" actually originate from the astral body.

The Astral Body

Whilst man identifies with his emotions he will be linked to the intelligence of the astral or animal body.

This body is associated with survival and hence reproduction. Therefore, in pure animal terms, there is often a tendency towards competitiveness, aggressiveness and defensiveness.

Without the influence of the logical mind or of the intuition, the astral intelligence has a tendency to react without prior thought to the sensory input that is received.

I find that people who are locked into this form of intelligence manifest many diseases whose origin arises from the astral level.

The Etheric Body

Another major seat of disease or disharmony is the etheric body which receives and transforms the collective intelligence of the other bodies and then passes this into the physical body for transmission.

Unfortunately, the intelligence which underlies this body, is not sufficiently sensitive to recognise which electromagnetic energies are harmful to man.

Therefore, over the past few years there is increasing evidence of the damaging effects to health from overhead electricity pylons, underwater streams and electrical equipment in the home.

These effects are seen within the nervous system which is the counterpart of the etheric body.

The Physical Body

Although the physical body often manifests the disharmony or disease, it is rarely the origin of the imbalances for it is purely the vehicle for the

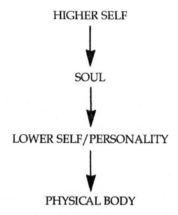

HIGHER SELF

SOUL

LOWER SELF/PERSONALITY

PHYSICAL BODY

energies transmitted from the other bodies, manifesting thought into action.

■ Description of the Bodies

The Mental Body

This body is the seat of the will of the soul; the starting point from which the soul can attempt to integrate its intelligence with that of the personality.

It is the seat of logic or analytical thought.

It is the place where the impulses of the higher self, under the guidance of the Universal Laws, pass from the soul and are transformed into thoughtforms and then into action.

Such thoughtforms may occur during sleep, in the form of dreams, during meditation, as a daydream or may slowly develop as an idea which enters the conscious mind as an achievable goal.

To a certain degree, the individual has the opportunity to deny the thoughtform and to bury it in the deep recesses of the sub-conscious mind. However, if this impulse is important to soul growth then it will be offered at different times and in different ways until it is manifested into action.

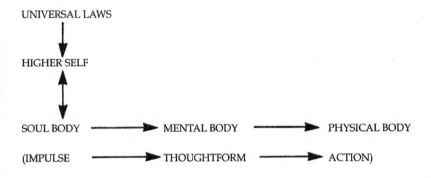

I know there have been times in my life when I have avoided a particular impulse which has usually involved some degree of change only to find that, slowly but surely, I have been "persuaded" to move by external events.

For example, one morning on going out to the car, I found that one of the tyres had a puncture. Annoyed that this would delay the start of my day I proceeded to change the wheel. At that moment, the telephone rang in the house and, on going to answer, I was invited to a meeting which ultimately led to major changes in my life.

I believe that nothing happens by chance ... if you wish to believe in coincidences ... that's fine ... but you may be missing some golden opportunities!

New ideas need fresh soil. Therefore, before an idea is manifest in the physical world, time may be required to prepare the earth and to remove old roots or weeds which may stifle the growth of the seedling. This is the concept of "spring-cleaning" when that which is old, and no longer valuable to the present life, is released to make way for the new.

In spiritual man the response to the manifested action is fed back through the mental body where it is given form through the use of memory. It then passes to the soul where wisdom is applied and the results are then compared with the original impulse.

The outcome of the action and the assessment by the soul governs the "character" of the next impulse.

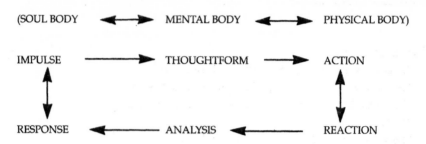

The soul's assessment is based on intuition which is influenced by the power to discriminate. Pure logic on the part of the mental body tends to rely on judgement which is usually biased in favour of the personality.

When man is purely identifying with his mental body, there is little impact from the soul's energy.

Therefore the results from an action are analysed into a "black and white" response and are granted the position of rules. These rules form the basis of "belief systems" which are then the main impulse for future activities.

Rules and laws are not necessarily laid down to make life difficult; they are fact.

For example:
It is fact that if you choose to walk in the middle of a busy motorway there is a good chance that you will get hurt.

It is fact that fire burns.

It is fact that if you do not eat you will eventually die.

Rules are there for our protection. If we go outside the law, then our safety and survival cannot be guaranteed.

The first rules laid down are those provided by parents, guardians and teachers who essentially wish to offer protective guidance within the earthly environment.

Such rules are often accompanied by the words "should and should not" or "must and must not". They teach us about the danger of fires, of

roads, of walking too near the edge of a cliff, of talking to strangers, and this advice is good and helps us to feel secure.

Unfortunately, in many cases the rules are flavoured with the biases, the emotions and the experiences of the adviser and therefore the rule does not follow a logical pattern.

For example:

"If you are not quiet, then I will not love you."

"If you do not stop crying, then you will miss supper."

"You should not/must not talk, speak, act, like that."

"Why?"

"Because I say so!"

"Do not let the neighbours know our business."

"Keep it in the family."

"Be a brave little boy."

"Grow up" ... often said to a two year old when the newest baby arrives home.

"Go and play on a motorway!" ... said in apparent jest!

"You should have done better."

"You must try harder."

These are often described as family sayings or mottoes and, as belief systems, may influence the recipient for the rest of their life.

Other sayings, which are meant to be helpful, may be misunderstood by a child whose mind is unable to differentiate one application of the law from another.

For example:

I remember hearing of a child who became hysterical when he was placed in a plastic humidity tent which is the treatment for croup.

When eventually he was taken out of the tent and calmed down he said that his mother had always warned him against placing his head in a plastic bag.

Another child became hysterical when being told that, in order to have his tonsils removed, he would be put to sleep.

It was then revealed that the previous week he had gone with his mother to have his dog "put to sleep" by the vet.

Logical thought develops with age and experience and therefore children often take things at face value until told otherwise.

Seven Year Cycles of Life

The most vulnerable time of an individual's development is the first seven years of life. It is during this time that mental processes are formulated and the basic rules of life are laid down.

Without an adequate spiritual link, many erroneous belief systems become the ground on which the concept of self-consciousness is based.

One of the main reasons why this occurs is that during these formative years, a child is totally dependent on its guardians or parents for food, warmth, clothing and love. He or she cannot go out to earn a living.

Therefore, if a child is told that he will not receive food unless he is quiet, then he will be quiet.

If he is told to be brave and not to cry and then he will be loved, then he will not cry.

Such belief systems are stored in the memory and years later may still influence the actions of the individual.

There will come a time, however, when it is necessary to challenge the wisdom of these beliefs and to see whether they still hold true in the present environment and are in harmony with the individual's own inner truth.

If there is disharmony then conflict develops which in the teenage years is described as the "rebellious stage".

Here the young person is trying to determine what is true for the individual and what belongs to their parents.

They may go overboard with wild hairstyles, outrageous friends and unrecognisable music. This is their attempt to present the other pole of existence to that expressed by their parents.

Between 14 and 21 years they tentatively formulate their own belief systems and apply them in the years between 21 and 28.

By 28 years they re-introduce certain of their parents standards which now appear to have some relevance and combine these with their new belief systems.

However, there are many individuals who pass quietly through the teenage rebellion, only to see it emerge in their 40s and 50s.

Hairstyles change (even though hair may be at a premium), wardrobes are re-equipped and there may be a change in partners or jobs.

In astrological terms such changes follow the seven year cycles of the planet Saturn, which is the planet linked with the power to restrict, but through this to learn. It could be said that at this time we review all those things which are holding us back and choose whether or not we are ready to change and to let go.

Starting Out Afresh

Setting out new parameters from which to work can often appear quite daunting as the "tried and tested" feel familiar and comfortable.

There is often a fear of "going behind the adviser's back" especially if the latter is a parent. There may also be a fear of failure and of trusting one's own new instinct.

The words "I told you so" or "Don't say I didn't try to warn you" are not helpful when we are setting out alone.

When the belief system involves repeated messages concerning one's self-worth, it can be very hard to start to develop some degree of self-identity and self-valuation.

The only role left to such an individual is often that of believing that all that happens is their fault and that they will never succeed in anything that they attempt.

As they begin to develop a small degree of self-worth, they may even feel guilty for denying that which they have believed for so long.

They can become both the victim and the victimiser and growth becomes static.

In truth, they are the only person who holds the key to unlock themselves from their gaol ... many can offer support but the "victim" needs to unlock the door to allow friends to enter.

Everything takes time and one of the ways of sabotaging any forward movement is to set the goals too high and therefore fulfil the subconscious belief that nothing is possible.

Whatever the reason, it is often difficult to change the "record" or belief system which is stored in the memory bank and to replace it with a new one.

However, if the time is right, change will occur, in compliance with the Law of Balance and Equilibrium, and we can go willingly or kicking and screaming!

I can think of a number of 50 and 60 year old men and women whose actions are still ruled by the belief systems of their parents.

How they should act; what they should wear; how hard they should work; what they should read; what they should eat.

All sensible and good advice at the time, but which may not be appropriate now.

Whenever I hear the words "Should, ought or must", I know there is a problem.

It begs the question:

.. "Who says?"

… The answer is rarely "I say."

It is far more common to be a throw back to childhood when love, food, warmth and clothing were conditioned by obeying the family rules.

For example:

Maria was a successful 55 year old woman who was a perfectionist. She worked all hours and then wondered why her mind was overactive and prevented sleep.

We talked about relaxation and recreation and she said that this was not part of her schedule as this meant that valuable time was lost.

I asked her about the source of this strong work ethic and she told me that her mother had always told her that she would never be any good at anything.

For the last 50 years she had tried to prove her wrong.

She was not capable of looking at her own achievements and congratulating herself … she still sought approval from her mother.

During times of change it is perfectly valid to go back to old patterns of behaviour for short periods until the new paradigms are well "worn in" and the old belief systems no longer fit the new image.

Deepak Chopra in his book "Quantum Healing" states how difficult it is to change old patterns of a lifetime … not impossible but it requires a "quantum leap" in thought which means letting go and trusting.

Laws and Rules

Laws of the universe and of the land in which we live are there to prevent chaos and to offer security.

Rules and belief systems, however, need to be assessed from time to time to check that they are still in harmony with the wisdom of the higher self.

Such wisdom comes through the development of the intuition and will reflect that which is good not only for the individual but also for humanity as a whole.

Chapter 3

The Subtle Energy Bodies ... continued

■ The Astral Body

This body is linked with the expression of one's impulses or desires in the form of the "emotions".

In spiritual man these desires are derived from the soul and enter the etheric body through the heart chakra. However, if there is no firm connection with the soul, the energy passes down to the solar plexus where it is expressed as the desires of the personality.

The energy of the astral body follows the Law of Attraction which reveals that through our emotions we will attract towards us all that is needed for soul growth.

In this way the emotions produce both the actors and the stage leading to the transformation of the impulse into action.

An analogy

The desire of a plant to spread its pollen leads to the creation of petals of a certain colour and the release of a particular scent into the air.

Insects, attracted by the colour and smell, come to feed upon the nectar.

Whilst resting on the plant the pollen becomes attached to the legs of the insect. In this way the pollen is transferred to another plant where fertilisation takes place.

Thus the survival of the plant is assured and the desire of the plant is fulfilled.

In a similar way, we are the creators of our own world in order to grow and to expand the field of our existence.

All that we sense or experience has been created for a particular purpose in our life whether on a personal level or as a member of the human race or of this planet.

The impulse of our inner world is reflected in the existence of our outer world.

For example:

If I feel happy on waking, I will dress and act in accordance with this inner impulse.

During the day I will find that most people I meet will offer a smile and kind words which will enhance the good feelings about myself.

However, if I feel miserable and feel that the world is against me, I will no doubt meet several people who will reinforce my own feelings of self-doubt.

The Transformation of Thought into Action

Emotions are outgoing; **E-motion** is to set this energy (E), or impulse, into motion.

This is achieved by using the different vibrational energies of the five elements (earth, air, fire, water and ether) to manifest the impulse in the physical world.

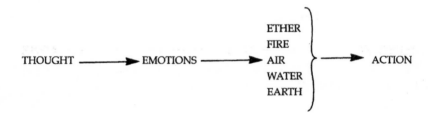

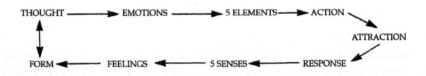

This manifested impulse will then attract a certain response which is recorded by the five senses and linked with memory within the astral body to provide an expression of the message in the form of "feelings".

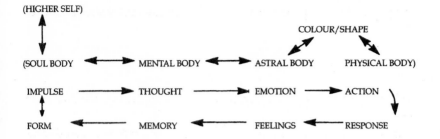

Feelings are incoming; they are a reflection of the situation.

Through the mental body, the feelings are given form and compared with the original impulse.

The astral body contains therefore both the seat of feelings and of emotions; one could say that which is expressed by the emotions is registered by the feelings.

If there is a match between the impulse and the response then harmony is recorded and the consciousness of the soul is expanded.

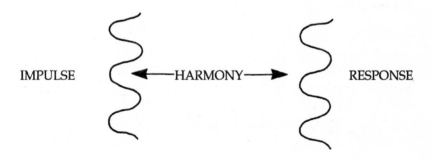

An analogy

An actor plays his part and at the end receives warm applause. He sees the smiling faces and hears the clapping and, on matching these sensory impulses with those stored within the memory bank, he realises that he has performed well.

This means that he has fulfilled the contract which he made when accepting the part and he experiences a feeling of harmony.

However, if the match between expectation and result is poor, ie. the actor does not receive the acclaim or does not feel satisfied with his own performance, then disharmony is registered and the process will be repeated, with alteration in the form of expression, until harmony is achieved.

IMPULSE ◄—— DISHARMONY ——► RESPONSE

The emotions are therefore more than just the verbal expressions of anger, joy and sadness; they also include the manner, the dress and the attitude of the person.

The "Colour" of Emotions

Colour is a powerful form of expression and hence an attracting force. The colours we wear add an extra dimension to the mood of the individual.

For example:

The girl in black may wish to appear mysterious . . or may be in mourning.

The women in red trousers contains much pent-up energy and nobody should stand in her way!

The man with the yellow tie feels vibrant and full of new ideas.

The colours that we choose to wear or surround ourselves with in our home reflect those colours which we need for soul growth and which may be absent from our aura.

(It may also reflect the only clean clothes in the wardrobe!)

Apart from colour, the visual senses will also record non-verbal communication which can be a powerful method of expressing a message: A smile, a laugh, the lift of an eyebrow can speak volumes.

The tone of voice, the inflections of speech, the use of gestures, can provide the listener with a wealth of information concerning the state of mind of the speaker.

The Link Between Memory, Senses and Feelings

Stimulation of the senses often leads to recognition of an emotion that is stored within the memory banks.

For example:

The smell of summer flowers may take us back to our childhood which reminds us of happy carefree times.

Conversely, the smell of ether may never fail to elicit the fear of the unknown and of being alone.

Smell is registered in the limbic system of the brain which is the seat of our emotions.

In a similar way, when the other senses such as sound, touch and taste are stimulated, there may be a recollection of a memory that has been well and truly buried.

For example:

White walls may remind a person of the time, aged three, when they were "deserted" by their parents and left in the hands of white, sterile people living in white, sterile wards ... being told that their parents "had only popped out for a few moments".

These children and then adults learn to distrust the words of others, especially those in white coats and aprons.

Such a memory may well influence the individual's ability to enter another hospital or to seek orthodox help, despite serious signs and symptoms.

It should therefore be remembered that memory is only a guide and not law and should be updated with relevant information. As has been stated before, changing the memory of the cells is not easy and requires much courage and perseverance.

The greater the contact with the soul, the easier it is to view things in perspective and to change the "record" that has been playing for years to one that is more in tune with the identity of the inner self.

Emotions are a Necessary Part of Life

Emotions cannot be defined as "good or bad". It should be akin to saying that night is bad or day is good ... which would certainly be untrue for there are many who rely on the night-time for their work.

They are a form of expression which is only relevant to the particular situation in which they are found.

Anger, sadness, resentment, jealousy are all part of human nature. They are part of who we are.

What is more important is that the emotions do not become the ruler of the individual's life, whether they are expressed or suppressed.

Many men and women function from the astral body and never move any higher.

The Basic Problems in this Area Include:

a) **Over-identification with the emotions.**
b) **Under-identification with or suppression of the emotions.**
c) **Identification with the desires of the personality rather than with those of the soul.**

Taking one at a time:

A) OVER-IDENTIFICATION WITH THE EMOTIONS
Some people are described or describe themselves as being "emotional". This usually signifies that they are easily brought to tears although other emotions may be just as evident such as anger, depression, happiness, jealousy or resentment.

When questioned about their state of health they will reply:

"I'm depressed." "I'm happy." "I'm angry." "I'm resentful."

Such a statement, if repeated many times, starts to create an identity rather than just a state of being at that time.

"I'm a depressive." "I'm an anxious person." "I'm an angry person."

It would be more accurate to say "At this moment I am manifesting anger" etc.

Emotions and feelings are there to be registered whether externally or internally expressed and then to be used for the purpose of learning and understanding by the soul.

Once they have been registered they should be released just as clothes are changed to represent a particular situation.

If I feel angry ... I register the anger and then ask myself "My anger represents an energy block which needs to be released. What can **I do** to change the situation?" This change may be physical or result in an alteration in the way that I view a particular experience.

Such awareness often comes only when we step out of the role of the actor and become the audience, allowing the mind to reach a state of peace from whence the answer will come.

Physically there may not be an easy solution ... grieving is a natural process of "letting go" and needs time ... but there may come a time when grief turns into self-pity. Such a state is damaging to both the "sufferer" and to those around them.

In other cases, it may be necessary to come to terms with the situation and to accept that this is "the way things are" and that such acceptance releases the individual to move forward even though the steps may be faltering at first.

I have seen many cases where over-expression of the emotions hides a fear or resistance to move from a point of the "tried and tested" ... such people are stuck in a rut and this may be seen physically in conditions where there is immobility such as osteoarthritis and some of the neurological diseases.

"I'm too busy being emotional to think about changing!"

Even someone who is permanently "happy" may be avoiding looking too deeply inside for fear of finding their shadow.

This over-identification reveals the two aspects of polarity ... the excessive outflow of emotions externally reflecting the inner suppression of forward movement along the spiritual path.

Eventually the Law of Balance and Equilibrium will create a situation where change will have to take place.

This may come about through changes in physical health but more commonly through the need to release one's own emotions in order to help others.

Many well-meaning folk have struggled to try to bring a friend, partner, relative or client out of their "emotional" state whether it is anger, depression, jealousy or even inappropriate happiness.

The harder the "rescuer" pulls, the greater the resistance to change. Sometimes the helper becomes the victim, trapped in the web created by the original victim who is now the "victimiser", leading to stagnation of movement for both individuals.

At other times the rescuer marches off in disgust which reveals the underlying motive of the abortive attempt which is to change someone else rather than to look at their own need to change.

We cannot change others or carry them along their path or ours. All we can do is to offer a supportive hand which can be taken within the free will of the individual.

Many people are very happy being depressed. They thrive on their misery and enjoy regurgitating past hurts and resentments. Just as some people are dependent on cigarettes and alcohol, these people are dependent on their emotions.

By using the principles of duality, those who wish to help such "victims" need to encourage the area of the victim's life which is lacking rather than try to discourage their emotional status without which they would feel totally insecure.

An analogy

If you want to dissuade a toddler from using a dummy, it is best to offer something which is more appealing rather than berate the child for its "childish and shameful" ways!

B) UNDER-IDENTIFICATION WITH THE EMOTIONS

The opposite extreme is the suppressor of emotions.

Such people always start the conversation with: "I think" rather than "I feel".

They answer the questions clearly and precisely although they never mention a feeling. They deal with logic and fact and may even look down on or criticise those who are "over-emotional".

In many cases the emotions have been suppressed due to their reactions to earlier experiences which may have occurred in the first seven years of life, at birth, prenatally (within the womb) or during earlier passages on this earth.

For example:

A child brought up in a household where there is anger and violence may learn to suppress its own anger.

Conversely, a child may grow up amongst a family of "non-expressers" ... not uncaring but not necessarily sharing feelings.

When asked "What makes you angry", the answer to follow is usually "Nothing."

However, if the question is changed to: "Do you ever feel irritated inside?" the answer is usually "Yes."

These suppressors are often the peacemakers; they avoid conflict where possible. They are the "listeners"; everybody tells them their problems .. but they rarely relate their own.

They may feel resentful but rarely complain as there is often now a fear of releasing their own anger in case they cannot control the problem.

In physical terms this anger becomes buried into the liver area and in acupuncture terms creates problems along the liver meridian.

In other cases crying may be suppressed as this was seen as a sign of weakness. The message was to "be strong" in a situation where the child had to learn at an early age to be independent and brave.

Crying, as with anger when used appropriately, is a natural release of energy ... both are part of the grieving process which enable the individual to "let go" of a situation which has been completed and to make room for new experiences.

Restrained tears appear in the physical body as excess fluid as in catarrh which drips down the back of the throat or in swellings of the extremities.

Others fear losing control of the situation through becoming too emotional. The emotions become the shadow which should be denied as long as possible.

But that which is not expressed externally will, through the Universal Law of Balance and Equilibrium, need to be expressed internally to restore harmony.

Therefore I see cases of skin rashes (unexpressed irritation), asthma (unexpressed speech), diarrhoea (unexpressed fear), fat intolerance (unexpressed anger) and many other conditions. These verify that so much of disease is only reflecting an underlying obstruction to the normal flow of life.

The soul will always attempt to find a method of relieving the system of excess energy either through the physical body or through external circumstances.

For example:

You hate your job. It is boring and this leads to frustration. You become irritated by those around you but do not have the courage to look for a new job.

Suddenly you are made redundant. You are angry with the company who employed you and then become depressed as the days at home drag into weeks.

In desperation you start to sort out your cupboards and find some art work which you had enjoyed in the past but because of pressure of work was laid aside.

Soon you realise that this is more than a hobby and decide to set up your own business selling your own creations.

The energy of the anger has now been turned into something creative and can now be used for soul growth.

Once there is awareness of the block in energy then this can be gently but consciously released without requiring physical illness, external changes or a cathartic experience.

Static energy leads to disease.

Awareness leads to freedom.

Shock

In some cases the strength of feeling that is received in response to the action is so great that the individual is overwhelmed by the experience.

In physical terms such shock leads to a state of fainting or unconsciousness which disconnects the conscious mind from the sensation of pain.

As a medical doctor I can achieve the same result, ie. disconnection using anaesthesia and if I require the patient to remain conscious then I will give only a local anaesthetic. This will result in loss of feeling or numbness and loss of movement or rigidity. However, it is now well-documented that although the pain is not felt consciously it is recorded subconsciously.

Such "pain" whether emotional or physical can be carried throughout life and even brought forward from another lifetime.

I believe that the result of these suppressed emotions is seen in the form of physical ailments where there is unexplained pain, numbness, rigidity or loss of movement.

Such patients may require the help of well-trained psychotherapists to unlock the buried emotion and bring the feelings from the astral body, through the mental body and to resolution on a soul level.

Once on the soul level, the individual can see the "shocking experience" for what it was ... a learning process, however painful, along the way to soul expansion and can release the energy which has been blocked for so long.

The Inappropriate Expresser

I remember asking one of my patients who complained of pains in the region of the stomach.

"Do you express anger?"

"Yes, all the time; I'm terrible at work and my family have learnt to duck as the plates fly across the room!"

"What about your mother, do you show her anger?"

"Oh no, it would only upset her. And yet it is she that causes me to feel angry. So instead I take it out on everybody else."

It is probably true that her mother would not understand the sudden onslaught of anger directed towards her, but the message behind this situation is that it is the daughter who has to change, not the mother.

The daughter described the mother as "pernickety" for whom you could do nothing right. And yet the daughter was still going to visit her mother with the subconscious hope that someday she would receive approval and hence love from her mother.

"She makes me so angry."

Or more appropriately: "I feel angry at myself for allowing her to rule my life."

Anger is the fire of the emotions; it is the power that will help us move forward. Anger says "You must do something about this situation."

In this particular case the daughter saw that her need for approval from her mother was outdated and that she was now old enough to praise herself.

With this insight, the attitude of the daughter towards her mother changed. She saw her mother as a woman who had not reached fulfilment in her own life and therefore found it difficult to give praise to others.

As the daughter's feelings of self-worth grew, her stomach pains subsided and she was able to give praise to her mother which eased the situation between them.

Other examples of inappropriate expression are seen when a husband shouts at his wife when she is lying ill in bed.

In this case it is not uncommon to find that the husband does not feel angry but rather fearful. He relies on his wife to be strong and cannot bear the thought that he may have to cope alone.

I find it sad that even in this day and age we need to hide our true feelings rather than show our fears and anxieties.

One other group of individuals to be mentioned are those brought up in an insecure or dysfunctional household where there are unpredictable mood changes on the part of the parents or guardians which may result from some form of addiction or chronic mental or physical illness.

These children learn to become chameleons changing their face, clothes and emotions to suit the moods of others. In this way they become depersonalised and often have to assume an adult perspective on life in order to survive and even to take on the role of "parenting" the unpredictable parent.

As they grow they lose themselves further and become total reactors to the outside world. This leads to severe insecurity and feelings of low self-worth. They are wonderful at mimicry and may even take up acting as a career. They become inappropriate expressers as their gift of reading the other person and reacting accordingly may become blurred by the outpouring of their own suppressed emotions.

All members of this group, unlike those who over-identify with their emotions, need to be encouraged to express their emotions whether verbally, physically, through writing, art or other means of creativity.

But it should be made quite clear that such expression must start with the words "I feel ..." and not "You make me ..." Nobody makes us do anything. In the end, whether consciously or subconsciously, the decision is ours.

The main aim for this group is to learn that emotions can and should be expressed freely and appropriately and then released. Any reaction from those nearby is the property of the reactor and not of the expresser.

If the expresser chooses to take notice of the reaction then that is their choice. So many children learn to suppress their emotions when their expression leads to a flurry of negative reactions.

For example:

"Don't cry ... it gives Mummy a headache."

"Don't cry/be angry ... it upsets me."

"Why do you always have to make Daddy angry with you."

"Please make Mummy happy and be quiet."

"You don't care that your behaviour upsets me."

This is emotional blackmail and can rule someone's life for a long time. For many their desire to please and to be liked overrules all rational thought.

Such reactions threaten the peace and tranquillity of the external world and this is worth maintaining despite the inner turmoil. We must all own our emotions and see them as messengers rather than rulers or jailers.

C) IDENTIFICATION WITH THE DESIRES OF THE PERSONALITY RATHER THAN THE SOUL

This is the commonest problem.

The first two examples describe the expression of two poles of existence around a common theme; over or under-expression leads to obstruction, often due to fear, in the movement along the path.

The third problem relates to the registration of the feeling by the mental body but failure to pass the message on to the soul for an objective view of the situation.

The result of this "short circuit" is that new impulses do not come from the soul but rather from the personality whose desires or impulses are based on belief systems which derive their origin from previous life experiences.

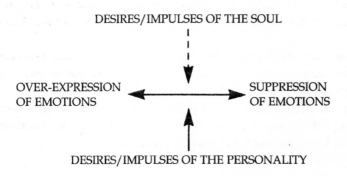

For example:

I believe or think that I am happy. I dress myself in bright clothes and go out into the world feeling happy; I smile and have a jaunty lift to my step. I express happiness.

However, despite my appearance, the first person I smile at has had a bad night and looks and feels miserable.

Due to a lack of deep feeling of contentment, I immediately take it personally and, despite the happiness that I experienced when I set out that morning, I now feel miserable.

Next morning I go out feeling miserable; I look miserable. Nine people tell me how wonderful I look. The tenth says ... "You do not look happy."

At last someone is speaking the truth!

"I am miserable" ... and in some ways this then makes me feel happy!

Such concepts concerning our state of being are often deeply sown from an early age. Therefore our reaction to each new situation can already be tainted by memory of previous experiences:

"You'll never make anything of your life."

"Stop reading and do something useful."

"Be quiet" … which amounts to "Don't exist."

"Don't question."

"So you were second, why weren't you first?"

"You are bound to fail, as always."

"Your father and I never wanted any more children."

How difficult it is to overcome such deep opposition in order to begin to believe in oneself. To add to the problems, the Law of Attraction guarantees that we will always attract towards us that which we project.

I feel miserable … I'll attract misery.

I feel happy … I'll attract happiness.

In the eyes of the soul there is no failure, there is only movement. But within the personality we are faced with two poles of existence:

Success or failure.

Express your needs or keep quiet.

Joy or sadness.

Be active or be lazy.

If I do not value myself, I will continue to meet people who will remind me that I am "no good".

If I feel insecure, I will continue to meet people who are also insecure and are looking for someone who has even less confidence so that they may feel better.

We truly are the creators of our own illusions.

We are stuck on a merry-go-round of acting on the basis of our reactions.

There is an alternative: to look up towards the place of the soul which is non-judgemental and gives unconditional love.

Here we can say: "I may not be perfect, but I'm alright."

Here we can learn to stand back from situations and to realise that other people also have problems. We can then allow them to express their emotions without becoming personally involved.

Here we can see that it is "fine" to express emotions of sadness and joy, to be busy and to relax, to talk and to be quiet. They all represent different aspects of the complex but beautiful organism called man.

Stepping away from the desires of the personality requires the individual to become aware of their own intuition and to become confident of its ability to guide them to areas where there is scope for the expansion of consciousness.

Learning to rely on one's intuition may take time but in the end its wisdom is seen to be more reliable than listening to the judgement of others.

Constructive criticism will always ring a chord with your own inner truth.

An analogy

I am walking along my life path when I come across a beautiful horse which stands in my way. I mount the horse and slowly it begins to move.

Initially I am thrilled by the feeling of the wind in my hair but as the horse starts to gallop faster I begin to feel unsafe. I try to slow the horse by pulling on the reins; but there is no response and I start to shout for help.

The speed of the horse is now so fast that there is no way of distinguishing individual structures in the surrounding scenery and I become completely disorientated.

At that moment someone shouts "Jump." But the fear which accompanies the thought makes me cling on more tightly.

Eventually I become so dizzy that I can feel my grip on the reins loosening and I fall unconscious from the horse onto the soft ground.

When I come to, I look and see to my astonishment that my beautiful horse is only part of a merry-go-round.

It was all an illusion. Staying on the horse could only take me round and round in circles. The faster the animal moved, the more fearful I became, disorientated and out of control.

Leaving the horse, however frightening at the time, led to the re-instatement of control and the freedom to move forward again.

Dis-orientation literally means to be "away from the East". In native American teachings, the East is said to be the site of enlightenment. Re-orientation leads to re-alignment with our own source of inspiration which is the soul.

Sometimes the only way of moving from a static position to one of freedom and movement is through a thorough shake-up of the original pattern allowing a new design to form under the guidance of the energy of inspiration.

Nothing is ever wasted or lost but sometimes it helps to look at things from a different angle.

We are not our emotions, just as we are not our material possessions or our belief systems. We use our emotions to express the energy of the soul and through this we grow.

■ The Etheric Body

The main function of the etheric body is to connect the physical body to the incoming energies of the astral body, the mental body and the energies of the higher self.

Such sources are sometimes termed "the life force" as they animate all life whether human, plant-like or planetary.

The vitalisation of the physical body by the etheric body occurs mainly through its counterpart, the nervous system and in particular through the autonomic nervous system.

The etheric body is described as consisting of a complex network of transmission lines or "nadis" which run all over the physical body in a similar way to the nerve fibres, arteries or veins. Every cell is touched and vitalised by this energy force.

In this way, the etheric body also acts as the blueprint for the construction of the physical body; the force of energy emitted and its rate of vibration determining the cellular formation required in order to create organs and systems.

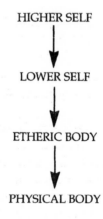

HIGHER SELF

LOWER SELF

ETHERIC BODY

PHYSICAL BODY

An analogy

If I turned a light on outside in the dark, after a while moths would form around the light until all that could be seen was a mass of moth.

Not knowing any better it might be thought that there was no light but just this ball of "moth".

On turning the light off, the moths disperse and nothing remains.

This analogy is symbolic of the effect of the etheric body on the physical body. When the "force" is active, we experience life. When the force is switched off, we experience death.

As has already been stated, the etheric body also links the individual to the electromagnetic force emanating from the etheric body of all life forms. In this way a network is created which spans the planet and even the universe.

The etheric body could be said to link all matter whilst the soul body links all spirit.

In recent years, technology has expanded at a tremendous rate leading to the widespread inclusion of electrical and computerised tools within our homes and workplaces. For some people this electromagnetic energy with its positive ions, is creating disharmony within their etheric bodies causing disease especially of the nervous system.

Such sensitivity to electromagnetic fields will depend on the state of the other bodies at the time, but I believe that more care needs to be taken to diffuse the energy of these positive ions in order to reduce the increasing number of diseases now affecting the nervous system.

■ The Physical Body

The splitting of the atom revealed that behind an apparently solid structure was a dynamic interplay of electric particles all expressing different aspects of the energy field.

With this knowledge, the physical body can no longer be viewed as a solid, static form but should be seen as a complex, synchronised mass of moving energy particles, each giving shape and form to the composition of the body, as expressed by the presence of cells and organs.

In terms of spiritual man, the physical body is a product of, and a vehicle for, the combined energy of the other bodies.

It possesses an excellent range of talents such as flexibility, agility, creativity, regeneration, transformation, extreme sensitivity and a very efficient communication system.

It relies on optimal nourishment not only from the food that is eaten and from the air which is breathed but also on the "intelligent" input from the lower and higher minds.

The appearance of disease within the physical body usually signifies disharmony at a deeper level. Ideally it is preferable to redress the balance at the deepest level possible and hence to eradicate the disease in the physical body. Sometimes, however, the physical changes are irreversible and adjustments need to be made in the deeper levels to accommodate the change.

An analogy

The function of a car is not dependent on the outer form but on the inner workings of the engine and on the activities of the person in the driving seat.

If a wire becomes loose and one of the headlamps fails, then a wise owner will seek the help of an expert who will recognise the fault and reconnect the wire.

However, if advice is not sought or not available then the driver will be unable to drive safely in the dark and this will handicap his performance.

Failure to take note of the initial warning signs may lead to the need for more serious signs to manifest in order to attract attention.

The physical body emits an electromagnetic force which can be measured and used as a guide to assess the functioning capacity of the body. This force is seen in **Kirlian photography** which has been used to outline areas of disharmony within the body. Such photography also recognises the subtle interplay of energies between two individuals who are in close physical contact. This is particularly relevant in the healing arts where the therapist's own energies will inevitably influence the well-being of their client.

Much work is now being carried out to enable practitioners to be able to record the energies emanating from the other bodies.

The physical body is the sacred temple of the soul; without it, our journey on this earth is finished. It should therefore be treated with the respect that any sacred object deserves. It is said that the heart has the capability to survive for 400 years; man can destroy it in 40.

It saddens me that the physical body is used to carry not only all the good things in life but also all our hatred, bitterness, resentment and hurts. These forms of pollution destroy our temple far sooner than any external pollution.

Loving this vehicle is the first stage towards total love and hence wholeness.

The Causal Body

Prior to death the impulses of the higher and lower minds are withdrawn causing the disintegration of the etheric body which leads to the inability of the physical body to survive.

The positive aspects of the astral and mental bodies which have been developed in this lifetime form the causal body. Those more negative aspects of our life are transformed into a positive energy to be used at a later date.

The building of the causal body takes many lifetimes and eventually will form the temple of the soul. This permanent vessel acts as the spiritual counterpart to the personality, carrying the soul between the various lifetimes on earth.

The Aura

Despite the fact that the bodies have been described individually, it should be remembered that they are integrated and that their energies intermingle.

This combined energy is termed the "aura".

To a clairvoyant, the aura is seen as a cloak of moving colours surrounding the individual. The colours will exhibit a variety of shades and will vary in their degree of expansion from the physical form.

The greater the harmony between the bodies, the larger the aura. Prior to death, the aura reduces in size as the life force leaves the physical body.

We are all, to varying degrees, subconsciously aware of the auras emanating from other people. Where we chose to sit or stand may be due to the sense that a particular person has a "brighter" aura while that of another is "darker" and less welcoming.

In view of the fact that the energy of a healer's aura will influence their healing abilities it is vitally important that anyone in the caring professions works at expanding their own consciousness before attempting to help others.

The Four Functions and the Bodies

The psychologist Carl Jung proposed four psychological functions which represented essential mental attitude ... sensing or perception, feeling, thinking and intuition.

These can be linked with the four elements: earth, water, air and fire respectively and with the four bodies as shown below:

> **SENSING eg. touch, taste, vision etc. ...**
> **PHYSICAL/ETHERIC BODY**
> **"I sense ..."**
> **FEELING eg. anger, joy, sadness etc. ...**
> **ASTRAL BODY**
> **"I feel ..."**
> **THINKING eg. analysis, logic ...**
> **MENTAL BODY**
> **"I think ..."**
> **INTUITION eg. unconditional knowing ...**
> **SOUL BODY**
> **"I know ..."**

Most people express themselves through one or two characteristic mental attitudes eg. feeling/sensing or intuition/thinking.

We should function within all four attitudes since the suppression of any one function may lead to its manifestation as disease in the physical body.

Exercises:

1) List three or four family mottoes which you can remember from your childhood;

For example:
> "Don't let the neighbours know."
> "The Devil makes work for idle hands."
> "Don't speak until you are spoken to."
> "Always wear clean underwear just in
>   case you have an accident!"

a) Are these still relevant in your life?
b) Have you passed these messages on to your children?
c) Are any of these no longer relevant?

We receive much sensible advice from our guardians but sometimes that which was relevant as a child is no longer needed. Fear is often the stumbling block. Decide to have the courage to move beyond the out-of-date belief system.

Many times we reject the advice given in childhood only to find ourselves repeating the same statements to our children.

Check to see whether your advice is warranted.

2) Listen to your own conversation:
How often are the words: "should, must, ought to, have to" used?
Ask yourself who is giving you the directions? Your higher self or the personality which may still be ruled by the past?

3) Look at the colours that surround you in your home and in the clothes that you wear.
What are they saying to those whom you meet?
Are you happy with this statement?
If not, maybe this is a time for change. Nothing rash, but moving in another direction.

4) Listen again to your conversation for the following phrases:
"I feel", "I think", "I sense" and "I know".
Which two do you tend to use when starting a conversation?

For example:
"I think" and "I sense":
As explained in the text, suppression of the other functions can lead to energy blocks which may manifest as physical disease.

Choose to express these latent functions by starting your sentences with "I feel" and "I know".

It is amazing to see the transformation in the content of a conversation just by altering the first few words.

Chapter 4

The Chakras

Within each of the six subtle bodies are found seven main centres of energy or "**chakras**" which are closely aligned in anatomic terms to the path of the older brain and the spinal cord.

The energy within the chakras moves in a spiral fashion much like that of a firework, the Catherine wheel.

The names of the major chakras and their positions are as follows:

CHAKRA:	POSITION
The CROWN:	TOP of the HEAD
The BROW (Third Eye):	FOREHEAD
The THROAT:	THROAT
The HEART:	CENTRAL CHEST
The SOLAR PLEXUS:	EPIGASTRIUM
The SACRAL:	LOWER ABDOMEN
The BASE:	COCCYX and SACRUM

There are many other more minor centres located, for example, behind the knees, in the hands and feet and around the ear lobes. These provide further sites through which a therapist can connect into the chakra system.

The position of the eighth chakra varies according to the text which is read. Some say that it is the energy centre located above the head which represents the link with the higher self and is often called the "starchild".

A chakra could also be seen as a multi-petalled flower with the central position being occupied by the energy of the soul containing its links with the higher self. From the centre outwards, the petals consist of the mental body, the astral body and the etheric body.

The more open the flower, and hence the chakra, the more in tune the individual is with the soul energy and the underlying spiritual attribute linked to that centre. The degree to which each chakra is open, and therefore active, is dependent upon the level of soul consciousness of the

THE CHAKRAS

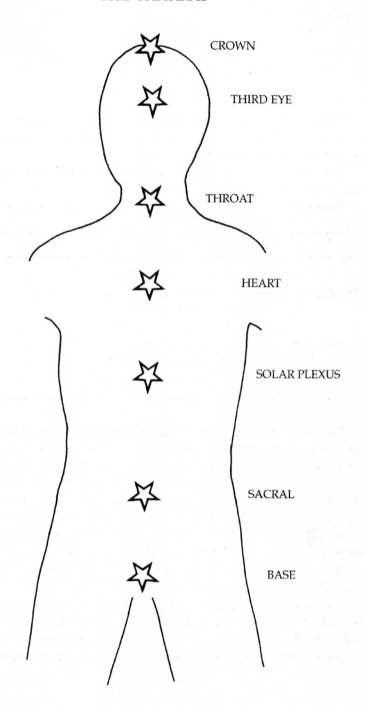

CROWN

THIRD EYE

THROAT

HEART

SOLAR PLEXUS

SACRAL

BASE

MENTAL BODY

SOUL
●
BODY

ASTRAL BODY

ETHERIC BODY

individual and of mankind as a whole. At present the greatest contribution of energy entering the chakras is from the astral and etheric bodies.

Until recently not all the chakras were active, with the majority of mankind working through the energies of the base, the sacral, the solar plexus and the throat centres, ie. those mainly below the diaphragm, while the crown and heart chakras were relatively inactive.

However, the advent of the Aquarian Age, bringing its own energies to our solar system, has led to changes in the consciousness of man through the activation of the heart and crown centres.

This has been expressed physically by an increase in the illnesses relating to the thymus gland which reflects the heart chakra. These include AIDS, allergies, cancer and auto-immune problems.

Schizophrenia, Parkinson's disease, S.A.D. (seasonal affective disorder) and depression are diseases related to the crown chakra and are now medically being allied to the hormones released by the pineal gland. (Illnesses often occur when changes are taking place.)

The illnesses have also prompted scientists to take more interest in these glands which until recently were considered to be relatively inert after puberty. Research now shows that several hormones are released from these glands well into adulthood.

The Passage of the Impulse through the Chakra

The energy entering each chakra from the different bodies intermingles until a combined force passes into the etheric body.

This body, consisting of its network of "fluid energies" or nadis, acts as the link between the energy emitted by the chakra and the physical body. Through it the brain and the autonomic nervous system are activated leading to the stimulation of the endocrine glands to produce hormones.

These hormones are then carried around the body, via the blood stream, to particular target sites where the impulse originating from the subtle bodies is manifest into action.

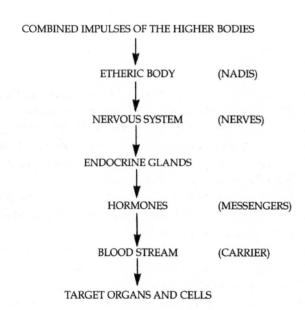

COMBINED IMPULSES OF THE HIGHER BODIES

↓

ETHERIC BODY   (NADIS)

↓

NERVOUS SYSTEM   (NERVES)

↓

ENDOCRINE GLANDS

↓

HORMONES   (MESSENGERS)

↓

BLOOD STREAM   (CARRIER)

↓

TARGET ORGANS AND CELLS

Each chakra is linked with a particular endocrine gland as shown overleaf:

ENDOCRINE GLANDS

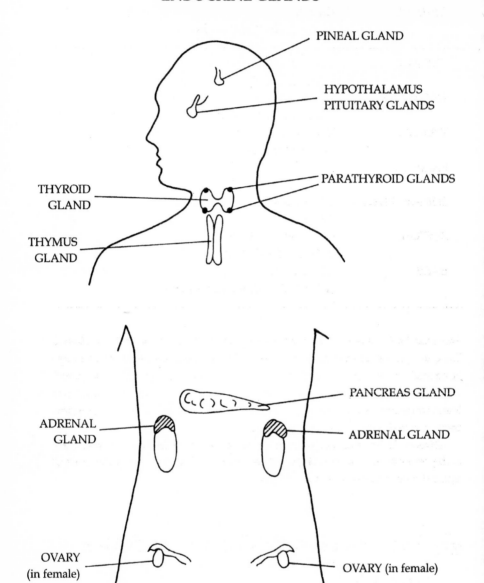

PINEAL GLAND

HYPOTHALAMUS
PITUITARY GLANDS

PARATHYROID GLANDS

THYROID
GLAND

THYMUS
GLAND

PANCREAS GLAND

ADRENAL
GLAND

ADRENAL GLAND

OVARY
(in female)

OVARY (in female)

TESTES (in male)

CHAKRA	GLAND (RELATED HORMONE)
CROWN	PINEAL (MELATONIN)
THIRD EYE	PITUITARY (STIMULATING HORMONES)
THROAT	THYROID (THYROXINE)
HEART	THYMUS (THYMOSIN)
SOLAR PLEXUS	PANCREAS (INSULIN)
SACRAL	OVARIES/TESTES (SEX HORMONES)
BASE	ADRENALS (CORTISONE/ADRENALINE)

The resultant effect of the hormones upon the individual is then relayed back, via the blood stream, to the originating glands. From here the message is passed through the nervous system and etheric body to be compared with the original impulse from the subtle bodies. This comparison then leads to neural and endocrine adjustments so as to bring about harmony between the impulse and the response.

Through this process, the function of the physical body at any one time is dependent upon the activity of the chakras which in turn is dependent upon the energies of the subtle bodies.

■ Spiritual Attributes and the Chakras

Each chakra also relates to a specific spiritual attribute which, when combined with the others, symbolises the aspirations of the total human being.

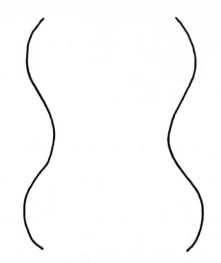

TWO POLES OF EXISTENCE

THE ATTRACTING POWER OF LOVE

UNITY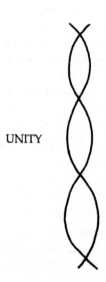

CHAKRA	ATTRIBUTE
CROWN	SELF-KNOWING
THIRD EYE	SELF-RESPONSIBILITY
THROAT	SELF-EXPRESSION
HEART	SELF-LOVE
SOLAR PLEXUS	SELF-WORTH
SACRAL	SELF-RESPECT
BASE	SELF-AWARENESS

The total expression of these seven soul attributes is achieved through the unification and harmonisation of the two poles of existence which surround the attribute. This is brought about by expressing, experiencing, recording, recognising and accepting the two poles of all situations.

The acceptance brings the opposites together in the name of "love" leading to unity.

For example:

In the case of the attribute of self-worth, I first need to experience times of worthlessness and then times when I feel very sure of myself or could be said to be egotistical or even selfish.

To take the first case:

Someone who has no self-worth or who cannot value themselves often takes on the role of the pleaser, always wanting to help others as this will give them an identity ... they have a need to be needed.

They demand praise even though this is initially in a fairly subtle manner: "Was that alright?" "Is it as you wanted?" "Do you like my ...?"

Unfortunately any amount of praise will not raise the level of self-worth unless the individual starts to believe in themselves.

After a while their constant need for reassurance, and their denial of the support offered, leads to a state of "self-centredness" which was the very thing they believed they could not achieve!

Conversely, the egotist who enjoys being the centre of attention often feels lacking in self-worth unless he commands his space in society. He may need to boost his confidence with a few drinks after which he becomes the life and soul of the party.

This example shows that, following the yin/yang principle, no state of being is static and each has the potential to transform into the other.

Indeed, according to the Law of Balance and Equilibrium, such a transformation must occur to prevent the existence of extreme states.

The ability to value oneself at the level of one's own inner being no longer relies on external identities.

Transformation of the Energies

The base, the sacral and the solar plexus chakras are related to the personality, while the heart, the throat and the crown chakras are related primarily to the soul. The third eye acts as the intermediary between the soul and the personality.

The personality is the vehicle for the soul's journey whilst it lives upon this earth. Therefore development of the lower three chakras is vital to ensure a full expression of the soul's energies.

The Divine Aspects

There are three main aspects required before there can be manifestation of an impulse: the will to act, the ability to create a plan, and the ability to attract the tools and materials required.

For example:
I think of making a cake ... **the impulse**

I have the will to proceed ... **the power of will**

I choose or design a recipe ... **the power of creativity**

I collect the ingredients ... **the power of attraction**

I make the cake ... **manifestation of the impulse**

The Will
The base chakra receives the will of the personality.
The crown chakra receives the will of the soul.

The Creativity
The sacral chakra receives and expresses the will of the personality.
The throat chakra receives and expresses the will of the soul.

The Attraction
The solar plexus attracts towards it that which is needed to satisfy the desires of the personality.

The heart attracts towards it that which is needed to satisfy the desires of the soul.

(The power of attraction is the power of love.)

As the soul becomes more deeply incarnate into the physical form, the lower three chakras receive their higher counterparts and the two energies, ie. that of the personality and the soul merge as shown below:

BASE CHAKRA ENERGY MOVES ...

INTO THE CROWN CHAKRA.

Awareness of self as part of life on earth transforms into Awareness or Knowledge of Self as part of the Universal Source of Creation. The will of the personality becomes that of the soul.

SACRAL CHAKRA ENERGY MOVES ...

INTO THE THROAT CHAKRA.

Creativity and its expression, moves from that of the personality to that of the total spiritual being, the inner Self.

SOLAR PLEXUS ENERGY MOVES ...

INTO THE HEART CHAKRA.

Desires of the lower self or personality, which are often conditional, transform into unconditional desires of the higher self.

The **THIRD EYE** acts as the sensory and activating force to guarantee the integration of the energy within all the chakras.

This can also be expressed in terms of two poles of existence becoming one. See diagram top p. 82.

In cellular terms, this integration is represented by the two strands of DNA (deoxyribonucleic acid) which constitute one chromosome. A

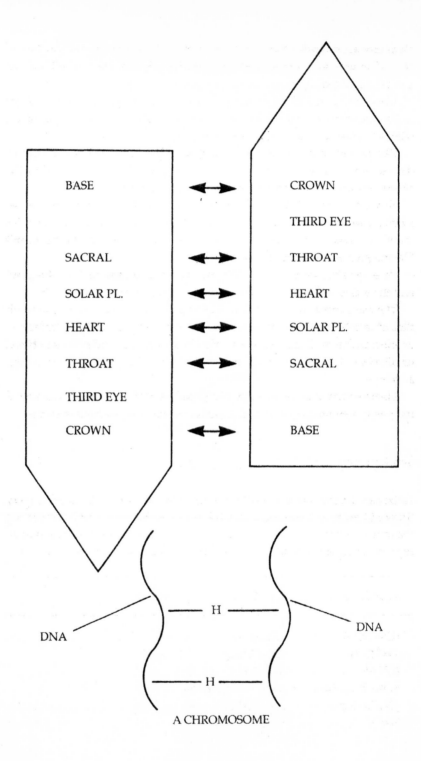

chromosome provides the basic blueprint for the structure and function of an individual and mirrors the spiritual design contained within the message of the chakras.

The connection between the strands, which in chakra terms symbolises unity, is seen in the physical body to be represented by the hydrogen atom, which has the atomic weight of one. See diagram (bottom) opposite.

The present increase in the understanding of the genetical causes of disease supports the concept that to correct the imbalances within the chromosomes, by physical means, will lead to perfect health.

However, we are still a long way from understanding the deeper mechanism which controls the function of genes. Esoterically, I believe this regulating force comes from the level of the chakras, and that these transmit the energies of the subtle bodies.

True genetical engineering therefore must include aspects of the mind and the spirit and until this happens deeper imbalances will remain.

The transformation phase, when the energy of one chakra merges with that of another, often creates a crisis point in the person's life leading to confusion, frustration and anxiety. This in turn may manifest as emotional or physical disharmony or disease, especially if there is resistance to such a change.

I believe that a more widespread awareness of these natural occurrences may well prevent the crisis point and ease the passage of the energies.

Polarity and the Chakras

Although the chakras contain the potential for unification between masculine and feminine qualities, they can be divided into those which represent the more masculine attributes, eg. outgoing and assertive, and those which represent the feminine attributes, eg. nurturing and receptive.

MASCULINE	FEMININE
(CROWN)	CROWN
THROAT	(THROAT)
(HEART)	HEART
SOLAR PLEXUS	(SOLAR PLEXUS)
(SACRAL)	SACRAL
BASE	(BASE)

As you can see (overleaf), the **Third Eye** is not included in this diagram as it directs the unification of the masculine and feminine energies.

I find that it is commonly the energy in the shadow side of the chakra which is blocked and needs to be released.

I also believe that the points at which the two energies cross will be found to be important areas for treatment.

In the physical body there are often strong links between those areas of the body which relate to the same polarity. Therefore, it is seen that the release of hormones from either the adrenal, the pancreas or the thyroid gland will influence the activity of the other two glands.

Similarly amongst the more receptive chakras. In animal studies on the pineal gland it is known that the hormones released from this gland have a strong influence upon the activity of the sex glands. In man, research is still proceeding to locate neurophysiological links between the pineal and other glands. There is no doubt however that information will be forthcoming, for endocrinology (the study of glands and their hormones) is an ever-expanding science.

Colours of the Chakras

The energy of each chakra vibrates at a different rate to the others. To a clairvoyant this energy is seen in terms of colour and the following guide shows the colours which relate to the particular chakra:

CHAKRA	COLOUR
CROWN	VIOLET
THIRD EYE	INDIGO
THROAT	BLUE
HEART	GREEN/PINK
SOLAR PLEXUS	YELLOW
SACRAL	ORANGE
BASE	RED

While the energy from the Astral and Etheric bodies is a dominant source of the energy entering the chakra, these colours will also be dominant. However, as the consciousness of the individual is expanded, incorporating the energies from the Higher Bodies, I believe that we will see a change in the colours presented at each centre.

Exercise

Find yourself a relaxing position in which to sit or lie, without the risk of falling asleep! Place a notebook and pencil nearby, so that you can record any feelings from the exercise.

Undo tight clothing, perhaps remove shoes and make sure that your neck and back are well supported.

Proceed through a relaxation technique moving from the feet through to the head, relaxing tense and stressed muscles and finishing with relaxing the breathing.

Next, symbolise an energy which represents your Higher Self above your head. Link with this energy and ask that you can be given the wisdom and understanding which will help you to become whole again.

Now, in turn, connect with the energy of each chakra starting with the base. Is there a picture, phrase, colour or feeling which represents this chakra?

When you are ready, make a note of your findings. Having done this, once again link with the Higher Self and then move up to the next chakra.

Continue in this way until you have reached the crown. Then linking with the Higher Self, bring down the energy of this force through the spine, through the feet and deep into the ground. As you do so, feel the ultimate peace and unconditional love which abounds from this source and allow it to enter every cell of your body.

In your own time, bring this energy up from the ground and down from above your head and place the love within your heart. Once again feel the peace and contentment. When you are ready, bring your aware-ness back to the room by taking a couple of deep breaths and moving your fingers and toes.

If you have a large sheet of paper and some crayons, it is now useful to draw your visualisations from the base to the crown. Using words often limits the concept and you do not receive all the information sent by the Higher Self.

When visualising the chakra, it may be that a different colour appears from the one which normally represents that centre. In this case it is the concept behind the colour which is important, ie. what does the colour mean to you?

You may well be able to analyse your own feelings and pictures but you may find the chapter covering the links between the chakras, the emotions and disease will enhance your understanding.

■ Affirmations and the Chakras

The following statements which relate to the individual chakras complete the cycle for spiritual growth:

CROWN: I am fully conscious of, and open to, the will of my higher mind.

THIRD EYE: I take full responsibility for my thoughts, words and actions.

THROAT: I am willing to express my true Self and hence fully participate in my own creation.

HEART: I love myself and others unconditionally, both in the giving and in the receiving.

SOLAR PLEXUS: I am worthy to live my life to the fullest, without fear or guilt, listening only to my own inner voice.

SACRAL: I respect my needs and the needs of others in any relationship and will act accordingly.

BASE: I am fully aware of my position on earth and know that my basic needs will always be met.

When the chakras are in harmony they resonate like a chord of music, the highest chakra of one body linking with the lowest chakra of the next.

Our total structure and function on this earth is dependent on the energy received and sent by the chakras. Linking this energy with psychological and endocrinological functions will, I believe, lead to a whole new branch of medicine, the beginning of which we are starting to see in the science of psychoneuroimmunology.

Chapter 5

The Meaning of Disease

If we accept that everything comes from the One Source, then disease itself must be part of the Greater Plan rather than a mishap which occurs along the way.

So what is the cause or, more appropriately, the purpose of disease? Is it as many believe a sign of failure or weakness? If that is the case, why do we say "Only the good die young". Does the fact that you are still here signify success or that there is unfinished business to be carried out upon the earth?

The more I study disease, the more I recognise the complexity of the subject. There is no one cause and each case must be taken on its merits. However, I believe that we are given clues to help us to unravel the mystery. Such clues come in the shape of the presenting signs and symptoms, the area affected, the pathological changes and in understanding the background history of the individual who is manifesting the disease.

Such a background must include cultural, religious and social beliefs whose roots pass deep within the structure of being even though on a conscious level they may have been discarded.

From a psychospiritual point of view, I have formulated the following statements which I believe encapsulate this aspect of the disease state.

1) Disease is just another manifestation of life representing a time for change and opportunities for soul growth. Conscious awareness of the experience can enhance the healing process as long as the consciousness does not remain purely in the head. Every cell of the body needs to become aware of the changes that are taking place and to release old patterns of behaviour.

(It is not necessary to re-experience these old patterns but only to acknowledge their existence.)

Changes will occur without conscious awareness and may be even more successful as they are then not hampered by the will of the personality!

2) In most cases dis-ease or disharmony appears in the mind before it appears in the body. We can choose to deal with it on the mental level or

we may need the physical evidence before we decide to act. Despite warnings, most people do not think that disease will manifest in them.

Physical illness also provides a legitimate reason for one's feelings of disharmony; in the eyes of many, mental distress represents malingering or weakness.

3) If the disharmony is not resolved within the mind, then physical disease appears representing one pole of existence held in an extreme state with the exclusion of the other pole. Such an imbalance can occur on any level and it often represents fear of entering the shadow or suppressed area rather than the desire to stay in the extreme state.

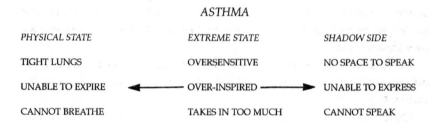

ASTHMA

PHYSICAL STATE	EXTREME STATE	SHADOW SIDE
TIGHT LUNGS	OVERSENSITIVE	NO SPACE TO SPEAK
UNABLE TO EXPIRE ⬅———	OVER-INSPIRED ———➡	UNABLE TO EXPRESS
CANNOT BREATHE	TAKES IN TOO MUCH	CANNOT SPEAK

The ultimate goal is to acknowledge and accept all parts of ourselves and with this to regain wholeness or health.

4) The signs and symptoms expressed by the body provide the message that something is amiss and direct the attention of the observer to this area of disharmony.

We can choose to ignore the message by "removing the bulb from the flashing red light" but in the end the messenger will be heard.

5) The message can be used to treat the physical cause alone or, if there is a deeper psychospiritual understanding, can be deciphered and used to treat the whole person.

6) Disease provides not only a message but also the means by which total harmony can be restored. This may be difficult to comprehend when considering diseases such as AIDS, cancer and multiple sclerosis, all of which are associated with a degree of suffering and a poor prognosis.

However, many people who are manifesting these diseases describe their illness as an experience which changed not only their body but also their view of life, in many cases, for the better.

However, if the question is changed to: "Do you ever feel irritated inside?" the answer is usually "Yes."

These suppressors are often the peacemakers; they avoid conflict where possible. They are the "listeners"; everybody tells them their problems .. but they rarely relate their own.

They may feel resentful but rarely complain as there is often now a fear of releasing their own anger in case they cannot control the problem.

In physical terms this anger becomes buried into the liver area and in acupuncture terms creates problems along the liver meridian.

In other cases crying may be suppressed as this was seen as a sign of weakness. The message was to "be strong" in a situation where the child had to learn at an early age to be independent and brave.

Crying, as with anger when used appropriately, is a natural release of energy ... both are part of the grieving process which enable the individual to "let go" of a situation which has been completed and to make room for new experiences.

Restrained tears appear in the physical body as excess fluid as in catarrh which drips down the back of the throat or in swellings of the extremities.

Others fear losing control of the situation through becoming too emotional. The emotions become the shadow which should be denied as long as possible.

But that which is not expressed externally will, through the Universal Law of Balance and Equilibrium, need to be expressed internally to restore harmony.

Therefore I see cases of skin rashes (unexpressed irritation), asthma (unexpressed speech), diarrhoea (unexpressed fear), fat intolerance (unexpressed anger) and many other conditions. These verify that so much of disease is only reflecting an underlying obstruction to the normal flow of life.

The soul will always attempt to find a method of relieving the system of excess energy either through the physical body or through external circumstances.

For example:

You hate your job. It is boring and this leads to frustration. You become irritated by those around you but do not have the courage to look for a new job.

Suddenly you are made redundant. You are angry with the company who employed you and then become depressed as the days at home drag into weeks.

The Message of Disease

A) You are late. You run to catch a bus, slip, fall and break your ankle. The physical diagnosis is a broken ankle and the treatment is to place the bones in a plaster cast.

The psychospiritual diagnosis is that you are always trying to fit too many things into too short a space of time and this time you "missed the bus!"

The deeper issue behind this diagnosis is that you only feel worthy when you are busy and hence the permanent running. You feel that you are wasting time if you sit down and that you are neglecting your responsibilities. Your self-worth is related to the degree of visible action.

The broken ankle requires you to rest, leaving two options open to you:

a) To use the time berating yourself for being so clumsy, being angry with the medical staff for diagnosing the fracture and to continue to walk on the ankle despite advice to the contrary.

b) To realise that you were careless but that this happened because you are so hard on yourself and never give yourself time to rest.

During the days at home you find that you can organise your day more constructively if you give yourself time to rest.

You learn that self-worth comes with valuing yourself for who you are and not for what you do.

B) Doris was 65 years old when she lost her husband. Despite a large and loving family she was desolate and now had no time for the grandchildren who previously occupied much of her life.

She started to complain of physical symptoms such as shortness of breath and bowel disturbances. But despite rigorous medical tests no physical cause was discovered for her symptoms.

Over Christmas her family became desperate and agreed that their mother should be admitted into a psychiatric unit. By this time she felt her world was black and could think of little else except her own problems.

One day she was coming back from occupational therapy when she saw herself in the mirror. "My goodness" she exclaimed, "What a miserable looking woman!"

From that moment on things changed and she was soon home again with her family.

One month later she had a massive heart attack and died.

I believe that she made peace with herself and was then ready and able to leave this life.

Many strive constantly to change their lives using extreme levels of willpower. However, change often creeps up on us without warning and when we are least expecting it. It can literally occur in seconds but may take a lifetime if we are unwilling to relinquish our hold on old ideas and emotions. The deathbed is the favourite place for making amends and for granting forgiveness, whether for others or for ourselves.

C) Joan came to see me complaining of pain, redness and swelling in the right knee. This was made worse by her daily trips to see her elderly father who lived in a village 10 miles away. Joan did not drive and therefore the journey was particularly arduous consisting of two bus rides and a long walk.

Her father was crippled with arthritis but refused any help from the social services. He relied on his daughter for everything and in the past six months had had several falls which had increased Joan's anxieties concerning his care.

Joan had two children plus a husband and found her days were so busy that there was little time for herself. She admitted that there were moments when she felt that she could not go on and even times when she resented her father for being so demanding. She realised that although her visits were full of good intentions, her resentment undermined her actions.

She resolved to try to persuade her father to accept some outside help and to reduce her visits thereby guaranteeing some respite for her painful knee.

At her next visit her knee was much improved and she told me that circumstances had overtaken her proposed plans; her father had fallen again which had necessitated a short stay in hospital. Following this he had been persuaded by the doctors to accept extra help and Joan now had more time for herself. (I am always amazed by the course of external events which support our decision for change.)

But, despite this good news, Joan looked downhearted. "What do you want to do now?" I asked.

"I have started many things in my life but always fail to finish them", she said. "I fear that I will fail again."

It then became clear that Joan's dedication to her father was not entirely altruistic. It provided a perfect excuse to avoid placing herself in situations where she may fail. She was now having to face her own fears without her father being there to protect her.

We talked about the setting of goals and how important it is to start with targets which are achievable. When I last saw her she had just finished a short course in creative writing and proudly presented her completed article.

When looking at the **message of disease**, redness and pain represent suppressed anger. In Joan's case this was initially towards her father and then towards herself at her own inability to change the pattern which existed.

The site of the redness, ie. the knee, represents humility which for Joan was excessive with a need to "rise from the position of kneeling" and to show more pride in her own self-worth.

The knee also provided an acceptable way out of a difficult situation when words may have given the impression of an uncaring attitude ... **the opportunity for change**.

If the deeper fear of failure had not been revealed then the painful knee could then have been used as an excuse for her inability to develop her own talents in the future ... **the secondary gain**.

Illness commonly masks a fear and may provide the means by which the individual can avoid facing or expressing that fear. Removing the symptoms without dealing with the emotion will inevitably lead to the emergence of further symptoms or lead to the failure of appropriate treatment to act.

In some cases it may be necessary to ask:

"Do you want to get better?" or "What would you do if the illness were no longer present?"

The fact that the patient consults a practitioner is not definite proof of the desire to return to full health. In some cases the ability to outwit a member of the medical profession, or to prove to their family that they really do have a problem, is satisfaction enough and is worth the suffering .. secondary gain.

When I see a patient referred through their relatives or friends and who appears poorly motivated I am not surprised to see that the results of my treatments are minimal.

Other patients whom I find respond poorly to help are those who claim poverty despite appearances and ask for discount on the consultation. It is sad to say that such poor monetary motivation often reflects poor motivation in their healing process.

I have found that in the case of private complementary medicine in the United Kingdom, those who have saved the money to afford the treatment and have been motivated to find a practitioner are often half way to a cure before they enter the consultation room. Motivation is the key to progress and although someone like Joan may be highly motivated in one area of their life, their "busyness" may be hiding a lack of movement in another area.

Here are further examples which I have met in my travels.

a) **A wife pulls a muscle in her back** and can no longer undertake the household chores. Her family rally round, relinquishing their hobbies at this time of family crisis.

As she recovers, they drift back to their other interests and she is alone. The following day she is flat on her back again.

This is a fairly common scenario when attention and love are sought through illness. It is often learnt at an early age when the child may feel neglected due to home circumstances and find that a minor ailment leads to the attention they seek.

With this information now stored sub-consciously, the pattern is repeated into adult life whenever insecurity or lack of love surface.

b) **A successful but stressed businessman is having problems sleeping** due to an overactive mind. He requests sleeping tablets from his doctor but is advised that he would do better to take a holiday and spend less time in the office.

He replies that he has far too many people relying on him and that the only thing that would slow him down would be a broken leg. The following week he falls down …

The internal drivers such as "try harder", "be strong", and "please me" are often so ingrained from childhood that it is difficult to break free and act on the guidance of one's own inner voice.

In this case, the businessman was unable to step off the treadmill voluntarily and circumstances had to take the upper hand. The period spent in bed would provide time to reflect on life and he would probably discover that in his absence others, unfortunately, coped very well!

Nothing happens by chance.

c) **A child with behavioural problems and asthma is brought to see the doctor.** She is a middle child, between two very verbal siblings. She tends to prefer to go off and play alone.

When the mother is asked about other stresses in the child's life she hints that her own relationship with her husband is not always harmonious and it becomes apparent that the child's bad behaviour is exacerbated at times of the parents' arguments.

Here, the child has become the scapegoat for the family's problems. Such an individual is common in many families … the butt of the jokes or the receiver of pity.

If the scapegoat decides to change their role, it threatens the basic structure of the family and therefore attempts will be made by the other members of the family to keep that individual in their designated position.

For example:

If the scapegoat is the plump child with nicknames such as "fatty" or "piggy" then everybody knows their place until that individual decides to go on a diet.

Initially there is encouragement until it becomes obvious that the status quo in the family is affected.

From then on everybody tries to persuade this new slim child to eat and tells him that he was much more attractive when he was fat!

If the scapegoat has the strength and the courage to hold on to their own self-worth then remarkable changes will occur within each member of the family until equilibrium is once again restored.

Such cases often benefit from family therapy where each member is given the time and space to express themselves as individuals and not just in the role which they have been given.

They can then start to understand each other's needs and work towards reaching an honest compromise which leads to harmony within the home.

d) **A mother has multiple sclerosis** and is practically bed-bound. Apart from symptomatic relief, nothing seems to halt the disease process.

As time passes, it becomes obvious that instead of her children becoming hampered by their mother's disease, they in fact grow and gain from the experience using the knowledge in their own lives in the years that follow.

Positive secondary gain of illness often stretches beyond the patient, affecting family and friends, those in the caring professions and even those who hear the story second-hand.

At the time, it is often difficult to see that any good could come out of illness and suffering, and the initial reaction of the observer is often anger and bitterness.

In the long term, however, such reactions create their own problems and do very little to alter the initial event. Eventually, conscious acceptance must occur in order to create space for forward movement.

Only in retrospect is it possible to see the wisdom and strength which occurs in those affected by the illness of a friend or relative.

e) **A man who owned a business** always found it difficult to receive help in any venture whether at home or at work. He believed that for a job to be done well, he had to be in total control of the situation. He became irritable and impatient towards those who were slow to understand simple instructions and who made mistakes.

One day at work he collapsed, paralysed down the right side of his body. He had suffered a stroke. His recovery was slow, hampered by his bitterness that his body had failed him.

He had to rely heavily on others for dressing, feeding, walking and even making himself understood through his affected speech.

He became frustrated by his dependence on his friends and family but was amazed by the tolerance shown by others towards him.

I commonly see strokes occurring in those who like to be in control and who tend to be great organisers but poor delegators. To give away such power is very threatening but the body's paralysis necessitates such a move. For this man, it took an illness to gain insight into his own character and, through this, was given the chance to allow others to share in his life in a more positive fashion.

f) **A woman was found to have terminal cancer.** She was hard working and often denied herself luxuries for the sake of her family which she had brought up single-handed following the death of her husband.

Unfortunately, her two sons had fallen out over a business deal and rarely made contact with each other.

When the woman was admitted to hospital the boys purposely avoided each other during visiting time. However, one day they found themselves on either side of their mother's bed and could no longer ignore the issue.

Their mother pleaded with them to talk to each other and because of their love for her they agreed to meet in order to discuss their differences and to see whether they could reach a compromise.

Their mother had never looked so happy.

That night she died peacefully in her sleep.

In this world no action occurs which does not have repercussions on other individuals. All our lives are intertwined and the ability to help others comes from the ability to change ourselves.

Until we are able to see death as a time of moving on into another plane of life, we will still hold the view that it is a time of loss and failure rather than that of growth. This woman had never asked for anything for herself until the evening of her death. Her ability to ask her sons to talk together for her sake was a great step forward and one which allowed her to move to another dimension of life through the door of death and rebirth.

The old adage that "The operation was successful but the patient died", should now be replaced by:

"The operation was successful **and** the patient died."

Psychology and spiritual understanding must, I believe, be part of any undergraduate medical or complementary therapy training for without it our treatments are barely scratching the surface.

The Signs and Symptoms as the Messenger

For a long time the signs and symptoms of disease have been seen as the enemy to be ignored or to be silenced at all costs instead of appreciating their deeper significance and the message that they bring.

An analogy

If the postman (messenger) brings a tax claim (the message) ignoring him or hoping that he will go away will not solve the problem.

He will eventually make his presence felt using his voice, his hands or even force.

You could shoot the postman but another messenger will be sent. Some people try to bring the postman into their home to make him part of their life ... but ultimately the problem, the tax claim, is still unresolved and unpaid!

The initial problem is to be able to interpret the message which is being expressed by the signs and symptoms of the body. I believe that this can only be achieved through the use of a "wide-angled lens" which encompasses all facets of the individual, including those seen and unseen.

On many occasions the clues are obvious if only we have the eyes to see, the ears to hear and the wisdom to understand.

1) The Spoken Word

I have found that the words which are used by a patient to express their social conditions at that time are often strongly linked with the physical symptoms.

For example:

The woman with a boil within the nasal passages:
   "My sister got up my nose."
The man complaining of an aching neck:
   "My partner is a pain in the neck."
The woman with a bout of shingles:
   "My mother gets on my nerves."
The wife with a burning rash around the neck:
   "I am so frustrated with my husband's actions but cannot tell him."

The mother with severe pain in the lower back:

"**I feel that I just cannot take on any more responsibility.**"

The girl with constant nausea:

"**I'm sick to death of my job.**"

The man with a painful abscess around the anal opening:

"**My boss is a pain in the backside!**"

In other cases the words which are used to express the symptoms may give guidelines to the underlying cause:

a) "**The rash is so irritating**" from the woman who has become irritated by the fact that nobody carries out her housework exactly to her specifications.

b) "**My hips are stiff so that I find it difficult to move in the morning**" from the man who is now retired and feels that he no longer has an identity in society. Physical immobility often represents mental immobility and the fear of moving forward.

c) "**I am so constipated that I may only go to the toilet once a week!**" This woman denies any other problems and likes to appear totally in control. She rarely expresses an emotion or a motion!

d) "**My dizziness causes me to be totally unbalanced and I have to lie down**" from a man who lives with an anxious wife, three active teenage children and a neurotic dog.

e) "**I hate myself for the fact that all I seem to want to do is to eat chocolate**" from the girl whose husband has just walked off with her best friend.

In each of the cases cited above it can be seen that the physical body is being used to balance an extreme state which is present on other levels, ie. within the astral, etheric or mental bodies in accordance with the Law of Balance and Equilibrium.

Seen in this way:

a) The woman with the rash is extremely fastidious and likes to see that everything is neat and tidy. The rash represents that part of her which is imperfect and this in her eyes is extremely irritating.

b) This man is feeling insecure and frightened now that he has no specific role in life. Such feelings of being out of control internally have caused him to become immobile externally.

c) This woman has a fear of letting go and of perhaps becoming vulnerable, which causes her to hold on to everything very tightly.

d) This man's external life is so hectic that the dizziness allows him to find peace and quiet within his bed.

e) This girl feels unloved and unlovable and tries to nurture herself with chocolate.

Although all the conditions given above can be relieved through orthodox treatment, I believe that the relief of symptoms would be more permanent if it included guidance in psychospiritual awareness.

Many forms of complementary medicine do in fact look at the whole person in their diagnosis and treatment and can achieve long-term relief of symptoms without the patient becoming consciously aware of the deeper issues.

However, I have found in my own experience that patients not only respond faster to treatment when their condition is discussed with them but also welcome this discussion so that they can take some responsibility for their own healing process.

I have also found that such awareness leads to the patient recognising the warning signs of future disharmony at an earlier stage and that they can then act accordingly to stop the disharmony manifesting as disease.

2) Body Language ... The Visual Message

Throughout the day our eyes register a variety of images, many of which are lost if the image cannot form a useful connection within the brain. Over the years as a doctor, I have learnt to use my eyes, both my physical and my third eye, more and more, not only to study the presenting sign of illness but also to observe the individual sitting before me.

These new images allow me to see the whole person and to treat accordingly.

Many books have been written on the subject of body language and I will only give a few guidelines at present. Much of this information links with my understanding concerning the chakras and will be expanded upon in later chapters.

Examples

a) **A young teacher crosses her arms over her solar plexus (across the waist)** when talking about the stresses involved with her work and the way that she is affected by the plight of some of the children.

The solar plexus is the area through which we receive information concerning our environment especially on an emotional level. Some people who are very sensitive to the world act like sponges, attracting all manner of emotions from their surroundings until they are totally overwhelmed.

Subconsciously they protect themselves using their arms as a guard against unwanted energies.

b) **A child is deserted by his friends in the playground because he refuses to play their games. He stands with his arms tightly held over his chest and looks sullen.**

The heart within the chest is the area where hurt is registered. To nurture a broken heart or to prevent further damage we once again use the arms as a form of defence.

c) **A nervous interviewee carefully winds her legs around each other in order to feel more secure.**

In this way, the girl protects a part of herself which is often seen to be vulnerable especially among women. A man who sits with his legs wide apart is saying that he is secure in himself and challenges others to come close.

d) **A nervous young boy answers his teacher with his hand partially obscuring his mouth.**

It is almost as if the boy is afraid to let others hear his answer and reflects his lack of confidence concerning his own abilities.

e) **The furrowed brow of a businessman warns others to approach only at their peril!**

Non-verbal communication is a very efficient and speedy method of making yourself understood. We are all able to communicate in this manner receiving instruction at a very early age. This is confirmed by watching a baby smile back at its smiling parent and then become solemn when the smile is replaced by a frown.

It is now clear that most babies receive messages from their mother in utero and the essence of this message, at such an important time of development, can shape the life of that individual.

It is no longer appropriate to say:

"Out of sight, out of mind."

f) **The watery eyes of the woman telling you about the death of her husband, shows that the grieving process is incomplete.**

Our actions often belie our words which makes face-to-face contact invaluable to the practitioner. Such a non-verbal signal needs to be explored, carefully and with the full co-operation of the patient.

g) **The foot of a man jerks as the practitioner asks him to speak about his marriage.**

Such movements are usually involuntary and it appears that the subconscious is now joining in the conversation.

h) **A boy clenches his hands together until the knuckles appear white as he talks about his anger towards his father.**

The boy's hands are acting out a subconscious scene where their combined strength would be sufficient to strangle the father. Thankfully his conscious mind prevents such an action but nobody is left in any doubt as to the depth of his feelings.

All these signs give important clues to those who can see and can combine what they see with wisdom. It is not the place of the practitioner to overstep the boundaries set by the patient in his enthusiasm to promote his own ego.

It is easy to offend people by innocently commenting on their words and actions. They may then feel vulnerable and even judged and may refuse to co-operate with further questions. It is also wise to take all the evidence into account before making a decision as to the possible cause of the problem.

Man is a complex animal and over many years learns to apply one layer of behaviour on top of another until his appearance is similar to that of an onion! In view of this, we should all strive to find the inner core of the problem and not be tricked by the outer covering.

The following chapters reveal other ways in which the message can be deciphered, through the pathological signs and through an understanding of the chakras.

Chapter 6

Disease Through the Chakras

Each chakra is related to the adjacent area of the physical body with a few exceptions which will be discussed below.

When disharmony occurs, it usually affects a number of centres but it is common to find that one centre is predominantly involved, with the bulk of the signs and symptoms being found in this area. Following the balancing of this centre, the others may be sent out of balance and require tuning to the new vibration.

In today's world much disease relates to the lower chakras which highlights the problems facing the individual of retaining a true sense of spiritual identity whilst maintaining an acceptable position in society.

As has been stated earlier, many problems of spiritual man are still focused in the astral body and expressed as physical disease. Therefore the chakras are described in terms of their spiritual and emotional qualities and the way in which the latter can be transformed into a new level of awareness.

7 Chapter

The Base Chakra

■The Base Chakra

Position:	Base of Spine
Spirtual Aspect:	Self-Awareness as a Human Being
Basic Need:	Security, Confidence
Related Emotions:	Fear and Courage
Endocrine Gland:	Adrenal (Cortisone)
Associated Organs:	Kidneys, Bladder, Rectum, Vertebral Column, Hips
Colour:	Red

Spiritual Aspect ... Self-Awareness as Human Beings

From the moment we are born, our soul's intention is to project the impulses of our spirit down the spine until our soul (sole) reaches the ground and we can stand firmly in our own power. As spirit and matter merge at the base chakra, we are committed to living wholly (holy) on this planet and to express all that we are: to reflect our "will to be".

Such union allows us to appreciate the joy of being held between our sacred Father and Mother bringing with it a deep sense of **purpose, security** and **acknowledgement of one's participation in the Greater Plan;** of becoming, at last, a **human be-ing.**

Then the fun starts, for sitting at the base of the spine is the celebrated **serpent,** the **kundalini,** waiting for our spirit to activate its powerful, intrinsic energy. Encouraged by the soul's longing to experience life to its fullest, the snake begins to unwind, moving in a spiralling fashion between different poles of existence (masculine and feminine, good and bad etc.), allowing us to honour and absorb the energies of duality. At each turn of the spiral, pure light is generated, revealing the true extent of our light or subtle bodies.

When the serpent (the agent of transformation) reaches the crown chakra, self-realisation occurs, the crown and base now united by two passages of energy; one conducting spirit into matter and the other, by its passage through life, revealing the beauty of that manifestation. The finale provides the twist in the tail, for the ultimate goal is to release one's attachment to this state of realisation and during the sacred marriage between soul and spirit, allow a third force to emerge, bringing total enlightenment.

However, the journey to the base chakra and beyond is not without its problems; remember all the obstacles you've met on your path to self-realisation. This is not the legacy of one generation but follows centuries of teaching and conditioning which reflect that, as a race we've forgotten our prime purpose and have become so isolated from each other that competition is now valued far more highly than co-operation.

Indeed, drawing our energy down to the base chakra is like attempting to land a plane in unknown territory, searching for somewhere that can accept our presence whilst also providing us with a firm and secure ground on which to rest.

Not only do we have to deal with potential hostile environments such as mountains, rocks, trees and lakes but then we have to meet the natives who are not always friendly towards newcomers. They have their own set of rules and regulations built into cultural, moral and religious mandates which provide the family, society or tribe with structure and order which should, in theory, ultimately lead to security and harmony for all involved. Anybody wishing to join the clan needs to agree to honour and accept the conditions or be prepared to leave.

In a group, where the core is strong and confident, the special qualities of each individual can be nurtured and respected, for communal wisdom shows that all will benefit in the end. Here, guidelines are produced to support the creative essence of life. The members are allowed to contribute to the pool of consciousness through their individual thoughts, words and actions while the group's energy transforms naturally, without losing the strength from within its centre.

But where the leaders of the tribe or family are insecure and hence fearful, they draw around them those who are more insecure and vulnerable, keeping them in their place through criticism, restriction and control. They offer little room for manoeuvre demanding strict adherence to their rules leading to a false sense of security.

The reason such situations continue is that one of the greatest human fears is "not to belong", also expressed as a fear of being "rejected", "abandoned" or "isolated". And the cause for this conditioning? We have forgotten our true connections and that this Earth is as much part of our spiritual home as any other planet or plane of existence; in essence, it's impossible not to belong for, like it or not, we are all indelibly linked.

However, due to our tribal amnesia, we have cultivated other reasons for this fear. For instance, some believe that our initial banishment from the Garden of Eden left a permanent scar on our psyche whilst others feel that the deep sense of rejection stems from our expulsion from the comfort of the womb or from a place of peace and love outside this incarnation.

Whatever the cause, we have all experienced disconnection during our many lives, forcing us to seek evidence of our existence in the outside world because we couldn't find the way home to the core of our being. And what forms this core? Our essential spirit, a loving remembrance of who we are, an acceptance of our chosen path and a willingness to release our attachments to those things which fail to resonate with the truth as it exists at this moment.

So as we search for our place on Earth, we sink our roots into anything that will provide us with a sense of belonging and security which is as close as possible to our ideal at that time. Through attachment to work, material possessions, identities and other people and control over as much of our life as possible, we build a relatively safe basis for our existence.

And then in theory, as the spirit begins to move through us, we should naturally adjust our circumstances to meet the needs of the soul. However, if we have lost sight of our purpose and have little connection to the core, it's easy to cling onto old redundant sources of assurance most of which revolve around deeply engrained belief systems energised by fear.

Whilst acute fear is healthy and helps to maintain a positive status quo in our life, chronic fear has a paralysing effect on our psyche, creating bubbles of illusion which can hold us spell-bound for years on end. Remember the acronym for FEAR is:

False Expectations of an Altered Reality, where the truth is obscured from view.

What would you not want to lose for fearing of being out of control?
What would make you feel insecure if it was no longer in your life?
(money, job, freedom, family, your mind, health, an ability to be independent, partner?)

If our sense of security and control is based on our **attachment** to one of the above which we subconsciously fear losing, we will inevitably be challenged to loosen our hold and will never receive the pleasure of being with these "items" for we will always be awaiting their loss.

So as the urge from spirit intensifies, encouraging us to let go, trust and move towards our core, it's easy to expend enormous amounts of energy in the belief that we can remain still amongst the waves of change, imitating the ducks who paddle their feet frantically so as to stay in exactly the same position on the river. Even when the green lights are on "GO", we attract new reasons to stay. Such as:

Fear of Failure or Inadequacy

"If I fail, nobody will want me." Remember the child who was always last to be selected for team games due to their poor track record. In the end, the individual avoids situations where they could risk failure inventing one excuse after another to perpetuate the fear. Interesting, psychological studies have shown that those who fear **heights** usually fear failure. Could this be linked to the initial **fall from grace**?

Fear of failure also prevents us from **living in the moment** driven by the perceived failures of the past and anxious about the future. You can see these individuals going to work with their head out front and their buttocks still worrying about what they've left at home. The gift of a balanced base chakra is to be able to live comfortably in the present, knowing that the past is over and the future is still in the making, totally dependent on the thoughts of the moment.

Fear of Success

"If I succeed, I won't fit in anymore." What a strange world we inhabit where success is highly prized but those who achieve it often find themselves ostracised. Success can also bring the added burden of other people's expectations which produces another factor, the fear of failure.

Fear of Imperfection, of "Not Being Good Enough"

"When I'm perfect everything will be fine." Of course, that moment doesn't exist in the future but is present here now without having to change one iota of life; everything is perfect in a strange, imperfect manner.

However, the perfectionist persists in trying to control his/her world through statements such as: "There's a place for everything and everything in its place" which is not conducive to spontaneous, intimate relationships and they often find themselves in the very place they fear, alone. One typical story was of a woman who, when the party she was hosting was at full swing, decided to vacuum the floor. She commented: "It will save time later and I just can't bear mess"; the guests left soon after. To set the record straight there are also extremely untidy perfectionists whose outer world appears chaotic but who maintain a tight control on their emotions, letting few people into their private space.

Perfectionists are never still, driven by the need to finish just one more task and convinced that "If a job's worth doing, its worth doing yourself!" Due to their own insecurity, they use criticism as a means of keeping others in their place:

"The dress is lovely, shame you didn't lose those extra pounds." (A two-faced compliment.)

"This house is much nicer than the one you had before." (A comparison used to conceal the underlying censure.)

The aim of any criticism at the base chakra is to pull the rug from underneath the feet of the victim so they never feel more secure than the perpetrator of the act. However, perfectionists are also very hard on themselves keeping a large stick by their side so they can "beat up on themselves" when anything goes wrong. If they do accept the need to change (and it's a brave person who suggests it) gentleness, love and the ability to make mistakes, all ease the tension bringing lightness and laughter back into their life. Indeed, the loneliness is often the trigger which initiates change when a choice is required between "being best" and "being intimate".

Fear of Not Being in Control

"I hate it when I can't cope or when I'm faced with an unknown situation." These individuals usually believe that only when they're strong and in control will they be accepted by the tribe which unfortunately is often true: "It's not like you not to be strong, pull yourself together."

Unfortunately, if you control yourself, you tend to control others by setting strict rules of engagement often related to time and space. For instance, there are those who always arrive at least 30 minutes late to any occasion with a wonderfully contrived excuse usually involving a car, a cat and a piece of string! If you're insecure, you'll be generous with your allowances even if it means letting others down; if you're wise you'll start the meal without them.

Then there are those who arrive prematurely where control is attained by appearing at times of maximum inconvenience: "Sorry, am I too early?" True inner strength will guide your answer. Finally, other controllers have strict rules as to the space you're allowed to occupy, or exhibit patterns of behaviour which can be very difficult to follow if you're new on the scene.

Fear of Vulnerability

"I would hate for people to see me as I truly am, to see the worse of my character." The fear of loss of control often protects a underlying fear of being vulnerable or naked in front of others. What is strange is that we always imagine that:

a) people don't already know the darker aspects of our nature and love us more for it

b) that there is only bad at the core of our being when it is usually the richness we hide.

Adam and Eve's desire to cover themselves in the sight of God reveals the level of separation which had taken place even at that early stage of our evolution. I believe that true security only occurs when we are willing and able to be "naked" without the need to hide behind limiting identities.

Fear of Our Own Power

This last fear is common but often goes unspoken. Do you have an inner knowledge of immense power but are fearful to express it? And what is your fear? Is it the expectations that may follow, the changes that would be required, the need to handle such power wisely or the fact that if you were to accept such energy, there would be no excuse for not expressing your soul's purpose.

In the right environment, we receive encouragement, support and guidance from those who have found their own will-to-be and can happily share in our endeavours. This is beautifully illustrated by a teaching from

Inca tradition where the victor of any race is duty bound to instruct those he defeats until they are able stand as his equal. Imagine the changing face of education and business if we were able to follow such an example.

Security comes from knowing who you are on a deep level, loving yourself whatever happens, being flexible and yet discriminating in your choice of companions and realising that perhaps there is nothing you have to change about yourself except to enjoy the present.

Body Language

As every chakra represents a different psychospiritual aspect, each has its own body language to reflect an imbalance of energy. For the base chakra, where insecurity and defensiveness are common, these include:

a) The need to tightly cross one's legs when sitting, protecting the base.

b) The desire to wind one leg around the other when standing; an acrobatic feat.

c) Sitting sidewards on a chair whilst the top of the body faces forward; very defensive.

d) Constant fidgeting as if the individual isn't comfortable with their place on Earth.

e) The desire to curl one's feet underneath the body when sitting rather than placing the feet firmly on the ground.

f) The presence of excess fat over the buttocks and thighs often depicts insecurity with poor roots, with the added weight acting as ballast to keep the person earthbound.

It is worth remembering that by consciously changing our body language, our personal beliefs also transform.

Associated Illnesses

As you will notice, the number of illnesses described under each chakra diminishes from base to crown reflecting the high degree of pressure, stress and insecurity most human beings are feeling at this time.

1) Constipation
Constipation relates to issues of control which are revealed in the following ways. First, is the person who believes they can control their bodily

functions, like King Canute attempting to control the Seas. They become so focused on the external goal that they fail to recognise signs of strain in the more personal areas of their life such as their physical body and relationships. Eventually, the wheels of their existence become choked, stopping them in their tracks and forcing them to give priority to their basic needs.

The second group are masters of control over their emotions or "motions" (or so they like to think). They strive to appear cool, calm and collected never allowing others to see the irrational side of their nature, their feelings. Often perfectionists, they prefer everything to be clean and tidy with nothing to "disturb the peace". However, the outcome of such a situation often results in the very thing they fear, diarrhoea, pain and the passage of large amounts of embarrassing wind!

Such control can emerge from a childhood where there was criticism or poor communication and where the child learnt to hold onto their emotions and not to speak their mind. Unfortunately, such containment usually results in someone who retains memories of events years later, often down to the very last detail, holding onto unexpressed hurts, grievances and tears.

Diverticular disease is usually a consequence of chronic constipation and is caused by stagnant faeces creating small inelastic pockets in the colon which later become the seat of infection, spasm and pain. Many of the features described above in connection to constipation are seen in this disease especially the desire to control and retain old grievances.

The message of both of these illnesses is to learn to express, accept, forgive and move on.

2) Piles

Piles are blood vessels which become distended during straining and are then not given time to empty at the end of defaecation and time is the key word in the life of those with piles ... there is never enough time. Whether it is the busy mother with the constant demands of a family or the high-powered executive with unrealistic deadlines to meet, both experience the basic and little-spoken about problem called piles.

Time and space for the essential aspects of the self are vitally important, for in the end, I can guarantee the body will always have the last word!

3) Ulcerative Colitis

This inflammatory bowel disease is common in those between 20–40 years of age and leads to copious bloody diarrhoea with a stool passed as many as 12 times a day, leading to weakness, anaemia, chronic pain and disruption to a normal daily life.

There are many theories as to its cause and probably in the end the causative factors will include stress, over-sensitivity to certain foods, a viral infection and an auto-immune tendency (see heart chakra).

From a psychological point of view, my experience is that these individuals are sensitive with a highly developed intuitive and creative side to their nature (even though this may not have been given the space to be expressed). They are often perfectionists with a fear of failure and of criticism although they are commonly their most demanding task masters. Their family background usually reveals high ideals and strict controls which commonly lead to a deep-seated resentment towards those who activated the initial driving force.

David had experienced ulcerative colitis for 10 years and was on heavy doses of steroids in an attempt to control the disease although now he was suffering from osteoporosis, one of the side effects of these drugs and his hip bones were crumbling.

His childhood background had failed to provide him with an adequate level of confidence and he found work and relating very difficult. During the consultation, I asked him whether something positive had emerged from the disease and despite the puzzled look on his face, he replied: "Funny, for all the years I've visited therapists and doctors, nobody has ever asked me that question. Now I think about it, if I didn't have colitis I would have to go back to work and risk the pain of failure and isolation again. The illness allows me to pay people (the therapists) to be nice to me!"

This desire to "run away" is a common theme in colitis with the various trips to the toilet acting out the unconscious longing. David's crumbling hips will soon stop him running but unless he chooses to look at the deeper issues behind his disease, will only give him further reason to avoid his fears. These individuals need the space to express their anger and their fears and then have the courage to step beyond their own limited controls and take responsibility for creating a life they choose.

4) Diarrhoea

Simple diarrhoea, apart from that associated with food poisoning, is often linked to anxiety. As discussed previously, the individual may be someone who appears in control on the surface but is terrified inside, overly concerned about their performance and the opinions of others.

Through developing strength to stand their ground, imagining deep roots pulling their feet towards the centre of the Earth and remembering that those who cause the anxiety, such as examiners, audiences etc. are also human, life becomes fun.

5) Crohn's Disease

This inflammatory bowel disease also affects those within the age group of 20-40 but can involve any part of the bowel from mouth to anus. It's a particularly aggressive disease producing pain, bleeding, diarrhoea, malabsorption and passages (fistulae) between one organ and the next. The cause is unknown but like colitis will probably be associated with a variety of factors including food allergies and an imbalance of the immune system.

Psychospiritually, these individuals are perfectionists, fastidious (especially about cleanliness), goal orientated and determined to "get it right"! Fear is less of an issue than in colitis, replaced by a self-sacrificing nature, where love and nurturing are denied in deference to high ideals.

A young woman with Crohn's disease would sit demurely in my office whilst her mother discussed her daughter's illness as if we were talking about a household appliance which was broken; there was little sign of love and affection. One day, the mother was late for the appointment which gave me the opportunity to talk to the daughter alone. My passing enquiry about their relationship led to a tirade of anger from the daughter which must have lasted over 20 minutes: "I hate my mother; she shows no feeling and demands so much" etc.

The release of anger, a loosening of the controls she placed upon herself and the chance to go and travel the world with her boyfriend (disapproved of by the mother), saw the end of the disease which never returned. Only when we recognise that perfection is not something in the future but is present now and that "everything is perfect just as it is", do we start to enjoy the moment and appreciate the loving strength which is awaiting for us, if we only let it in.

6) Appendicitis

Infection and inflammation of the appendix can occur at any age but is more common around puberty or at other times of change. The appendix sits between the small bowel which absorbs and the large bowel which rejects and I believe the change from one state to another is significant in the aetiology of this disease. Psychospiritually, appendicitis reflects the pain of change and loss often linked to deep feelings of helplessness and anger which go unexpressed. I also suspect that the individual may see themselves as an "appendage" or "outsider" either in their family or amongst their peers, which intensifies the pain.

As the situation is acute, surgery is the treatment of choice but it would be wise to counsel the individual to help release any unexpressed feelings especially those associated with isolation.

7) Hypertension

A blood pressure reading is the pressure exerted by the circulating blood on the walls of the blood vessels. Medically, we are interested in two readings. The first, the highest, reflects the blood leaving the heart during its contraction phase (systole) and is raised when we are active or stressed. The second, however, is more important and relates to the period of heart relaxation (diastole). If this reading is raised above the normal level of 80 mm of mercury, especially 95 and above, hypertension is diagnosed and we recognise that both the heart and the individual have difficulty relaxing, even at times of rest.

You probably know someone like this; they claim to be really laid back whilst their inner observer is on constant high alert. And what do they fear? They fear being found out, being out of control, of the façade slipping or not being good enough in the eyes of those that matter.

Hypertension is a "secretive" disease with almost no symptoms, creeping up on the individual insidiously or exploding into their life in the form of a stroke. And as the outer world reflects the inner, I see time and again that those with hypertension possess a secret. Whether it concerns the hidden truth of their nature which no-one must see, a secret from the past which remains unresolved or even a clandestine love affair which, despite the excitement, leaves one exhausted, the tension builds up.

In the end, the need to protect the secret places so much pressure on the individual that release becomes essential. Any creative expression, such as dancing, singing, writing will ease the strain and, eventually, the ability to relax adequately and be oneself will be reflected in the blood pressure reading.

8) Cerebrovascular Accident (CVA): Stroke

The commonest causes of this illness are either an embolus or a bleed, the latter often occurring as a result of untreated hypertension. Both are sudden and will affect different parts of the body depending on the area of the brain involved. Psychospiritually, the episode is commonly seen in those with a controlling personality, affecting either their own emotions or other people and presents the individual with varying degrees of loss of control, both physically and emotionally.

The resultant disability, if there is one, challenges the individual to learn to let others into his/her life, become more flexible and less demanding of themselves and those around them. Some people are unable to accept their situation and remain angry and bitter towards the body which has failed them and, unfortunately, towards their carers who still have the use of a healthy body.

Strokes that last less than 24 hours are called **transient ischaemic attacks** and are a warning to the individual to slow down and relax their control on the beautiful flow of life.

9) Nose Bleeds (Epistaxis)

A common cause of this condition in adults is hypertension where the excess pressure seeks an outlet through the fragile blood vessels of the nose. Treating the hypertension is the obvious answer whilst finding ways to reduce the stress which has accumulated within the individual. Learning to relax, reduce the controls placed on life generally, plus following the tips given above (see hypertension), can certainly diminish the incidence of these attacks.

In children, there are other causes of epistaxis such as an infection or allergy (see heart chakra) but it's also important to review the level of stress which the child may be experiencing but not expressing, remembering that play and speaking out when necessary help to reduce the pressure held within.

10) Hypotension

In this situation, the blood pressure is low with a diastolic reading below 60 mm mercury. Since blood signifies our life force, low pressure suggests someone who is failing to apply their full life's energy onto this Earth. As an illness which usually goes untreated, these individuals often complain of cold hands and feet and of feeling dizzy when they stand suddenly.

Psychospiritually, they appear to hover above the world often criticising its "imperfections" and claiming that they will join the rest of us when everything is beauty and light. This approach usually follows early personal experiences of "not feeling good enough", of criticism or control where escape from such attacks came from living in a fantasy world, avoiding connection at all costs.

Unfortunately, although providing a sanctuary from pain, the human soul cannot survive and grow in this rarefied atmosphere. Therefore healing comes from choosing to stay on this planet, avoiding meditation which allows one to float out of the body, walking barefoot on the grass and imagining roots developing from the soles of the feet which draw you into the earth. It also helps to find friends who are non-judgemental which include animals and nature and ask for strength to manifest one's own wonderful soul essence so as to make the world a better place.

11) Cold Hands and Feet

When an individual feels threatened they instinctively withdraw into a "shell" taking their blood supply from the extremities to the organs which will allow them to **fight or flee**. Once the danger is over, the blood should return to all parts of the body as relaxation takes place.

However, those who see the world as a place where people can't be trusted, never feel secure and maintain these defences leading eventually to permanently cold hands and feet and the possibility of developing the condition called **Raynaud's disease**. This auto-immune illness brings with it the added dimension of low self-esteem and the need to please others (see heart chakra).

Learning to relax, dance, laugh and trust the world and those in it, helps us to flow with life's experiences and not be constantly on guard from fear of failure or humiliation. Life is for living and the more present we are within it, the stronger we feel.

12) Frequency of Micturition (passing water too often)

The bladder of these naturally overactive people reflects their permanent need to be "on the go". They are unable to do one job at a time and even if their body is at rest, their mind is actively engaged in a myriad of worries and plans, ensuring they are never out of control.

Since their life is already stressed and rarely empty, any extra pressure sends them into panic mode. In a similar way, their bladder quickly becomes full and they have to run to the toilet. Such is their desire to stay in control that these people have usually ascertained the location of every toilet facility en-route long before their journey begins.

Their basic insecurity, especially in new surroundings, is threatened by being asked to stay in other people's homes or by the thought of a long journey, so they use their recurrent need for toilet stops as an acceptable excuse for staying within the comfort of their own environment.

13) Cystitis

This inflammatory condition of the bladder is characterised by painful frequency of micturition. Emotionally, there is classical fear and anger. "I'm so frustrated by my boss at work but I'm afraid to leave in case I can't find another job." There is a tendency to hold onto old grievances and regrets rather than go with the flow.

Healing often occurs when the individual takes responsibility for their future happiness and moves towards something which brings soul satisfaction and away from limitation and frustration. On many occasions decisions are forced through redundancy or separation although my advice is that it's far easier to make the moves under one's own steam!

14) Bed Wetting (Enuresis)

This problem, often familial, is more common than is discussed in public with one in 10 of all 10 year olds and one in 20 of all 20 year olds in the UK, passing urine in their sleep on a fairly regular basis. Apart from treating structural and infective problems, psychotherapy for both the child and parents has already proved to be successful in reducing the incidence.

There seem to be two psychological issues involved. One is that the individual is often a very deep sleeper, difficult to rouse at the best of times. Various methods have been used over the years to awaken the child but a better understanding of sleep states would enhance the treatment potential. The other factor to be explored is that wetting the bed is seen as the child's way of exerting their power when they feel helpless and impotent during the hours of waking.

This may well be true, as my experience is of meeting individuals who are either shy and insecure purely due to their personality or have become withdrawn through the presence of oppressive control often in the form of sexual or emotional abuse. It is therefore important to obtain a clear picture of life at home and deal with the problems where appropriate and then to make it clear that this is not a condition to be punished but rather a state which usually recedes when the child or adult begins to stay away from home for longer periods of time.

15) Incontinence

The involuntary loss of urine can be very embarrassing and again affects large numbers of people who never speak of their problem. **Urge incontinence** is related to a weak bladder neck and is often associated with frequency of micturition with the problems of insecurity as described above. **Stress incontinence** affects many women after childbirth where the pelvic floor loses its strength and with it goes bladder control, especially when the muscles are stressed such as during jumping, sneezing or coughing.

Apart from medical and surgical interventions, psychospiritual factors must be addressed, as there is a tendency for the individual to rely upon their partner, career or family to provide the foundations for their security as it is often lacking from their inner life. Strengthening one's sense of identity and independence may not restore muscle tone in the perineum but will establish a stronger personality.

16) Kidney Stones

A stone anywhere in the body denotes a collection of material which, for some reason, cannot be eliminated by the body often because it is present in excess. The emotion related to the whole urinary system, including the kidneys, is **fear**. My observation is that renal stones occur more commonly in those who hide their fears behind a façade of calmness or coping.

One man, with recurrent stones, told me that over the past two years he had watched his business fail and knew that it was almost time to accept defeat. And yet, he had managed to keep the impending doom and his anxiety from his family by always appearing cheerful and optimistic at home. Whether the family had been fooled by this charade, I'm not sure, but once he brought the matter out into the open, the stones dispersed.

Fear relates to the base chakra and demands the opportunity to be expressed. As therapists, we actively encourage the release of anger and grief but commonly distract our clients away from rising fear, probably because we have difficulty dealing with our own.

Fear is a natural sensation and denotes appreciation that something is approaching which is new, shocking, unknown and probably involves the breakdown of some part of our world. Children spontaneously express their anxiety through screaming, crying, shaking and asking for hugs. As adults, we believe that such behaviour is beneath us and we "should be able to cope".

When fear is recognised as a powerful ally allowing us to step bravely into a new challenge, we can then harness its energy and give expression to its voice.

17) Impotence

The external sexual organs, such as the penis and clitoris, are under the control of the base chakra, the seat of our inherent power, with the serpent coiled in expectation of a wonderful awakening, the orgasmic release. However, the rise of this energy can also be savoured in any situation where we experience a state of "bliss", "ecstasy" and "oneness" such as watching a beautiful sunrise, being amongst loved ones or reaching a place of deep peace in meditation. At that moment there is no separation, no fear but rather a place of security and unconditional love.

Impotence or powerlessness is a state which reflects not only a reduction in sexual prowess but also reflects lack of self-worth and personal security. Here the snake is trapped in its lair unable to reach its full height through fears (such as failure, rejection or humiliation) or through tight controls (such as guilt). So much emphasis has been placed on a man's ability to "perform" that it's not surprising that impotence is on the increase.

Over the past 20 years, we have seen an increase in competition, performance audits, women becoming the hunter gatherer, all of which deeply challenge the role of men within the world. However, healing will not occur through burying one's head or blaming others but by reassessing one's gifts and talents and regenerating that inner strength so that self-confidence can be restored and the snake can once again rise.

18) Vaginismus

This is a condition where the vaginal muscles are in spasm making intercourse extremely painful if not impossible. There are many causes for this problem and it is important to eliminate structural problems or those caused by infection, both of which can lead to severe pain. Any history of sexual or physical abuse in childhood must also be explored for this would naturally explain why a woman would choose to close down this place of entry.

All abuse reflects a sense of powerlessness exacerbated by any restriction to the throat chakra where words and sounds go unexpressed and are then painfully held within other muscles of the body. When we look beneath the surface of any society, abuse is not uncommon whether emotional, physical or sexual. In all cases, power is taken away through fear, low self-worth or pure innocence, and the deep impact of such an insult means that it can be a long journey back to the place where you believe in yourself enough to say "NO".

Through the help of loved ones, therapists and other professionals, it is possible to move through the pain, guilt and anger, to find one's voice, regain inner power and allow into life all those things which bring deep soul pleasure.

19) Candida

This very common condition, found in both men and women, affects many chakras including the solar plexus, sacral and throat, but needs to be mentioned at this level. Candida is a yeast which normally lives in harmony with us in our gut. But when the internal environment changes such as after the use of steroids, the pill or antibiotics or after prolonged stress, then the yeast's survival is threatened and in response it produces spores which lead to the symptoms which we relate to candida.

These include bloating, increased wind, sore throats, white discharge from the vagina, pain on intercourse, increased sensitivity to foods such as bread and sugar and extreme tiredness. There are additional symptoms and this condition often accompanies other illnesses especially those of the immune system such as ME and allergies (see heart chakra).

The important point to understand is that the "disease" occurs only in response to another problem and although a restrictive diet will help, the underlying cause needs to be addressed. From a psychospiritual point of view, these individuals are highly sensitive to atmospheres and other people's emotions with low self-esteem and a desire to please. They have very poor boundaries between what is their issue and what belongs to someone else, easily becoming overwhelmed by other people's problems.

The ability of their small intestine to correctly absorb those things which are healthy for the individual and reject the rest is deficient and hence the increased incident of associated sensitivities to foods.

Finally, the vaginal irritation reduces the desire for intercourse which often reflects a need for protection in situations where the individual feels threatened, out of control or overwhelmed. It is obvious that the condition will persist, despite treatments, until inner strength and adequate boundaries are restored often requiring honest communication.

20) Vaginal Herpes

This increasingly common infection, spread during intercourse, leads to severe pain and ulceration during an attack. As part of the base chakra, its presence relates to insecurity and fear of rejection, often from the tribe, and is seen in those whose sexual activities have been connected, in some way, to the search for belonging and acceptance. Unfortunately, despite the desire for security, intercourse does not always lead to a deepening relationship, leaving the "roots" of the individual stranded and abandoned with no earth in which to flourish.

Only when we feel "good enough" about ourselves, do we stop looking for others to provide our security and eventually find a home for the roots of our own inner being.

21) Osteoarthrosis of the Hip

Osteoarthrosis pathologically presents with pain, stiffness and limitation of movement. Our hips are the means by which we move forward and also provide us with a firm base to stand upon the Earth. Psychospiritually, this illness reveals someone who, subconsciously, is terrified by the fear of change and of losing their sense of security. They are often very good at motivating other people and yet balk at the idea that they themselves may have to change.

These individuals are helped by "taking a stand" personally, particularly one which involves their own well-being. A weight-reducing diet, so often required to lessen the load on their hips and knees, is an excellent way to start. However, as a therapist you may meet a few unexpected challenges to this plan.

I remember visiting an elderly patient who had previously denied the intake of any calorie-rich foods. There, stacked beside her chair, was a mound of sweets, biscuits and cakes. When questioned, she admitted to imbibing in these delicacies but only to please the family as they left the food to appease their guilt of leaving their mother alone. After a few tactful words the sweets disappeared and with the family's help, she started to lose weight and became motivated into finding ways to occupy her days to her own satisfaction.

22) Congenital Problems of the Feet

The feet are where spirit meets matter. When I see someone whose sole (soul) turns away from the Earth (**club foot**) or where it is very high (**pes** cavus) then I recognise someone who is extremely sensitive and not sure if they want to be on this planet.

Even in pregnancy, there will be stories of threatened miscarriages or problems with the placenta, with the birth overdue or difficult. Their reluctance to arrive may be followed by protests in the early years of life with crying, tantrums and physical problems.

These children need firm but loving support with encouragement to stay the course and not play the victim to **their** own pre-natal choice to incarnate at this time. It may not be, however, until their first **Saturn return** (age 28–29) when they are willing to place their soul's imprint on the world and take their place in the Greater Plan.

FLAT FEET AND FALLEN ARCHES. These people are definitely here to stay and feel the world through their feet. They are often "down to earth" individuals who may in fact be a little too structured! Once again, dance, movement and remembering the power of humour will help these individuals through life!

As for those adults who suffer from the painful condition of fallen arches, I see a tendency to stand above the world with high ideals and expectations. I remember a woman who was a cookery teacher who believed nobody could make a soufflé quite like she could. Then her arches fell and she was brought down to earth with a bang as she could no longer work.

Forced to sit down, her mind wandered to all the people who had let her down at different times in her life and the hurt she was still feeling. She realised that the pain in her feet was the pain of disappointment and it was time to forgive and move on. Within days of the release, her arches were restored to their normal position; a good job well done!

23) Athlete's Foot

This benign but troublesome condition mainly affects the feet, although other areas of the skin may be involved and leads to weeping skin, blisters and cracks in the heels. It is caused by a fungal infection which prefers damp and unprotected areas of the body, reflecting the personality of the individual who has poor boundaries and is anxious not to place his/her feet on this Earth for fear of failure and rejection. They often see the world as critical, unfriendly and competitive when all the while, these views are hiding their own insecurity.

By standing tall and "naked" in our own light, the feet can be allowed to heal.

24) Osteoporosis

This softening of the bones found in both genders, although affecting more women, commonly leads to fractures of the wrists, hips and vertebrae. The structure of the bones is laid down in the early months of life and continues until the bones stop growing around the age of 20. Any hormonal disturbances during this time will affect bone growth including diabetes, anorexia nervosa and intake of steroids.

Esoterically, bone reflects the basic structure of our life through which we receive support and if this was psychologically deficient in those early years, I believe that osteoporosis will be more evident in later life. Therefore, I would be interested to carry out a study to see whether those with osteoporosis had more periods of insecurity in early childhood, such as moving home regularly, chronic poverty, break up of the family or deaths of close relatives, as bones carry the memory of our life story. I also suspect that fractures or collapse of the vertebrae occur at times when the support or feeling of security is threatened by circumstances outside the control of the individual.

25) Panic Attacks

These very frightening attacks occur in all ages and both sexes. The common symptoms include rapid, shallow breathing, fast heartbeat, butterflies in the stomach, shaking, tingling in the fingers and toes and around the lips and feelings of faintness.

In my experience, panic attacks occur in those who are controllers and who like to appear cool and able to cope. Then something happens from outside their control and panic sets in. It is as if the lid has been taken off the pressure cooker which has been locked for so long and there is a great sigh of relief from the body. Unfortunately, there is a natural tendency to try and control the situation by telling the individual to "pull themselves together" which obviously just exacerbates the problem.

It is important to reduce the attack in whatever way necessary but afterwards there is a need to show the individual how the tight reins on their life, and probably on those around them, leave them vulnerable to a recurrence. Learning to lighten up, be more spontaneous, changing patterns to those less demanding and laughing, greatly enhance one's inner strength.

26) Insomnia

Sleep disturbance affects millions of people around the world presenting with a variety of patterns which may involve regular waking throughout the night or the inability to sleep during a certain period of time, which can persist for many years. Sometimes there is an obvious physical or psychological cause such as anxiety or hot flushes but on other occasions no immediate pattern can be elicited. In my experience, there is a strong connection between insecurity and the fear of losing control during the unconscious sleep state which can also be present in those who fear a general anaesthetic.

Insomnia is certainly more common where the roots of our existence have been suddenly shaken and the only way of holding onto reality is by staying awake. This can be seen after loss of a loved one, separation, moving home or country or being forced to change jobs. At other times, the history of insecurity goes back over many years such as the woman who now only sleeps fitfully, but remembers as a three-year-old child being lifted in the night by her parents to flee the invading troops.

Others relate stories of abuse occurring in their childhood bed where the need to stay awake and alert became an issue of survival. I might say that I also meet those who forced themselves to sleep rather than face the shame and pain of abuse and many of these individuals still fall asleep at the hint of anything that appears threatening.

As you can see, insomnia has many faces and certainly requires more than a few tablets to deal with problem.

27) Anaemia

A low haemoglobin features in many illnesses and it's not possible to look at all of these in turn. But suffice to say, esoterically, haemoglobin carries the life force or joy around the body and therefore anaemia represents a lack of basic joy in our life often due to insecurity caused by circumstances changing which are out of our control and which highlight the underlying low self-worth. Any exhaustion is exacerbated by the stress caused by the individual desperately trying to correct the situation in their own way.

Apart from receiving the appropriate medical or complementary treatment, it's important for the individual to find time to rest, reflect on their life, let go of the past (especially any shock) and start to build a solid framework from within, recognising the uniqueness of their existence.

Suggestions to Balance the Activity of the Base Chakra

1)   Learn to relax and take time for all the basic needs such as sleeping, eating, making love and laughter.

2)   Do one thing at a time without the distraction of telephones, television or work.

3)   Create opportunities to walk in Nature, especially barefooted. Find a tree that really attracts you and lean or sit against it. Get in touch with its strength, foundations and height and imagine your roots firmly planted in the earth while your arms are stretched high into the sky.

4)   If you know you are a controller, critic or perfectionist, ease off. Learn to hold your tongue, counting to ten before you speak and concentrating on the relationship rather than on proving that you're right!

5)   If you recognise your need to be perfect and it bothers you, do one or two things which shake that pattern. Wear your watch on the other wrist, wear odd socks and giggle when you look down, don't wash up that last cup before bed, don't make the bed before going out, and take up belly dancing. Spontaneity and flexibility are keys to a healthy base chakra.

6)   Put away the stick that "beats" you when you get something wrong, everything is perfect, even our so-called mistakes. Our own self-punishment is far worse than that at the hand of others. Write it down or speak it out if it helps and then start to forgive, learning from the experience and using the newly-gained wisdom for the future.

7)   Rather than accepting other people's criticism of you, either confront them: "Why is it every time we meet you need to make a comment which sounds critical?" or choose to accept what they say without becoming defensive: "You're stupid" to which you reply: "Yes, but I'm happy with myself. Please accept me as I am rather than trying to change me."

8)   Dancing, gardening, walking, pottery and sculpture all help us to ground the energy. Try not to set tasks against time; so many miles in so many hours. Enjoy the experience.

9)   Choose to stay on this planet and to do it in your own unique way without the need to prove anything. Standing tall with your knees slightly bent and shouting: "YES" really states your claim on life.

10) If a particular situation makes you feel insecure, place your feet firmly on the ground and imagine magnets pulling the soles into the Earth. This strengthens your base chakra and you can speak or act from a place of greater authority.

11) The colour red relates to this chakra. Take your awareness to the base of your spine and allow your intuition to choose a shade which seems to strengthen this area. If necessary wear red clothes over the lower body but remember too much red can exhaust you, so take care.

The Sacral Chakra

■ The Sacral Chakra

Position:	Lower Abdomen
Spirtual Aspect:	Self-Respect
Basic Need:	Creativity within Relationships
Related Emotions:	Possessiveness, Sharing
Endocrine Glands:	Ovaries and Testes
Associated Organs:	Uterus, Large Bowel, Prostate, Ovaries, Testes
Colour:	Orange

Spiritual Aspect ... Self-Respect

If the base chakra says: "I am" then the sacral chakra says: "I am in relationship to ... my partner, work, family, religion, friends, nature, money"; it is the centre of all relationships. Anything we are willing to interact with in order to find ourselves becomes an intimate partner. It asks us to open ourselves to the world and be willing to exchange energy so as to experience our essence to the very depth of our soul. The outcome of such a union is that we create something which is totally unique, for no two situations are the same in the presence of time and space.

Relationships are not limited to people and especially not only to one individual. Every moment of our life, even during sleep, offers us opportunities to meet and interact with different aspects of Universal energy, whether of the animal, plant or mineral kingdoms or with our own sub-personalities, higher self or guides. Here we reach a place of communion (common union) where, for a moment, the two parts create a greater whole benefiting all concerned, consciously or unconsciously.

Even when we admire an exquisite bloom on the stem of a rose bush and lean over to smell its perfume, we're in relationship with that plant. We receive the gift of beauty and delight which instantly changes our mood but unbeknown to us, the rose also benefits from our appreciation, being stimulated to enhance its aroma and colour. Just as we respond positively to compliments so does Nature, which is worth remembering next time you walk in your garden.

When we stop relating and connecting, we stop growing which causes great sorrow to the soul which asks: "What needs to change ... the situation or attitude?" Do we need to change jobs, start to study again, take time to be still, be more forgiving or review close relationships? In marriage, it's not uncommon to reach a point when the euphoria, joy of exploration and creative energy have fizzled out, leaving apathy and the only thing in common being the roof overhead.

In most instances, the partners are willing to address the issue often seeking inspiration from outside the marriage which encourages the spark back into the home and creates a forum for re-connection. At other times, larger adjustments are required which, although painful, release the soul from its paralysis and inevitably brings new growth and happiness.

Relationships demand time, space, commitment, respect and the willingness to honour the essence of another to the very deepest level of their being.

Independence versus Dependence

The base and sacral chakras perform together in the most intricate dance where the essence of "who we are" is commonly formulated by the nature of our relationships and in return, relationships are greatly influenced by the identity we chose to present at that moment. In other words, we cannot find that place of inner security demanded by the base chakra living in isolation on top of a mountain and yet, if we attach our sense of self to our relationships with people, work, material objects or concepts, we will invariably feel insecure and lack confidence.

Indeed, jealousy and possessiveness occur where one member looks to find themselves through outer symbols of assurance and finds the other party lacking. They then enforce a strangle-hold on the relationship craving the feeling of specialness which, in the passion of a new relationship, can initially be met. But unfortunately, this doesn't appease the basic problem of insecurity and as the conditions of the alliance tighten, the co-operative partner starts to withdraw so as to maintain their own equilibrium.

The inevitable feelings of rejection and isolation felt by the wounded party are commonly projected beyond the relationship and out into the world. But it's only when the individual has the courage to look within and recognise their basic insecurity that they are willing to take responsibility for developing firmer foundations so that their roots can be truly nurtured and their inner strength developed.

Of course, the opposite scenario is also common with the individual appearing so capable and in control that they have little need of attachment and prefer to present the "face of independence" to all concerned. They often find themselves in relationships with those who are unavailable either mentally or physically, such as with someone who is married, lives abroad or who rarely shares their feelings. None of these demand commitment or true intimacy and hence independence can be maintained without losing control. But as discussed in the previous Chapter, anybody who needs to hold onto such a strong identity is not secure and is, in fact, fearful of being challenged in any alliance that potentially represents change, vulnerability and most of all, love.

The whole matter of **independence** versus **dependence** is the key issue when viewing the sacral chakra where ultimately both need to become absorbed by an even greater facet of relationships, INTERDEPENDENCE.

As spoken by the Prophet (written by Kahlil Gibran) when talking about marriage:
>Give your hearts, but not into each other's keeping
>For only the hand of Life can contain your hearts.
>And stand together, but not too near together:
>For the pillars of the temple stand apart,
>And the oak tree and the cypress grow not in each other's shadow.

Interdependence allows each to know and walk their own path whilst happily supporting a common beam, the relationship, in honour of the greater journey.

BALANCED RELATIONSHIP

It follows that, if you have nothing in common, you have no relationship, whether we're talking about a person, job or belief. Interestingly, sometimes the only thing that keeps a marriage alive is the participants' dislike for each other, and when one party dies, genuine grief is expressed for this dysfunctional relationship.

Other relationships can appear extremely symbiotic and comfortable but are bound by a co-dependency agreement which states: "I'll be what you want me to be as long as you are what I want and nobody steps out of line." I call this a "tent" relationship where the only supports are the ropes, tautly pulling in opposite directions to maintain an inner tension which is not immediately apparent to the outer world. This arrangement works perfectly well until one member chooses to expand their horizons. Immediately the rules and regulations of the tribe/family are challenged and every attempt is made to restore the status quo, often through manipulation or fear: "If you loved me ... ", or "I'll be glad when you've finished finding yourself and we can return to the old ways."

This is a common problem at this time of change when so many people are searching for greater meaning to their life and finding the old models failing to provide the flexibility required for self-expression. But any relationship built on love and respect is committed to allowing the breakdown of old structures, the introduction of new ideas and encourages dialogue to maintain a healthy connection.

I think we all know of relationships where it seems almost inconceivable that one partner could survive without the other due to their close bonding. When the separation does occur everybody watches in anticipation. Occasionally, what was predicted happens with one death following the other but, more commonly, the remaining individual sways and then starts to straighten, drawing on their own inner reserves and, despite their grief, prepares to carry on. Indeed, a totally new personality often appears, coping in a way that defies previously held beliefs surprising even the individual.

So to reiterate, this chakra brings up issues around **respect, space, flexibility** and **commitment**. Can we find a place within our relationships where everybody feels nurtured, respected and heard and if necessary, are we willing to do this for ourselves rather than waiting for the world to provide? The latter scenario is exemplified by the "damsel in distress" who is prepared to wait forever at the top of the tower for her "knight in shining armour", little realising that he is waiting downstairs if she would just take the time to make the first move towards commitment.

An analogy

There are two porcupines living in the Arctic; it's very cold and they decide to huddle together to stay warm. As they move closer, their needle-like spines start to injure the other's skin, so they move apart and become cold again. They then move backwards and forwards until they find the place where they can give each other warmth and nurturing without causing pain.

This is the perfect relationship!

The Creative Process

There are three phases of this process which embody our relationship with the Earth and our Creator and represent a large part of our life's purpose, revealing that we are co-creators of all of our experiences. In women, this is enacted every month in the form of the menstrual cycle but is also described in every individual by the in- and out-breath of respiration, occurring approximately 18 times per minute.

1) Birth, Inspiration and Taking a Risk: the Energy of the Virgin

The first stage of the creative cycle, represented in women by the maturation of the egg, reflects the ability to be inspired. This is the time to acknowledge and develop one's dreams, one's passions, one's ideas and to hold onto the belief that they can reach maturity and be manifest into the world. Everybody has dreams, the highest form being those which emerge from our inner wisdom or intuition, and the fulfilment of those dreams is, I believe, our soul's purpose.

Such a belief is challenged by the "fear of taking a risk" which is often compounded by the opinions of others whose life purpose has involved maintaining a equilibrium which is safe but boring! Such fear emerges either from the base chakra: "I won't be good enough" or from the solar plexus "I need someone else's approval before I can start." But when the creative urge is denied, problems such as infertility, ovarian cysts, hormonal imbalances and depression arise and the individual fails to appreciate the pleasure of seeing a seed they have planted take root and eventually develop into a tall and wondrous tree.

What are you willing to risk for your dream, for love, to be all that you are? What are you willing to let go of so that your dream can be manifest?

2) Life, Fertilisation and Intimacy: the Energy of the Mother

The second phase, represented by release of the egg at ovulation, involves the quest for fertilisation of our dream, idea or seed, for it's only when they impact upon the world of matter that they can truly be said to be realised. The ecstasy of the orgasmic release during sexual intercourse reflects the exquisite nature of this interaction with two people coming together and, through love, willingly releasing their hold on separate identities in order to merge. Here they cherish the ultimate bliss of connection not only with each other but with Universal power and love. This is the very essence of this phase: to be able to share yourself, your dreams, your thoughts, your body and your soul so completely that you experience and know God's love.

It is a time of "co-operation" not "coercion", beautifully illustrated by the baby growing in the womb, dependent on the mother for support and nourishment whilst allowing the spirit within to create the blueprint for life. This symbiotic partnership shows that the energy of every successful relationship flows in two directions where each receives from the other, with the result being that the more we give, the more intimate the connection and the more we ultimately receive.

Where force or persuasion is involved, even so called harmless nagging, the relationship can quickly become abusive where one party feels used, unheard or betrayed and chooses, as a defence, to withdraw trust, commitment and love. I often hear said about a partnership: "We never talk any more. Any time I start to discuss something, he/she disappears; it's so frustrating!" But when asked what it is they want to discuss, the answer usually sounds like a barrage of criticism and judgement and bypasses any concept of loving communication or respect. I can then fully appreciate the partner's reaction to the words: "We need to talk!"

The essential aspect to understand in any relationship is that we can only develop ourselves, our dreams, our desires, our insights by appreciating the invaluable gifts of the other person or the world around us. This means we need to recognise and honour **their** soul's path and not just see them as a means to an end. Every relationship offers us an intimacy which is life changing whether at work, with our partner, parents, children or with ourselves.

What it requires is the willingness to:

- trust
- connect and be intimate
- be vulnerable and "naked" in front of others
- be nourished and supported
- be flexible and receptive to whatever occurs
- be out of control and meet the unknown
- and finally, to change.

Many people, however, are happier "to give" than "to receive", often fearful of a deeper commitment to the relationship and hence to themselves, giving reasons such as:

- "People think of me as strong; if I receive I'll look weak."
- "I like to be in control and I don't like being vulnerable."
- "I feel I'm too much for other people so I hold back from asking."
- "They'll probably want something back later and I may not be able to provide."
- "I don't like being in debt."
- "They may say 'NO' and I can't stand rejection."
- "Nobody ever gives me what I want (doesn't live up to my expectations), so I've stopped asking."

These wonderful excuses allow us to maintain a distance and hence avoid the passion and ecstasy of love where there is no separation. And what is the greatest intimacy we avoid? That love affair with ourselves. This phase of the creative cycle is particularly poorly developed in those who have cultivated a strong wall of independence following the experience of being let down, hurt or even abused after trusting someone else with their dreams, their feelings, their body and even their heart.

In men, it has been considered weak to "ask for help" especially in the area of emotions which has led to an enormous strain being placed on the body, personal relationships and to the chance of experiencing the joy of union. They have often been badly hurt when their love was rejected and, in response, drew the energy of love down into the groin rather than risk a heart connection and further pain. Sex then became purely hormonal but emotionally "safe" (see prostate disease).

These independent individuals attempt to "nest" their ideas alone, avoiding delegation and often pushing on with willpower (throat chakra) or sheer determination (base chakra) and then wondering why they become exhausted, disheartened, depressed and anaemic, with their dreams poorly realised. Co-operation and connection are the keys to happiness.

This same one-sided offensive is seen in personal relationships where the fear of further disappointment and pain leads to someone falling in love with the perfect partner and then "trying to change them"! Perhaps by holding an image of someone who cannot exist in reality, but still persisting in projecting it onto everybody, keeps us safe from committing to intimacy. Initially everything is wonderful, until the veil of illusion starts to thin and our partner's true self (which was always present) reveals itself and we realise we've fallen in love with our dream and not with the individual.

Thankfully in most cases, enough of the relationship is sound and therefore able to withstand the diminishing initial euphoria whilst allowing us to adapt and grow closer to the truth of love. But there are those who never get over the shock of their scorned expectations and live a life of continual disappointment applying it to anybody and everything they meet.

And finally, who or what do you trust to support you?
Who shares your dreams when they emerge from the depth of your soul?
Who do you turn to when the going gets tough?

We all need someone or something that we can trust to be behind us especially when we grow tired of "doing it alone" or at the end of the day when we are so bone weary. Apart from people, some choose a warm bath (very solid and nurturing), others look to a tree or Nature for solace, while "having enough money" can provide a secure but dispassionate support. Pets have, of course, for generations been the unconditional companions for many during lonely and troubled times.

And what of God, the Masters, our guides, our loved ones who have passed over: do we call to them for assistance and more importantly do we trust the support they offer? So many times we feel deserted during our most desperate moments and fail to recognise that other-worldly help comes in many ways, often through the most surprising messengers and always focuses on the bigger picture and not on something we want "fixed" immediately.

Universal support moves us closer to our own centre and enables us to hear our inner voice more clearly. The question is: "Do we want the sort of assistance that could involve change and greater insight or do we prefer the type that supports us in our pain and keeps us in the dark?" The choice is ours.

And finally, there are those we call close friends who we turn to for love and support both during our good times and bad. They may come from within the family or from outside and these are the people who:

- know all facets of your personality, including the difficult ones and love you more
- are present for your triumphs and disasters and celebrate both
- allow full expression of your emotions without trying to "fix you"
- know what you're feeling without being told
- will tell you when you're wallowing or becoming a martyr
- are honest in response and truthful when requested
- trust you when you head off in a direction they don't understand
- know when to remain silent and listen
- offer a hand or arm of love without being asked
- hug you for no particular reason
- reflect the pleasure of being together even if only for a short time after many months.

Who do you call a friend?

As Kahlil Gibran says about friendship:
And let your best be for your friend.
If he must know the ebb of your tide, let him know its flood also.
For what is your friend that you seek him with hours to kill
For it is his to fill your need, but not your emptiness
And in the sweetness of friendship let there be laughter, and
    sharing of pleasures
For in the dew of little things the heart finds its morning and is
    refreshed.

3) Death, Expiration and Release: the Energy of the Crone

This final stage of the creative cycle, the expiration or death is represented by the menstrual bleed and asks us to release that which is complete whether our ideas were realised or not. Everything has an end, death is inevitable; it is just a matter of timing. Women's bodies are intimately tuned to understand the cyclical and rhythmic nature of human existence, appreciating that, like the phases of the moon, life waxes and wanes. It is inherent in every woman to accept death every month and see it as a time to let go of the old and prepare for the new.

And yet, among many Western societies, both men and women fear death and hold on relentlessly to that which is dead or needs to be allowed to die. Here I am not only talking about the physical body but also past relationships, unrealistic expectations, unfulfilled dreams, unrequited love, failure in business, redundant images of ourselves and even our attachment to our children.

It is so easy to become entangled in the grieving process, holding onto the past through fear: fear that there is nothing else, fear of the void and fear of our own inadequacy re-enforced by low self-worth. The feminine side of our nature has become so suppressed that we've forgotten that inspiration faithfully follows expiration just as day follows night and this is reflected in the steady increase in breathing problems as people attempt to hold their breath against the inevitable tide of change (see throat chakra).

I remember listening to a relationship counsellor who said that you only make space for someone new in your life when you are able to let go of, not only things which were negative in the previous partnership, but also those that were positive. This seemed hard at first but on reflection, death requires us to move on and not live in the past.

But remember this stage can, and should, be a great time for celebration, for it's the completion of a cycle and much has been achieved. It is harvest time when the fruits of our labour are picked and eaten and we, as the creative force and nurturer, are nourished by our own creation. It reminds me of the mother animal who eats the placenta of her young recognising the importance of being nurtured herself in order that her life-giving force should continue. Every plant that produces seeds or fruits not only shares these with the world but also absorbs some of the energy back into its own structure so that its ability to produce new life next season, is enriched.

Have you enjoyed the fruits of your labours before moving on to plant a new seed?

Like proud parents we can rightfully stand tall and watch with pride as the spirit of our creation makes a life of its own and frees us to move on. Whatever happened during the first two phases of the process has changed us just because we choose to participate in life itself.

Body Language

In the sacral chakra, the issues of lack of nurturing and trust show themselves in the following ways:
a) The commonest place for women to lay down fat is over their sacral chakra often reflecting a desire to be nurtured but fear of allowing anyone too close.
b) Women and some men will hold their hands over this area when they feel dejected and unloved. They seek care and attention although are often unable to voice their needs for fear of rejection. It is therefore important to reassure them that they and their space are respected.

Associated Illnesses

1) Irritable Bowel Disease
This condition, also known as "spastic colon", leads to bloating, alternating diarrhoea and constipation, abdominal pain and the passage of excessive wind. It can affect any age and both genders equally and may be linked to hypersensitivity to certain foods or an overgrowth of candida.

Psychospiritually, the attacks are associated with relationship issues, especially those of a parent/child nature, where there is an initial desire to invite others into our space and then resentment when then they fail either to meet expectations or demand too much of our time.

Many of these individuals are "nice, uncomplaining people" who have learnt to swallow their concerns and anger rather than "rock the boat". They prefer to tie their guts in knots and leave their body to express the explosive nature of their hidden emotions!

By managing to let off steam gently but consistently and to voice their needs through respect for all concerned, the pressure fails to build and a balance can be found between closeness and suffocation.

2) Lower Back Pain

As this is such a common problem, it is included in this section and not with the other musculo-skeletal problems. Most of the symptoms arise from muscle tension although it is important to have an adequate diagnosis before embarking on psychospiritual healing. The spine represents "support" which, for most individuals, involves other people although some prefer the comfort and safety of money. When the support is withdrawn for whatever reason, the lower back starts to complain.

The problem is that these patients can be very difficult to help for three main reasons:

1) They do not receive easily preferring to be the one who gives. So when asked: "What can I do to help?" the reply is: "Nothing" (followed by a long, winsome sigh). And yet when you turn to go, the cry goes out: "Don't leave me!" They are often stoic types who prefer that someone should read the signs, rather than simply voice their concerns.

2) They are perfectionists with the motto: "If you want a job well done, do it yourself!" So as they lie upstairs listening to the mayhem occurring down below they can't resist the temptation to control all the proceedings from their sick-bed and eventually are forced to stagger downstairs to restore order, as only they can.

3) They have high ideals of what support entails and therefore find themselves frequently disappointed. They fail to appreciate that perhaps they need to look at ways to nurture their own needs and are therefore often heard to say: "Nobody cares for me!"

Healing is enhanced by the individual learning to receive even in minor ways such as when they are asked: "Would you like a cup of coffee?" Replying: "Yes" rather than the usual: "Don't bother, I'll do it myself!" And even if the coffee is cold or too sweet, letting go of the need for perfection and remembering the love which accompanies the beverage.

The damsel in distress, who is often present in lower back problems, needs to find a balance between nurturing herself and learning to ask for help. By lowering her expectations of others and committing to her own care, she will find greater joy and a definite reduction in the pain of chronic disappointment.

3) Problems Related to the Reproductive System

This is an area where we can meet disturbance in the three phases of the creative cycle as described above.

First stage: Inspiration

INFERTILITY

Some causes of infertility are present at birth, in both men and women whilst others are due to hormonal imbalances or follow infections such as mumps in men and chlamydia in women. In some couples, no cause is found and other interventions are offered.

In my experience, whatever the cause, it's important to look at the psychospiritual background of the individuals so as to be able to rule out any significant contributing factors which, undoubtedly, will have an effect on attempts to achieve a successful pregnancy. Professional psychological support may be required, as long-buried issues often arise during initial discussions into this matter.

Personally, I have heard many stories of abuse in childhood, usually sexual, that so scarred the individual that there was a deep fear that they may repeat the pattern, and hence, they had unconsciously attracted infertility. Others had lived in such dysfunctional families that their role model for parenthood was distorted, and hence, they found it difficult to picture themselves as parents. Finally, I have worked with women who are caught between their desire to have children and their ambition for a career. Interestingly, I also hear that it's messages from other women, especially the mother, which often provoke the dilemma. By looking at our images connected to "becoming a father or mother", it soon becomes clear which belief systems need to be changed.

One woman who came to see me, presented a slightly different scenario. She had been trying for a pregnancy for the past four years without success. Since her father died six years previously, she had become very close to her mother who continually stressed how important their relationship was, and how it was giving meaning to her life. However, this dependency was now placing a tremendous strain on the daughter who, feeling as if she was now parenting her mother, also felt she could not usurp her position by producing another baby!

After much discussion, it was clear that the situation had to change and that the daughter needed to lessen her feelings of responsibility for her mother's happiness. By allowing her to become involved in the pregnancy etc., the mother started to release the past and move smoothly into the role of grandmother.

A) FEMALE DISORDERS

a) AMENORRHOEA The loss of periods within the reproductive phase of a woman's life is usually hormonal and as this stage represents the planting of the seed, it's not uncommon for the periods to cease at times of change such as getting divorced, leaving home, taking exams or in the midst of grief. It is also a feature of **anorexia nervosa** (see heart chakra) when the body weight falls beneath a certain level and changes occur to the function of the pituitary gland. One aspect of this illness is the wish to stay as a child which reflects the desire to avoid the risk of being asked to plant one's seed and be seen by the world.

The other common cause of amenorrhoea relates to increased levels of **male hormone** which may be part of **polycystic ovary disease**. In the case of the latter, a fine fibrous sheath grows around the ovary preventing release of the egg at ovulation. At the same time, there are signs of excess male hormone such as hairiness, change in fat distribution and acne.

On a psychospiritual level, there may be deeply engrained cultural beliefs around femininity or a history of sexual abuse where, in both cases, the shroud around the ovary protects the woman from her own sexuality. I remember one girl who came from a mixed home of Islam and Christianity where the modern style of living did not require her to wear the veil. Yet something deep within her psyche was disturbed by the blatant presentation of her sexuality and without consciously owning her dilemma, she had solved the problem by cleverly "veiling" herself with body hair which also made her less attractive to men.

After some discussion, she decided to talk to her family and started to dress in accordance with her inner feelings. Slowly, the hair subsided and the periods returned.

b) ENDOMETRIOSIS In this condition, the endometrium not only lines the uterus but is also found in other sites in the pelvis causing severe pain and menorrhagia when it bleeds, alongside the normal loss from the uterus.

There is much medical debate as to the cause of this disease but psychologically there are two possible theories. One is that misinformed sex education was offered at the time of puberty with old-fashioned concepts such as the "curse" or fear of pregnancy being instilled into the mind of the young girl. The second is that there is an overriding desire to become pregnant and indeed there is much evidence to show that after giving birth, the disease is much less aggressive or even absent. The presence of a child certainly negates all negative beliefs about femininity and allows the uterus to reveal its true and wonderful purpose.

Both theories may have a part to play in the development of this illness and it's wise to examine all underlying beliefs concerning womanhood in any healing process.

c) OVARIAN CYSTS It is not uncommon for women to develop isolated cysts on their ovaries many of which disappear without causing any further problems. However, psychospiritually, those that do persist, represent a block in creative energy which accumulates to form the cyst. As discussed above, the cause of the blockage is often a sense that: "What I have to offer is not good enough", accompanied by fears of failure and success. This belief has often been re-enforced by others who controlled or criticised any creative efforts, as a form of emotional abuse.

Without encouragement and self-confidence, it is hard to plant "our precious seeds" fearing their vulnerability. Any healing of ovarian cysts must include removing limiting beliefs surrounding one's own capabilities and gifts and encouraging their expression.

d) OVARIAN CANCER The ovaries contain a powerful creative force that needs to be expressed either through giving birth to children or to our ideas and dreams. Individuals with cancer often have a poor sense of self and therefore are easily swayed by comments which say: "Your feelings don't matter" (which really says "you don't matter"), "I know what's best for you" or "You'll never be good enough". Unfortunately, because of their poor self-worth, they fail to challenge these statements with any sense of conviction.

I have also seen those women who, through unfortunate circumstances, have been denied pregnancies (or none with the partner of desire) and this suppression of creative energy plus unexpressed anger, has accumulated inside until the disease became manifest.

This precious area of a woman's life needs to be respected and it's important that women find ways of honouring this sacred gift whether through the bearing of children or through other creative and fulfilling outlets.

e) CERVICAL EROSION, CERVICITIS AND CERVICAL CANCER A cervical erosion and cervicitis do **not** predispose to cancer and are common after childbirth, the pill or due to an infection. It is important, however, to recognise the cervix as the entry point to the sacred womb and hence any disease in this area may be linked to a history of abuse (emotional or sexual) or feelings of shame, and these issues need to be explored for healing to occur.

Cervical cancer has become more prevalent and aggressive in the past 10 years affecting a much younger population with spread occurring over a shorter time. Research has shown that the cause of this illness is complex and includes early sexual encounters, smoking, the pill and the presence of a particular virus or wart in the area of the cervix. But once again, little attention has been paid to the psychospiritual factors which I believe have an important part to play.

In my experience, the issue of abuse (sexual, emotional or physical) must be addressed during any treatment process, for when a woman feels used, devalued or shamed, this gateway to her soul bears the brunt of the attack which is reflected in the abnormal cells of cancer. It's interesting to note that a wart-like virus is a probable causative factor, for warts always say: "What don't you like about yourself?"

Is it possible that low self-worth and transgenerational information about being a woman could disable a woman so much that she feels helpless to protest about the abuse? If this is true, counselling needs to accompany any treatment program otherwise the insult will reappear in another part of the body at a later date.

Second Stage: Nurturing

a) PRE-MENSTRUAL SYNDROME (PMS) The symptoms of this condition are irritability, clumsiness, bloating, food cravings, weeping and a desire to be alone. These signs all reflect a distortion to the natural instinct which is to create a secluded "nest" in which to nurture the maturing egg. This syndrome, occurring commonly in women in their late 20s to early 40s, is on the increase as the demands of modern living have changed the way a woman sees herself. So that:

■ She tries to be "superwoman", juggling her life between work and family whilst still seeking approval, unconsciously, that she is a good wife/mother.
■ She has become increasingly independent and self-sufficient but now has difficulty asking for help.
■ Childbirth is occurring much later with less time allocated for nesting and nurturing.
■ More and more women fail to find a suitable partner to father a child and the emptiness is revisited every month.
■ Despite the transformation in cultural identity, she still places herself low on the list of priorities when it comes to care taking.

■ She feels less able to find sacred space in her own home due to the loss of gender-specific roles and therefore can no longer hide herself away in the kitchen!

It is time for women to choose how they wish to progress in this modern environment, looking first at the drive to prove themselves within a man's world and then hopefully deciding to return to the rhythm of their own gender, allowing their intuition to guide them towards that which honours and respects their natural instincts.

b) FIBROIDS AND MENORRHAGIA Menorrhagia, or heavy periods, represent unexpressed "tears" often linked to a sense of feeling unsupported, unloved and taken for granted. However, even when support is offered, these women are often poor receivers, placing themselves on the bottom of the priority list for nurturing.

Life has often become a drag and far too serious with the child-like qualities of play and laughter lost in deference to responsibility and the burden of womanhood. When we add the issue of **fibroids** to the picture we see someone who takes care of everybody else but is unable to answer the question: "Who takes care of you?" There are usually growing feelings of resentment unexpressed behind a smiling face that says: "I can cope with anything; I have broad shoulders."

The enlarged mass of uterine tissue that comprises the fibroid, represents this resentment and may give the appearance of a pregnancy, as if the woman is attempting to nurture her own wounded, inner child. However, before this can happen, she needs to look at her deeper fears around being taken care of and what it would mean to let others into her life. It's so easy for us to take on the responsibilities of others or get lost in our work, so as to avoid acknowledging our need for space, love and closeness.

The first step is to look at one's life and start to empty the uterus, metaphorically, of people, expectations and feelings that need to be allowed to die and be released. Ask yourself: "Who no longer needs my help?" and "Who do I feel responsible for, purely through duty or pity?" Perhaps the ex-husband or the 25-year-old son? Remember nobody is ever going to turn down the attention of someone who always appears so capable; so become less available!

Then clear out the unrequited love, the expectations of others that never came to fruition, the romantic fantasies, the painful failures and the unexpressed grief. Write letters you never send releasing the thoughts and people to follow their own path, not yours. Now buy yourself some flowers and look around your home to check whether this is a place where you can be totally nourished; if not, do something (or get someone else to help!)

Then in small but steady steps, learn to reach out and trust others, gracefully allowing them into your sacred space and letting their love soothe your fear of vulnerability so you can move forward towards a healthy state of self-respect.

Third Stage: Release and Expiration

a) MENOPAUSE This is a subject on which many books have been written and for which many remedies are available to alleviate the symptoms which is strange, as so little is mentioned about the previous 30 years of menstruation. Anyhow, this time, which marks the cessation of periods and re-adjustment of one's hormones to enter the mature years of the elder or crone, affects different women in different ways.

The commonest symptoms are hot flushes (flashes), aching joints and muscles, tiredness, depression, irritability, weeping, lack of vigour of the hair and skin and increasing vaginal dryness. However, it's important to remember that not every women experiences symptoms and in some cultures, there is no word for the menopause, seeing it as something that is natural rather than something that needs "fixing". Despite my medical training and my understanding of the changes to the bone, tissues and blood vessels in the ensuing years, I do not believe that our Creator made a mistake by only supplying half of the years of our life with hormones and then said: "Let them create HRT to correct my mistake!"

It is well documented that following the menopause, a woman's body continues to produce some oestrogen whilst other hormones, such as androgen, play an important role in maintaining a state of well-being. However, there are other factors which also contribute to ensuring a healthy body and mind and reduce the symptoms of menopause:

1) **Hot flushes** are the way in which the body attempts to discharge excess creative energy that is not being actively used by the individual. At this time of change, we are given the opportunity to look back and ask:

"What seeds of my own soul have not been planted and where is my fear?" (See stage 1.)
"What of the past am I clinging onto that needs to be allowed to die?" (See stage 3.)

Many of the symptoms just described can be attributed to low thyroid function (see throat chakra) where change is avoided leading to heaviness and pain in the limbs, as the unexpressed energy builds up inside.

2) **An active mind and body** maintain the juices of our being. Exercise, mental stimulation and an enjoyable sex life are all known to keep us feeling fit and able to appreciate the advantages of this age.

3) **Dryness of the vagina** is painful and reduces our enjoyment of intercourse but fortunately there are medical and natural remedies to ease the condition. However, remember that there may be other psychological reasons why it's more comfortable to avoid an interaction with our partner, using vaginal discomfort as an excuse.

The menopause occurs in line with our second Saturn return (every 28 years) with symptoms tending to appear between 50–56 years of age. This is the time when this planet moves to its position at birth and says: "Where are you going? Are you living your soul's intention and following its blueprint?" This should evoke feelings of excitement not depression as we enter the domain of the crone or wise woman. Here we are given the chance to hand over the mantle of child-bearing to the younger women and allow ourselves time to rest while we explore what wise thoughts we would like to share with the world from our own personal experiences. And when we are ready, in an environment where elders are respected, we can then bring these thoughts into action and enjoy the experience of being a crone.

However, the natural cycles of life have been lost in the name of progress and convenience and I believe that health will only be restored to this planet when they are reinstated. I would love to see the return of the "rites of passage" when we honour the commencement of menstruation with flowers given by a newly created elder who is herself, entering a fresh and exciting creative phase of her life.

And to complete this subject, let it be known that men also have a menopause for they also have a Saturn return. Unfortunately, they are far less prepared for this transition and often find themselves either trying to hang onto the past or floundering at the thought of a future beyond work. It's time that men demanded to know and understand their own rhythms rather than being given tablets to resist the tides of change.

a) MALE DISORDERS
a) TESTICULAR DISEASE Over the past 10 years, we have witnessed a steady increase in testicular tumours. Like the ovaries, the testes contain

the creative life force and this energy needs an outlet by fathering children and/or ideas which express the powerful qualities we associate with manhood.

There are many contributing factors to disease in this area, but a common psychological theme concerns the appropriate use of this power as judged by the individual. If it is deemed to have been misused or a sense of failure was experienced, then disease may manifest.

Jonathan was 33 years old when he presented with testicular cancer. Uninvited, he immediately launched into the reason he thought he had cancer. His career in the legal profession had rocketed following university and, at 28, he landed a superb job where he was offered all the perks of a partnership, bringing his family financial rewards far outside that of his contemporaries. However, he soon realised that there was one catch: he had to "cook the books" (be dishonest) and keep quiet about it. He faced a major dilemma where his desire for all the good things in life clashed with his individual morality.

As he said: "The only way out was to get cancer!"

"And what now?" I asked.

"I can't go back."

"So you haven't got the balls to stand your ground?"

"No," he replied.

In view of his unresolved childhood issues which seemed to be linked to his lack of inner strength, I suggested psychotherapy. However, I later learnt that he left after a few sessions as the changes required of him appeared immense compared with staying with the disease.

Men's role in the world is greatly challenged at present and the young require strong role models who can lead by example and not by dictation. Unfortunately, for a variety of reasons, many fathers are absent from their son's upbringing, either physically or emotionally and the teenagers are forced to look to those in the world of music and sports for direction.

It's those men who have integrated their male and female aspects who will guide their own gender into the future encouraging the exploration and expression of the deeper core values which include love, respect and honour.

b) PROSTATIC DISEASE The prostate gland provides the nourishment for the sperm during its journey and can therefore be seen as the male equivalent of the uterus. In the Western world, 60% of men over the age of 60 suffer from prostate disease which is a shocking statistic when we consider how little is understood about the cause of the problem.

I believe that both benign and malignant diseases are related to an unnatural flow of energy during the sexual act. In simple terms, it is understood that during intercourse, the energy of the male rises from the groin into the heart whilst the female energy passes from the heart towards the groin. This accounts for the fact that women are more likely to require the right mood before participating in the sexual act whilst men are charged up and ready to go.

However, for a man to experience a full orgasm, the kundalini sexual energy must reach the heart where a soul connection is made with the partner and ultimately with himself. If however, the individual has experienced hurt and rejection around the area of love then the heart becomes a no-go area and sexual excitement and release remains in the groin.

The desire for different partners often represents a belief that one day someone will unlock the heart. But in truth that intimate connection can only be made by turning the key from the inside and releasing the unexpressed pain and sorrow so that love can flow in.

The *macho* image maintains the limited flow of energy around the groin and I can only hope that the young men of the day start to value the powerful force within their heart and refuse to settle for anything less.

Suggestions to Balance the Activity of the Sacral Chakra

1) Choose to respect yourself by creating precious space in your day for nurturing, sharing and time on your own. Rather than feeling rejected when others choose their space, be content that they feel secure enough to take it.
2) If you know you find it difficult to receive, start by asking for small things and work up gradually. If they say "No", at least you asked. Try to accept gracefully whatever is offered, letting go of the need for perfection. Restrict the use of sentences such as: "Don't bother, I'll do myself, I can manage", and say "Yes" with ease.
3) Look at the dreams and ambitions you've held from teenage days, especially those which were placed on hold because of lack of time. If the world were to end tomorrow, would you be able to say you were totally fulfilled or would there be regrets? Decide to put aside your fears (especially the irrational ones) and go for it; take a risk.
4) Make sure every day contains one aspect of self-caring; buy flowers, have a long, hot bath, go out with friends, have a quiet night in, spend quality time with your partner and pamper yourself.
5) Have a clear out, releasing all unrequited love, unmet expectations of others, romantic fantasies, painful failures and unexpressed grief. Write

letters you never send releasing the thoughts and people to follow their own path, not yours. Remember every relationship is a valuable gift and give thanks to these people for coming into your life.

6) Remember to take time between completion and the planting of new seeds to enjoy the fruits of your labour. Celebrate and drink in the pleasure of seeing what you have achieved manifest into the world.

7) Become more conscious of your relationship with Nature. Stop awhile and smell the flowers, feel the dew on the grass or listen to the birds sing and let it reach into your heart with pleasure.

8) If you are in the midst of a difficult relationship where communication is difficult, sit in a quiet space and close your eyes. Imagine meeting this person on top of a mountain (if that is too much, place them on another mountain) and ask to speak to their higher self.

Tell them what you want them to hear, remembering that you are no longer speaking from your personality and therefore only want the best for this individual. Hear their reply. It may be necessary to ask for help from the spirit world by saying: "Please would someone come and help ... as I am far too close to the situation and can no longer act without bias." Always complete by offering love and gratitude. Such a meditation, working through the ether, can have a profound effect on the relationship.

9) Orange is the colour associated with this chakra which can range from deep red-orange to peach. Intuitively choose a shade that attracts you when working to balance this chakra. Blue may also be useful when there is a need to communicate feelings and needs.

Chapter 9

The Solar Plexus Chakra

◼ The Solar Plexus Chakra

Position:	Epigastrium, Below the Ribs
Spiritual Aspect:	Self-Worth
Basic Need:	Valuing the Needs of the Self
Related Emotions:	Anger, Resentment, Unworthiness, Guilt
Endocrine Gland:	Pancreas
Associated Organs:	Liver, Spleen, Stomach, Small Intestine
Colour:	Yellow

Spiritual Aspect ... Self-Worth

So as we progress through the chakras we find that when the base and sacral are in balance we can say: "My inner strength and sense of belonging allow me to fully participate in any relationship recognising and honouring the creative process and my part in the Greater Plan."

To complete the triad which comprises the personality or ego, the solar plexus supplies the final dimension which exposes the power of our own uniqueness and reveals its manner of reflection in the outside world. This centre is primed to provide us with an identity which becomes the vehicle for the soul's journey during this incarnation, enabling it to work out its purpose with maximum effect.

Without such an identity or healthy ego, we are easily swayed to follow the views of others as there is no sense of the "I" present within our psyche, no sense of personal identity, and this, I consider to be a major factor in the causation of most of the diseases of the immune system. To compensate our loss, we seek roles within our family and society that offer an identity which, although superficial, enable us to feel some sense of self-worth. But unfortunately, when we are only feeding the needs of an inadequately formed personality, any acclaim and reward we receive for our activities, seems to purely skim the surface of a far deeper longing: the need to find and honour the self within.

Often, in an attempt to rectify the situation, we take on more work or care for more people, believing that this will bring the rewards we desire, but to no avail. One day, we wake up and realise that we're exhausted, burnt out (see ME) and still lost. Only with that realisation do we courageously begin the slow and anxiety-provoking process of discarding the garments of our artificial identities to reveal our true nature and build a solid foundation of self-worth for which we can be proud.

This chakra has a long history of development stretching far back into Atlantean times when the people of the day knew how to use its energy to attract towards them all they desired for their own personal needs and gratification. Unfortunately, there was no end to their greed, and the craving for individual power eventually outweighed the needs of the group and became one of the contributing factors in the collapse of that civilisation.

The solar plexus, linked to the astral body, is the centre where we develop and perceive our emotions, and the legacy from those ancient times is that many of us still use our emotions, often unconsciously, as the driving force behind our actions. Taken to an extreme, the ability to manipulate others and to persuade them to relinquish their personal power to another authority, relates strongly to this chakra and has been the mainstay of some families, most major religions and many dictatorships over the past 2000 years.

While individuals prefer to give their power away and choose to ignore their own inner guidance, the ability to evoke "guilt", a "victim state", "helplessness" and "martyrdom" in the name of God, one's leader, or the promise of a better life, will still have an enormous influence on this planet today. And why do we fail to hold onto that which is rightfully ours? I can only give a few suggestions:

1) Old habits die hard and we have at least 12,000 years of imbalance in this chakra, for while some of those in Atlantis were lining their own nests, others were providing them with the power. It could well be that those who were power crazy in the past have returned at this time to experience the opposite polarity, finding themselves with low self-esteem and at the bottom of the ladder. However, the grip of karma needs to be released so a healthy balance can be restored and we can learn to hold and use this power wisely.

2) The Age of Pisces was one of gurus and masters and always ran the risk that it could all turn out to be a grand illusion. Like shoals of fish there was always a leader and followers, which satisfied everybody until the dawning of the Age of Aquarius. This time promotes community, clarity of mind and self-consciousness and the cracks have started to develop in a dogma which, for 2000 years, has been the underlying cause of so many atrocities and wars, all in the name of: "My way is right and any other opinion needs to be scorned and if necessary obliterated."

But it takes many generations to change genetic consciousness and it's still relatively easy to detect the religious background of an individual, even if they don't attend church etc., just by their language: "I feel so guilty" (Catholic), "Nothing seems to work for me" (Jewish) and "I'm fine, I'll cope" (Protestant). These may be generalisations and I do not mean to offend, but rather to point out the strong link between our religious background and our inability to stand in our own power.

Remember, if you wish to be powerful it has, until now, been the pattern to find someone lacking in self-confidence, with low self-worth, and through manipulation, take something that is not yours. Of course, it's also important to keep these people ignorant of who they are by denying a proper education and applying limited rules of engagement with the Creative Force.

3) The feminine power of Intuition has been suppressed over hundreds of years because it challenges reason and control. It represents an inner knowing which is non-local and does not follow a sequence of events. It often appears out-of-the blue piercing through elaborate masks and false identities with razor-sharp clarity and determination.

In the last one thousand years, many women have lost their lives due to this natural gift, and yet in our schools and other teaching establishments, intuitive powers are still given little credence next to the rational, analytical mind. Recently, the business world has shown an interest but mainly so that they can use this talent to have dominion over their competitors.

But without acknowledging the power of the intuition which connects us to our own inner guidance and true purpose, we find ourselves wandering the world, seeking an identity and increasingly dependent on others to "tell us who we are" and to proffer their approval.

4) In many cultures, self-worth has been undermined by the tribe's need to remain secure and united. Therefore, if a member dares to step out of line and starts to own their personal power, they receive rebukes which say:

"Nobody likes a big head/show off. It's not nice to talk about yourself."
"You're getting too big for your boots."
"Remember those who are less fortunate; think of others before you think of yourself."
"We need to maintain equality in our society, so never be better or worse than anybody else."

Self-worth requires the ability to know who you are and to be able to say:

"I like myself, I'm good enough, I'm OK and I'm happy to celebrate my existence."

Power of Attraction

The powers of attraction found throughout the chakra system are as follows:

1) **Hoping, wanting** and **wishing** arise from the solar plexus and involve the creation of an idea or fantasy behind which we place all our passion, driven by powerful emotions. Like our ancestors, our needs are met but the longing doesn't necessarily abate: "If I just had more ... " Such hoping drives us into the future and usually reflects a belief that who I am in the world today is not OK. Unfortunately, this low self-worth and lack of contact with the present moment, can only attract limited success until we stand still and honour who we are now, allowing the energy to flow freely once again.

Much of the devotional energy directed towards a guru, teacher, leader etc. comes from this level which says: "I'm happy to give my power to you ... as long as you give me something in return", for I suggest that the only reason we devote ourselves to someone else is because we effectively desire their power. What is fascinating to observe is that when two or more are gathered together and focus their devotional intention onto a cause or person, they attract towards that object of devotion a similar energy from the collective consciousness. **As above, so below!**

Now the person/object is overshadowed both by the desires of their followers and by the immense power of Universal energy which symbiotically feed each other. It is easy to see how one man can change the world for better or worse, driven subconsciously by the power of the populace who are, in all innocence, unaware of their responsibility in world affairs.

2) **Believing, willing** and **trying** emerge from the throat chakra where our needs are drawn towards us through the power of the mind. This fire-like energy is far more conscious and focused than "hoping" and is the basis of "affirmations" and NLP. As will be discussed later in the section on the throat chakra, the use of the mind allows us to emerge from the plethora of irrational, emotional power games and become far more directed. But it is limited by the fact that we are still disconnected from the Source preferring to use "My will" rather than "Thy will".

3) **Knowing, merging** and **loving** are the attracting energies of the heart chakra where we lose our need to be separate and come home to the understanding that there is only one desire and that is to be one with ourselves and hence with the Source. We give up the personality-based struggle and, instead of disappearing into a void, we find ourselves carried gracefully along the highways of life, open and available to whatever it offers.

Psychic Powers

This chakra is also the seat of our psychic (but not intuitive) skills. This sixth sense allows us to enter the ether or vibrational force of the planet and link into other dimensions of consciousness. Through the use of clairvoyance (inner eyes), clairaudience (inner ears) etc., we can detect the subtle energies surrounding other people, especially their emotions, and this information then passes through our astral body into the solar plexus. This mechanism is commonly used by mediums and psychics while others rely on the same source of information and call it their "gut feelings".

However, the one problem is that the emotional centre it is prone to be highly charged by unexpressed feelings and associated memories. So when we receive a "psychic buzz" about someone else, we need to be clear where our life ends and their life begins.

Approval Seeking

With low self-worth, we can find ourselves seeking approval which can quickly transform into a "neediness", with powerful conditions attached such as:

"If I do ... will you then love/like/accept me?"

and when the conditions aren't met, we hear:

"After all I did for you, I would have thought …

The patterns that emerge include:

- The need to be needed, the "pleaser": "Please, let me do it for you."
- The need to be liked: "Do you like me/like having me around. Please say yes!"
- The need to rescue or fix others: "I know what you need, let me help; you can't do it without me" (commonly found in those who work in the service industry).

These are extremely addictive patterns of behaviour and probably far more difficult to curtail than any substance abuse due to their subtle nature and their widespread acceptance as a way of behaving in society. This co-dependency places a stranglehold on any relationship and the last statement is really saying: "Please don't get well too quickly as I need you to need me and if you do improve, don't forget me!"

Despite the outwardly pleasing charm which appears to offer so much, there is nearly always a catch to this conditional love which is usually unspoken but intended: "If I do this, I expect … in return."

As you can see, one of the greatest problems of this area is the enormous accumulation of expectations which these individuals carry around with them and quietly lay at the feet of those who accept their offer. In all probability, most of this manipulation is unconscious and truly arises from the belief that this is the only way: "I just want to be seen/heard/acknowledged or loved because I honestly believe I am nobody and therefore not important in the lives of others."

Unfortunately, when the need is not met, and of course it rarely is, because it's impossible to **make** someone else feel good about themselves and the expectations are too high, then there is deep **disappointment, hurt** and commonly, **resentment**. This is the seat of most of the pain which is felt in the heart area although it doesn't originate from that particular chakra.

Hopefully, the pain from the most recent disappointment which is so familiar, will not force the individual deeper into despair but rather show them how far they have strayed from the love they need to feel for themselves. With wisdom and insight, they can start to see that until they decide to believe in who they are and stop looking outside for approval, the hurt will continue as will the low self-worth.

A thousand people can tell you that you did a good job or you look great but with low self-esteem, you will always seek out the one who raises an eyebrow and says: "I suppose you were OK", and down you go again. Even when compliments are offered, these are quickly thwarted either by a mirror-image reply: "I like you too", or batted away with self-condemnation. For instance, you comment: "Your hair looks great", which meets the retort: "It's really a mess."

Intrigued by this behaviour, I often ask: "Who would need to tell you that you were OK for you to believe them?" and sadly the answer is that there is nobody they trust. When we can learn to hear the compliment without brushing it aside and say: "Thank you" when it resonates with our truth, then our self-esteem is starting to shine ... and that's OK too!

Shame

Behind this fear of receiving compliments is probably a much greater issue called shame. This deeply disturbing emotion which penetrates the very depth of our soul leads us to believe that we're not worthy of receiving love just for "being who we are", re-enforced by messages which continually expose our faults and failings and remind us we should be grateful for any favours shown towards us. Any comparisons made between ourselves and others also tend to emphasise that being a unique individual is not OK.

Most shame has been passed down through the generations, often referred to as the "Sins of the Fathers". However, such stigma is hard to eradicate from the consciousness of our genes. One only has to look at the women of today, to see the face of shame which has been forged over many generations. Some take up the mantle of defiance and attempt to prove themselves by competing in a man's world always needing to work twice as hard as the wound is so deep. Others offer no defence, giving their power away in submission and allowing the abuse to continue. Whatever the ploy, shame forces us hide away which can be through our work, at home, amongst family or even through illness.

It is not difficult to appreciate how those in authority have managed to keep this belief alive, especially with stories which emphasise our "Fall from Grace" and the "Original Sin". Even in these days of sexual enlightenment, many people are ashamed of their body and its sensuality whilst others are afraid to share their emotions and dreams, fearful of inciting humiliation. Shame, as a wound of the soul, reveals the vulnerability which comes from being human but also keeps us separate from ourselves. If we were truly made in God's image then there is nothing to hide for fear of judgement, for there is only love and acceptance and those who say otherwise are playing power games, driven by their own sense of inadequacy.

Personal power comes from the determination **not** to give our power away, to begin to be proud of our own achievements and to truly like the person we see in the mirror. So:

When did you last stand in front of a full length mirror and say: "Hi gorgeous"?
What have you done for yourself in the last few days which boosted your self-esteem?
When did you last have a celebration for personal achievements?

Prejudice

Some say that this is a time when we've become far too self-absorbed and yet I see this apparent obsession with ourselves as a defence against inadequacy and feelings of not being good enough. It's when we can stand in a crowd and speak clearly from our inner being or be with others and not feel judged or judging, that we know we've made it.

For low self-esteem encourages the need to make comments about others that are not always complimentary. Our "prejudices" and "biases" which have been passed down through the ages, are often inaccurate but go unchallenged. I'm sure everybody has been on the receiving end of such a situation where someone forms an opinion of you, based purely on their observations and you feel you've been typecast. The time has come to set aside such thoughts and choose to meet each individual anew with no preconceptions or hidden agenda.

Sensitivity and Boundaries

Our self-worth develops from a very early age as we quickly learn to decipher what we need to do in order to be liked and even more important, loved. Some children come into this life with a firm grasp of their own individuality and take little heed of the emotional ups and downs of adults. However, others are far more sensitive right from the start and even as babies can be seen to follow their mother with their eyes, observing how she reacts to their smiles and tears.

Their basic insecurity, especially in new surroundings, is threatened by being asked to stay in other people's homes or by the thought of a long journey, so they use their recurrent need for toilet stops as an acceptable excuse for staying within the comfort of their own environment.

13) Cystitis

This inflammatory condition of the bladder is characterised by painful frequency of micturition. Emotionally, there is classical fear and anger. "I'm so frustrated by my boss at work but I'm afraid to leave in case I can't find another job." There is a tendency to hold onto old grievances and regrets rather than go with the flow.

Healing often occurs when the individual takes responsibility for their future happiness and moves towards something which brings soul satisfaction and away from limitation and frustration. On many occasions decisions are forced through redundancy or separation although my advice is that it's far easier to make the moves under one's own steam!

14) Bed Wetting (Enuresis)

This problem, often familial, is more common than is discussed in public with one in 10 of all 10 year olds and one in 20 of all 20 year olds in the UK, passing urine in their sleep on a fairly regular basis. Apart from treating structural and infective problems, psychotherapy for both the child and parents has already proved to be successful in reducing the incidence.

There seem to be two psychological issues involved. One is that the individual is often a very deep sleeper, difficult to rouse at the best of times. Various methods have been used over the years to awaken the child but a better understanding of sleep states would enhance the treatment potential. The other factor to be explored is that wetting the bed is seen as the child's way of exerting their power when they feel helpless and impotent during the hours of waking.

This may well be true, as my experience is of meeting individuals who are either shy and insecure purely due to their personality or have become withdrawn through the presence of oppressive control often in the form of sexual or emotional abuse. It is therefore important to obtain a clear picture of life at home and deal with the problems where appropriate and then to make it clear that this is not a condition to be punished but rather a state which usually recedes when the child or adult begins to stay away from home for longer periods of time.

Handling Power

Perhaps one of the reasons we so readily give our power away is that we don't want to take responsibility for its energy. As discussed in the section on the base chakra, there are many who fear their own power, possibly due to past memories of misuse. But times are changed and no one person is more powerful than another, except by choice or coercion. We all have talents through which the creative energy can flow but each ability has equal importance in the greater scheme of things.

Some of the most subtle uses of power are seen in those who play the victim, martyr or guilt tripper in "power games" all of which attract enormous sympathy, especially from the rescuer, who is also looking to gain energy in the form of approval.

For instance, Pete was raised in a household where he became the rescuer to his father's alcohol addiction. Initially, his father responded to his encouragement but as soon as Pete left home, he returned to the bottle. Disappointed and feeling guilty that somehow he had failed, Pete entered one relationship after another, believing that: "One day I'll be able to make a difference." With the best of intention his belief really said: "I'm powerful enough to change your life."

Inevitably, Pete met his match, in the shape of someone he loved dearly but who was strong enough to walk their own path. After several arguments, Pete decided to leave at which point the two entered a new phase of the power game with the victim saying: "If you leave me, I'll ..." while Pete replied: "I'll feel guilty if you do." Eventually, there was only one way to resolve the issue for the good of all concerned and Pete had the courage to say: "I love you but I'm not that powerful to stop you doing whatever you choose." This was a momentous statement to make but in the end the only solution was to tell the truth as it essentially exists.

Finally, we will always attract towards us those who detect our weak spot, especially when it relates to low self-worth. In their presence, we become exhausted and, without awareness, will wander off for a coffee, cigarette or sweet in the hope to redress the balance. However, if we are willing to reflect on the situation, we will probably remember similar feelings in response to other people and understand that this hole in our defences will only be closed by changing the limiting beliefs we hold about ourselves.

In the meantime, some short-term methods of protection include:

- Imagine wearing a white cloak which stretches from the top of your head to underneath the feet or if colour is easier, a rainbow cloak.
- Cross your arms across the solar plexus when someone enters your space emotionally. If necessary you can also cover this area with colour, such as pink or green or wear a crystal which absorbs the energy, remembering to wash the crystal at the end of the day.
- Imagine a mirror in front of you with the reflective surface pointing towards the person whose energy is difficult to accept and let it return to them.
- Place yourself in a golden pyramid with a solid base, allowing the light to enter through the top. Then ask that all energies which are not good for your soul growth, should return to the source.
- Remember, however, the greatest form of defence is our own inner light and pure love.

Body Language

a) When talking about a sensitive subject, it's not uncommon to unconsciously cross our arms to protect the solar plexus.

b) A more permanent protection comes from laying down fat over this area seen as a "beer belly". I suggest that behind every man with a large stomach, attempting to convey confidence, there is a small boy who seeks approval.

c) In woman, comfort eating is used to boost confidence but unfortunately this is short-lived and often leads to extra padding over the solar plexus and the additional feeling of guilt.

Associated Illnesses

1) Diabetes

There are two types of diabetes; the first is where little or no insulin is produced by the pancreas and is an auto-immune illness (see heart chakra) and the second is where the cells are no longer responsive to insulin, even though it is in plentiful supply. In both cases, there are high levels of glucose in the blood stream but it cannot pass into the cells and be used as energy.

In esoteric terms, without insulin or an ability to benefit from its presence, we're unable to absorb and appreciate the sweetness of life, glucose. In both forms of diabetes, I see someone with low self-esteem who rarely complains and feels unlovable but shuns any love offered to them. Indeed, commonly they are surrounded by people who want to cherish them but because of old beliefs about themselves, cannot let love in. Alice Bailey calls it "starvation in the midst of plenty".

There may be a history of being special, the centre of attention, at some point in their early life but then this was usurped by the entrance of someone new into the household such as a baby or new partner. I've also seen individuals who are financially secure but living quite frugally, as if driven by a fear of spending anything on themselves that may bring comfort and pleasure in case it's taken away again.

As one can imagine, the particular regime of diet and medication often leads to further inhibition of spontaneity although some diabetics take this as an opportunity to take care for themselves whilst others, unfortunately, see it as additional control and even punishment.

In the older patient, there has often been a tendency to replace the perceived lack of love and nurturing in their life with "sweets and cakes". Such comfort eating eases the situation for short periods but, in the long run, doesn't enhance self-esteem and is definitely a factor in the development of diabetes in later life.

It takes time and courage to let love in and trust those who want to help. So often there is a tendency to reject such overtures leading to further isolation. But in the end, if we're willing to open the door to love, we'll find that it had never deserted us even in our most desperate moments.

2) Hypoglycaemia

I believe that low blood sugar is a symptom rather than a disease representing a more complex hormonal imbalance. The signs include irritability, clumsiness, slurred speech, agitation, sleepiness and a craving for instant food. The cause is usually associated with high levels of insulin (caused by stress) plus the inadequate intake of long carbohydrates such as the grains.

This condition is commonly seen in those who are highly strung, analytical and find it difficult to do one thing at a time (see base chakra) and therefore, rather than advising the intake of sweet foods which only give a short-term buzz, any healing program must explore the individual's stress levels and encourage relaxation.

3) Indigestion

Although this is probably one of the commonest complaints in the world, most people treat themselves with "over-the-counter" remedies, never seeking professional advice. But there are powerful psychospiritual messages behind the illness which include:

"What do you find difficult to digest?"
"Where have you bitten off more than you can chew?"
"What in your present life needs breaking down into smaller, more manageable pieces?"
"What are you worrying about unnecessarily?"
"Where do you feel helpless about a problem?"

"Worrying" has become an acceptable form of behaviour in most societies where it is equated with "caring": "It's because I care, that I worry." The problem is that adding worry to any situation rarely eases the problem and more commonly, magnifies it. Have you noticed that when someone says: "I'm worried about the trip you're about to make", it doesn't reduce your anxiety level! Respecting the path of another and trusting their abilities is a far more positive and loving affirmation.

For our part, we need to honestly assess whether we are using fear, anxiety and guilt to avoid making personal decisions, taking responsibility for our own happiness or standing in our own power. By becoming overwhelmed by situations with the resultant feelings of helplessness, we can ignore the need to take any responsibility for our actions. However, by reducing our problems into manageable pieces and then calmly dealing with each in turn, we gain confidence and the knowledge that we do have choices in our life.

4) Peptic Ulcers

If the stress continues, indigestion may subsequently lead to ulceration caused by thinning of the lining of the intestine due to poor blood supply and abnormal digestive-juice production. The two types, gastric (stomach) and duodenal, affect different sections of the gut and also have different psychological mechanisms.

Gastric ulcers tend to be seen in those who are extrovert worriers. In appearance, they often look nervous and restless with deep worry lines across their forehead. They commonly smoke, drink copious caffeine, imbibe in alcohol to relax and have a mind that never switches off.

The obvious answer is to find ways of relaxing which may require professional help such as hypnotherapy, yoga or Tai Chi. Through voicing their concerns and making them more manageable, stress can be reduced although it may be necessary to reflect on why they appear to attract so much tension into their life. Is it time to change a belief pattern that no longer serves them such as: "I'm only successful when stressed", or "Everybody needs me."

Maybe a useful question to ask related to self-worth and worry would be: "If you knew you were good at your job and loved by your family, could you relax and enjoy life?" If not: "What do you need to happen for you to worry less and is it achievable?" Changing patterns of a lifetime takes time but it's worth it in the end.

Duodenal ulcers more commonly affect those who hide their problems, preferring to appear in control and respond to any concern with a cheerful: "I'm fine." Then between two and four in the morning all the problems of the day emerge from the deep unconscious and the pain of the ulcer wakes the individual to the anxiety they are trying to avoid. They may also smoke and drink but will rarely show their feelings or lack of confidence believing that they "should be able to cope"!

These individuals need to learn to let others into their life and to share their concerns. Through delegation and co-operation the load of responsibility is lessened and the risk is reduced of these intense fears boring a hole through the lining of the intestine.

5) Cancer of the Intestine

Cancer overall will be discussed further in the section on the heart chakra. However, the need to "swallow" disappointment, anger and hurt behind a smiling, cheerful face is a common feature of cancer of the oesophagus, stomach, pancreas and colon. Some cancer patients do not attempt to hide these feelings but fail to release them, preferring revenge and pain to forgiveness.

Unfortunately, it has become popular in many societies and religions to pay great respect to those who shield their emotions from public view, despite the cost to their health. It is not a matter of whether you express or not but rather that you can appreciate the motivating force which is available to you, moving you through any situation to a place of greater understanding and enhanced soul life. Emotions are not the enemy; indeed, stagnation, ignorance and control kill many more people.

Unfortunately, I can recall many examples of repressed feelings being a contributing factor in the emergence of cancer of the intestine:

- The man who coped with the sudden loss of his job but couldn't cope with his wife walking away from the marriage, with his son, developed colon cancer but never got angry!
- The woman who never got over her unrequited love for a married man, developed pancreatic cancer, telling very few people of her deep love and subsequent pain.
- The man, whose business partner cheated the company out of thousands of pounds, failed to mention this when asked: "Has anybody ever hurt you or let you down?" developed colon cancer.
- The woman, raised in a violent household, who never expressed her anger, even when provoked, developed cancer of the stomach.
- The man who was latterly angry and cantankerous and who never forgave his father for making him join the family business, developed colon cancer.

The message is this: learn to express (through talking, writing, shouting, singing, dancing etc.) your emotions and then choose to move on. Anger is the emotion of movement and with it we must either "move our position" or "our attitude". If we stay in it or deny its presence, it destroys us.

6) Hiatus Hernia

This condition occurs when a portion of the stomach pushes through the diaphragmatic opening causing a loosening of the sphincter which controls the direction of flow of our food through the stomach. The individual may experience reflux of acid, heartburn and excess burping, all made worse by bending over or when lying in bed.

Esoterically, the hernia suggests laxity in the area of the solar plexus related to low self-esteem and feelings of not being "worthy of love". When extra worry and guilt are added to this dimension but not expressed, the pressure builds up and is experienced as reflux.

Expressing the emotions, delegating where necessary and giving oneself credit when it's due, may not correct the defect in the diaphragm but certainly eases the symptoms!

7) Coeliac Disease

In this condition of the small intestine, the ability is reduced by the lining of the bowel to absorb the healthy materials from the food, leading to malabsorption, diarrhoea and anaemia. Medically, we know that the gluten component of many grains exacerbates the problem but there is a psychospiritual aspect which also needs to be addressed.

Our intestine deals not only with food but also with life's experiences allowing us to absorb from situations those things which will nourish and enhance our being and to reject those which we no longer need. I believe individuals with Coeliac disease have often experienced one or more episodes of painful crisis which were "hard to swallow" and therefore difficult to understand or absorb.

This contributed to the changes which took place in the lining, with the message of the disease being: "I'm on guard against anything which may further hurt me, so I'll limit what I absorb into my life, even though that may restrict my intake of love, nourishment and joy."

The body's innate concern is to protect us from emotional pain even when this may lead to physical distress and disease. The way forward often requires professional psychological help to provide a safe place in which the pain can be expressed and then released, as well as advice given on healthy methods of coping.

8) Liver Disease

The liver performs many vital functions including manufacture, detoxification and storage. It is also strongly allied to the emotion of anger which, as discussed previously, is the energy that helps to motivate movement and make decisions. If we choose to hold onto anger, resentment or bitterness preferring to "please" others by seeking their approval, it's the liver and its associated organs which take the brunt of the impact. Therefore, if we look at the liver meridian (from oriental medicine) we see the following illnesses:

Gout: commonly seen in the joints of the great toes, denotes frustration.
Varicose veins: suggests a failure to accept the truth as it is, preferring to wear "rose-coloured glasses".
Pelvic problems: such as fibroids and prostate disease (see sacral chakra).
Gall stones: balls of anger seen in someone who is caught between the desire to see good in everyone and their resentment of being used. Both perceptions are correct and a compromise must be reached to bring healing to this area.

Hepatitis and cirrhosis of the liver: usually associated with a viral or bacterial infection but in my experience also linked to a predisposing tendency towards suppression of anger.

Alcoholism: this addiction relates to poor self-worth, over-sensitivity to the feelings of others and difficulty expressing anger appropriately. Drink becomes a way of increasing confidence, escaping from the world and more importantly, from oneself.

Throat or thyroid disease: the persistent sore throat asks: "Who are you angry with?" (see throat chakra).

Tense neck muscles or wry neck: unexpressed rage: "I'll kill him" behind an angelic smiling face, settles into the muscles of the neck. The wry neck, where there is an inability to turn the head in one direction, asks: "Who is the pain in the neck?"

Tight tempero-mandibular joints (TMJ – jaw) or grinding teeth: tension so easily gathers in this area and everything is expressed through a "fixed grin". Compliant children often grind their teeth at night in an attempt to regain control of their life (see throat chakra).

One woman had visited a variety of specialists over a period of ten years for jaw pain. During my consultation I asked: "When is the pain worse?"

"In the morning," she replied without hesitation.

"What's the difference between the night and morning?" I enquired.

"My husband is there!" she answered with a sigh.

Apparently, her husband worked late into the evening and therefore they had little time to talk. However, in the morning, she would attempt to hold a conversation over breakfast, at which point her husband would say: "I'm listening" and promptly disappear behind the newspaper. This infuriated her, for at work she was the boss and everybody listened!

I gently suggested other ways of communicating, preferably without the underlying anger and the following morning she announced: "You won't believe it but my husband came home last night and said that we need to talk and we continued long into the night. Look I can move my jaw without pain." Sometimes miracles do happen!

Eye problems: typically the bright red eye says: "I'm seeing red!" Other illnesses where there is infection or inflammation may be triggered by feelings of anger (see third eye).

Ligaments: sprains are far more common when we are tense with resentment or anger.

As you can see, anger is a factor in many common diseases and as a doctor I can remember many a patient whose varicose veins had been treated, their uterus and gall bladder removed, suffered from thyroid inactivity and whose eyes were not in perfect health.

Maybe if I had known then what I know now, I would have treated my patients in a very different manner. Everybody has their own preferred way to express anger. For example, some benefit from shouting (especially in the privacy of their own car or in Nature), others write letters they never send, whilst others believe there is a need to confront the person concerned. Different situations may require different responses, but at the end of the day, the release of anger should help to move you on so that the decisions you make bring the very best out of life.

And finally, from the study of the iris of the eye, we know that people with green or hazel eyes (the yellow of bile on the underlying blue eyes) have a greater propensity towards suppression of anger, so watch out!

9) Travel Sickness

Whether the nausea occurs in the car, boat or plane the problem is the same. Although the imbalance physically involves a disturbance in the inner ear, psychospiritually it relates to an overactive solar plexus where the movement of the vehicle increases its energetic activity causing the individual to vomit.

In my experience these individuals are highly sensitive and psychic and need to learn to close down their solar plexus and hence reduce the vibrations they absorb from their environment. At the same time it helps to move one's awareness down to the feet and fix one's vision onto something which is stable.

10) Diseases of the Spleen

Physically, the spleen is part of the immune system and acts as the cleanser of the blood. In esoteric terms, the spleen is related to the ability to "sift through" the myriad of thoughts which flow, often unconsciously, through our mind, and retain those which can realistically bear fruit, whilst destroying the rest.

There are two factors that can disrupt this function. The first is that the individual's mind becomes so overwhelmed with all manner of thoughts, with little discrimination, that the spleen experiences overload. The second relates to the manifestation of such thoughts which require a solid base in which to grow. If the individual is poorly grounded, out of touch with their feelings or unrealistic about the chances of these ideas growing to fruition, then the spleen will also suffer.

Fortunately, this organ is extremely resilient and can adapt fairly well to its environment showing early symptoms of strain as tiredness, mild anaemia, a low white blood count and poor resistance to infection. Any of these signs may require medical examination but at the same time the individual should look at their mental workload and start to filter out those things that do not reflect the soul's intention and therefore cannot reach a creative outcome.

Esoterically, the stomach works alongside the spleen and will often show signs of "overload" (indigestion) before any hint of disturbance to the spleen's function.

Suggestions to Balance the Activity of the Solar Plexus Chakra

1) Write a CV to God which includes six talents that you are proud of and state why He/She should employ you. (And don't just write down sociably acceptable gifts but include those that make you who you are.)
2) List three episodes from your life where, from a soul point of view, you achieved something that was personally difficult or challenging, e.g. returning to study at the age of 40, staying in a difficult relationship which in the end proved the right thing to do, giving up a job that was secure in order to fulfil a dream, learning to swim when you were 50 etc., and celebrate.
3) Congratulate yourself when you manage to say "No", rather than taking the easy way out. If uncertain, remember to use: "I'll think about it, I'll come back to you, I need to consult my diary."
4) Learn to receive compliments in style, remembering not to return them immediately but to accept them as a loving gift.
5) Use the short-term methods of protection mentioned under the section on "Handling Power" while making time to understand the deeper issues.
6) Remember to express the appropriate emotion at the appropriate time and if this is not possible, talk to someone else about the problem, write a letter you never send (and burn it) or let your feelings out in a safe place such as in the car, on a beach or with the aid of a punch-bag!

It is said that we have five days to express our emotions after which they become chronic and can become a contributing factor in the development of disease. Check where you are holding onto, suppressing or expressing the wrong emotion and choose to release it and move on.

7) Only give advice when requested, accepting others as they are, just as you wish to be treated.

8) Become conscious of your "victim, martyr, rescuer, pleaser or guilt tripper" and recognise the game you are playing with others. There is no winner in these contests and they are a waste of valuable energy; have the courage to get up and leave.

9) Yellow is the natural colour of this chakra although when the centre is overactive, yellow may intensify its activity, so try a few different shades and if necessary bring calming colours into your life such as green and pink.

Chapter 10

The Heart Chakra

■ The Heart Chakra

Position:	Centre of Chest
Spirtual Aspect:	Self-Love
Basic Need:	To Give and Take Unconditionally
Related Emotions:	Joy, Hurt, Bitterness
Endocrine Gland:	Thymus
Associated Organs:	Heart, Breasts
Colour:	Green

Spirital Aspect ... Self-Love

The diaphragm provides a natural division between those chakras involved in the personality and those which are transpersonal, allied to the soul. At this time in our evolution, both the heart and crown chakras are being activated by Universal energy, awakening us to our true purpose and bringing us in line with the transformation of consciousness which has been occurring on this planet since 1987. For apart from the planet's movement into the Aquarian Age and the end of the Mayan calendar in 2012, we as human beings are in the process of undergoing a much larger paradigm shift which is transforming our whole perspective on the Universe, especially in the area of time and space.

If the personality is secure and true, the changes will feel like riding the rapids interspersed with periods of calm when nothing seems to be happening at all. For others, the journey will appear more hazardous presenting the individual with many challenges which are urging them to seek the truth and light within.

The activity of the heart chakra is fundamentally important to these times for its energetic signal acts like a homing device which, through resonance, **reconnects us to our true centre**. It is the seat of **intuition** or inner knowing and dynamically has the function of adding the creative spark or **joy** to any idea or dream so that its manifestation is **en-joyable**.

If we're excited by a project then this is a good omen for its success, for it suggests that we are in harmony or resonance with the notion and that the excitement felt is purely an echo of the situation already being realised on another level of existence. If the thrill is not present then the time may not be right or the structure of the project may need revising.

Love and Forgiveness

So what is love? Throughout history, our poets, song writers, artists, playwrights and those less creative have attempted to depict their interpretation of love. Even within our own language, love has many different faces dependent on the object of our affection, with the same word being used to describe a state of being when talking about an intimate partner, sex, friends, our car, food and occasionally ourselves!

As spoken by Kahlil Gibran, in the Prophet when speaking about love:
Love gives naught but itself and takes naught but from itself.
Love possesses not nor would it be possessed;
For love is sufficient unto love.

And what of self-love? Apart from those who are narcissistic, most people find it easier to love others than themselves for we can always bring to mind a part of our nature or body which is less than perfect and certainly not loveable. Yet the statement in the Bible that says: "Love thy neighbour as thyself" (Matthew 22:39) is a theme which runs through all religions, implying a fundamental Law by which man should live. However, the phrase has often been interpreted as: "Love others first" which of course completely denies the latter section of the message and poses the question: "How are we able to love others when we have little or no notion of loving ourselves?"

Can we accept **all** aspects of our being, loving our crocked nose and offering forgiveness to ourselves when we "make a mistake" or when we do those things of which we're not proud. And can we do the same for others transforming our need to judge and condemn into compassion, understanding and forgiveness?

This does not preclude the need to express one's feelings and to release any pain endured, but the healing process reaches its climax at the moment of acceptance and forgiveness which by its very word means "making space for the new". To cling to the past through unexpressed emotions which have often been boxed up and placed in the attic, denies the soul the chance for full intimate connection with itself. Even though the packages are "out of sight" they are certainly not "out of mind" and their contents will eventually seep out of their hiding place and erode the very fabric of life especially our physical body.

And why will we not forgive? Probably because such a powerful release of old attachments would propel us into a transpersonal world where we would truly find ourselves in service guided not by "our will" but by "Thy will". Are you willing to take the risk to forgive and be loved unconditionally?

True, unconditional love is not about being soft and accepting any behaviour. It is best exemplified by watching the mother bird who instinctively knows when, with love, she needs to push her young from the nest. As they plummet towards the Earth, their wings still furled tightly to their side, they lament: "What did I do wrong, I thought she loved me?"

As their anger rises in response to this unjust treatment, they start to flap their wings and all of a sudden, they're flying. That is unconditional love! On these occasions, we're guided by our intuition to act for the good of all concerned even though they may not appreciate or understand our motives at the time. You cannot **give** unconditional love for in the giving, conditions are attached as seen in the solar plexus. It is a state of being which, when we are totally in alignment with our soul and resonating with the greater truth, labels become unnecessary.

Intuition

Both the heart and third eye are deeply involved with this innate power, the former contributing the quality of compassion while the latter brings wisdom. Love without wisdom lacks clarity, discrimination and detachment whilst wisdom without love can appear cold, callous and lacking empathy.

But together they create a force which is so strong that we will change our lives on the basis of its message. That moment of: "Ah-h-h" resonates so deeply within our soul that nothing can dissuade us from following its calling: "I can't explain but it just feels right." Many a time we will actually place our hand over our heart and tap gently to re-enforce the feelings of strength.

Intuition is our eternal friend who has never left us but who we desert when fear, desire or will take over our consciousness. It is the voice we hear in our darkest moments, during sleep-state and meditation. It also reaches us through a variety of messengers who provide us with an answer just when we need it most: friends, Nature, the media, messages on poster boards and strangers who cross our paths for a fleeting moment in time.

The intuition, also known as "gut feelings" or a "hunch", is not interested in our day-to-day affairs but will repeatedly guide us back onto our soul's path when we become entrenched in human matters which have paralysed the soul. It cannot interfere with our actions, for free will is always respected but, given the opportunity, thoughts will enter our mind or events be presented that will, hopefully, remind us of our true vocation.

Intuition asks us to live in the "present" moment rather than giving our power away to an obsession with the past and future. Caroline Myss, a gifted medical intuitive and author, says that when she reviews the energy threads entering the body of an individual, it's not uncommon to find that 80% are still attached to the past, 15% to the future, leaving only 5% interacting with the present. When I've asked people about living in the present, it has been fascinating to see that although there are wonderful altruistic views on the matter, I'm offered many more reasons why this state of affairs should be avoided.

Despite intensive enquiry, I'm still unclear why we have so much difficulty accepting, what I believe is, our birthright:

To love and be loved unconditionally
To find joy in the present moment
To achieve our heart's content
To feel secure in our place on this Earth
To enjoy the fruits offered in total respect to those who offer them
To be co-creators of our life

The intuition, the feminine aspect of the soul, relates to our feeling body and is therefore strongly connected to the five senses, the emotions and the psychic sense. I suggest that our preoccupation with the masculine qualities of the soul over many thousands of years betrayed and belittled this sensory body, separating us from our environment

and almost fatally disconnecting us from each other, ourselves and the Creative Force.

This cannot continue and it's inherent that the female within every soul should once again become sensitive and receptive to the world through feelings, our five senses and intuition. It is interesting to note that in our language we use bodily sensations to describe the intuition: "I feel it in my bones or water" or "He/she has a nose for these things."

I'm very hopeful that the situation can be reversed especially when I find that most people can recall feelings associated with their intuition, such as:

- tingling up and down the spine or on the top of the head
- goose bumps on the arms: "It makes my hairs stand on end"
- feelings of inner strength and determination
- clarity in decision-making; seeing the larger picture
- feelings of inner peace, joy and stillness,

and when they don't follow it, they feel:

- drained, sick in the stomach or shaky
- a sinking feeling which says: "Get out of this situation fast!"
- everything is a struggle or a drag.

The difference between these two lists shows how sensitive we all are to our inner guidance even though the subject is not discussed openly. For unfortunately, as mentioned in the previous chapter, intuition has been suppressed by those who needed to retain authority over others because it promoted the idea that you could "think for yourself" and this, they concluded, would create mayhem!

But the intuitive force cannot be destroyed through man-made edicts, coercion or by evoking fear. For this is a God-given gift built into the very DNA of our soul and linking us, not only to our own truth but also to that of each member of the human race, every facet of life on this planet, to the galaxy to which we belong and the worlds beyond, on a multi-dimensional level. And when we are in harmony with its "tone" and can feel that vibration in every part of our body, including our subtle bodies, then we are truly "in love" and there is nowhere else we want to be. Our life then becomes totally in tune with the creative energy and rather than intuition being another function of the mind, it becomes a "way of being" where there is only the present moment.

Merging with the Moment

As discussed previously, whereas the attracting force in the solar plexus is hoping and in the throat is willing, that in the heart is loving. I wonder if you're able to feel the difference in your own mind and body as we move from one energetic form to another? Love is both the vibrational energy which attracts us towards situations with which we can resonate and the state we enter when in that place of coherence.

The loving vibration is both gentle and accepting; it doesn't force or coerce nor does it exist in the past or future; it just is.

A symbolic form which represents this concept is seen in the Vesica Pisces as shown below:

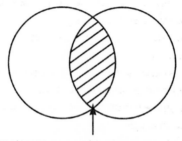

COHERENCE, BLISS, STILLNESS, ECSTASY, UNITY, THE VOID

This geometric figure reveals that when the circumference of one circle is drawn so that it touches the centre of another, the oval shape that is created between them is a sacred mathematical design with a vibration which equates to coherence, love, bliss and perfect unity.

Our aim, via the heart chakra, is to create relationships with other aspects of the Creative Life Force and reflect this exquisite union where **each circle remains true to itself and yet is touched in its centre by another**. This is love and in this place magic and miracles happen for we are totally connected to the God Force.

To achieve such ecstasy, our hearts need to be clear from any impediment that would prevent us from loving ourselves fully and embracing the entry of someone or something into our centre. One way that we've avoided such a state of connection is through the production of multiple forms of **disassociation** through which we've created an illusion of reality, similar to a "soap opera", where we can live undisturbed nursing our fear of losing ourselves to the bliss of love. So real is this world that in many cases we have become addicted, experiencing actual physical and psychological withdrawal symptoms when the bubble bursts. However, remember these addictions are **not** the problem but conceal a deeper fear of becoming immersed in the experience of love.

Some of the methods through which we can enter a state of altered reality, not in harmony with our inner being, include:

- Drugs, alcohol, gambling, smoking and excessive sex.
- Television, the computer, books and hobbies.
- Becoming a workaholic, so busy and so much in demand.
- Overly serious, or the opposite, making light of every aspect of life.
- Controlling one's world through criticism, cynicism and scepticism.
- Taking on the responsibility of caring, fixing and rescuing everybody.
- Provoking confrontation and remaining angry, bitter and revengeful.
- Becoming introvert, aloof and avoiding confrontation.
- Over-talking rather than being still.
- Over-analytical, always asking questions and living in the head, avoiding spontaneity.
- Living in a permanent state of anxiety about the future.
- Preoccupied with the regrets of the past.
- Playing power games with the rescuer, controller, pleaser, victim, martyr and guilt tripper.
- Being too busy saving the world to commit to oneself.

What methods do your use to avoid this deep connection with yourself and the Universe and what fears do you hold about being loved?

Entering the Void; Kali and Lilith

Some of our anxiety relates to a fear of annihilation, being totally absorbed by the experience and denied any sense of self. In most cultures, the archetype of this destructive or devouring energy is represented by a female figure such as Kali or Lilith, both of whom are seen to exert their power during moments of intimacy.

However, if we truly understand the nature of our interaction with these Goddesses we will realise that, like the woman who gave us physical birth, these ancient Mothers are, in that precious moment of bliss, removing everything in our life that prevents us from experiencing spiritual birth. Our willing and conscious acceptance of these Universal forces is essential for true enlightenment to occur and that their denigration to the dark side over thousands of years has been engineered by those who craved power and sought to prevent each human being realising their true state of existence.

And finally, what is encircling our heart that the Goddesses are attempting to clear and that prevents us reaching this deep state of union? Here we find the **pains**, the **shame**, the **disappointments**, the **hurt**, the **feelings of loss**, the **tears** and even the **deep feelings of connection** which overwhelm us. It is time to move on, allowing these feelings to surface, accepting their presence without judgement and absorbing them into our being with forgiveness and compassion.

Only then can the heart be free and unbounded and only then can we experience the exquisite and extraordinary power of love.

Body Language

1) As mentioned above, it's not uncommon to touch our heart chakra when speaking from the place of intuition re-enforcing the power of our words. 2) We've all seen children standing alone expressing their hurt by hugging themselves across the chest. This action is not restricted to the young, with many adults finding similar comfort. A hug from someone else is even more effective.

Associated Illnesses

It's not easy to separate diseases of the solar plexus and heart chakra as most of our efforts as a race are focused, at present, on raising our desires from those which merely serve our needs to those which serve the community; moving from conditional love to that which is unconditional.

Therefore the illnesses mentioned here could be attached to either chakra although the immune system is specifically geared to resonate with our soul/heart's desires and becomes diseased when these are not met. Some features of heart disease also relate to the base chakra but ultimately our deepest sense of inner security can only emerge from a true heart connection.

1) Disease of the Heart and Blood Vessels
A) MYOCARDIAL INFARCT (HEART ATTACK)
Still one of the major killers in the Western world, this illness has been the subject of intensive research for decades. From a psychospiritual point of

view, studies carried out in the mid 1970s showed that even though smoking, high cholesterol, diabetes and high blood pressure play a large part in the causation of a myocardial infarct, they are not always present.

What the researchers did find was that there was a common time for these attacks to occur that is, **between 8–9 o'clock on a Monday morning.** These findings were verified around the industrial world and intriguingly when questioned further, most respondents expressed a strong feeling of "lack of fulfilment" in their work with "heart-sink" when they woke on a Monday morning.

Further enquiry revealed a general sense that "dreams had gone unrealised" and "achievements had brought little happiness" but there was also a strong belief that they were powerless to do anything to change the situation. This feeling of limitation is reflected in the pathology of the illness where the blood vessels which feed the heart are restricted by the formation of "inflexible plaque" so that reduced amounts of blood, which carries the life force or joy, are able to reach the heart itself.

This sense of being driven into a "cul-de-sac" is evoked in phrases such as:

"My heart isn't in my work any more."

"My heart sunk when I saw the pile of letters I needed to answer."

"I just feel I'm not enjoying my life; my heart has stopped singing."

Accompanying these sentences are words of limitation which form a large part of the individual's language:

"I should/must/ought/got to ... I'm caught up in the SMOG!"

"I can't/it's not that easy/that's difficult/I'd love to ... but ... "

This ingrained belief system which deals with limitation, helplessness and control can unfortunately be passed down through generations of a family where all the men suffer a heart attack at the same age. Indeed, even the thought that your life may end in a particular year creates a limiting belief. I remember meeting a man who was convinced that he would die at 50 and therefore made no plans past that date. When he reached his 51st birthday, he was distraught: "What do I do now? I'll have to make a life for myself."

Moving beyond redundant belief systems takes courage, especially when it goes against the family and social background, but when we are committed to improving the lives of our children, the effort is worth it.

The next major factor in heart disease is "loneliness" and you can be lonely in a crowd! We all need to "connect", to be "intimate" and to "communicate" ourselves to others. The type A personality, commonly associated with heart disease, often values success more highly than friendship, finding themselves at the top of the ladder minus family and friends, or if they are still present, unable to communicate with them except on day-to-day matters.

On other occasions, work becomes an acceptable escape from difficulties at home where criticism is a large part of communication and where the heart has gradually closed down, expecting little intimacy from the relationship. In Chinese medicine, the heart is connected to the tongue and it is said that if the tongue does not speak from the heart, the heart will start to die. How many times do I hear someone say:

"I have spoken to you more in this hour than I have to my wife in 25 years."

"Nobody's ever been interested in what I truly felt and probably I've learned to keep quiet rather than risk scorn or humiliation."

It is well known that those who have a loving spouse at home have a reduced risk of recurrent heart disease. Unfortunately, heart disease among women is rising and I don't believe that it's all smoking related. Women are losing their natural art of connection through talking and sharing, often too busy with daily concerns and becoming more and more disconnected from their feelings. Women, more than men, need to resonate with the rhythm of the pulse in order to maintain a healthy heart.

Another natural medicine with very few side effects is a loyal and loving dog. The heart of many people has benefited from this special relationship as it provides unconditional love with a tail that wags whatever mood you emit. A dog also takes you for walks which is good exercise, eats the food you shouldn't, listens to your concerns without answering back and allows stroking to take place which is actually giving *you* healing. I would love to see every heart patient being discharged from hospital with a dog in tow under oath to take special care of this faithful friend.

And a final note on the matter of raised cholesterol. Eighty per cent of the cholesterol in our blood is made by the liver in response to stress, enabling the body to form cortisone, the hormone which helps us to deal with the problem. So when we become concerned about our latest reading, our body immediately makes more cholesterol to deal with the added stress and guess what, the blood level goes up! Relaxing, letting go of the tight controls on our life, laughing more and allowing everything in moderation certainly eases the pressure on the body and creates a better sense of reality. Truly enjoying one's life from deep within the soul is the best medicine for the heart.

B) PERICARDITIS

In this illness, the sack that encircles the heart becomes inflamed causing severe pain which is often confused with angina. The causative factor may be viral but there is usually a high level of stress involved where the barriers protecting our "heart" have been breached, leaving the individual feeling vulnerable and hurt.

Exploring who or what got inside our defences, and gently but firmly closing the "wound" accelerates the healing process.

C) ARTERIAL DISEASE

The blockage of arterial blood flow, mainly affecting the legs, is commonly associated with smoking and the presence of high cholesterol (see appropriate sections). However, it is also important to recognise psychologically where the full appreciation of life is restricted. "Where is the joy?" The physical pain due to the poor blood supply prevents the individual walking forward and reflects a deeper fear of walking into the future exacerbated by the pain of the past. Therefore, alongside any medical treatment, it is essential to examine and release old grief, hurts and regrets allowing forgiveness into life which can immediately open the way for more joy to enter.

2) Diseases of the Immune System

Medical science has seen an enormous increase in illnesses related to this system and indeed, our knowledge on this subject has quadrupled since the early 1980s, mainly in response to the worldwide emergence of AIDS. One modern branch of medicine, psychoneuroimmunology (PNI) makes direct correlations between the mind, the nervous system and immune system and has allowed us to understand that when we express emotions, small hormones (neurotransmitters) are released into the blood stream and cellular changes occur.

This is only the beginning of the age where ancient esoteric concepts meet science but it's an exciting start. One interesting observation is that where there is a weakened immune response, present both in infections and cancer, strong feelings of "helplessness" often precede the illness. These emotions which are evoked when we feel out of control and unable to cope, are made worse in the presence of "low self-worth" and a "poor social support system", meaning that we have few true friends to turn to.

As someone who has worked within the health system for many years, I recognise that the commonest times of feeling out of control are when we are unwell, where there is little communication, when the prognosis is unclear and when our identity has been stripped away from us. I would ask that those in the caring profession come to understand that psychological care of the individual is as important as any medical intervention. Let us remember the patient is a person first and not a disease and even though we may not have the answers, have the courage to treat them with respect and say: "I don't know."

A) ALLERGIES AND HYPERSENSITIVITY

Allergies, such as hay fever, are genetic, affecting many family members whereas hypersensitivity seems to occur out-of-the-blue. Whatever the situation, apart from removing the offending triggers such as house dust mite, grasses etc., I believe it's important to recognise psychospiritually that these individuals have an extremely vulnerable solar plexus. This means they easily attract other people's thoughts and feelings which cause them to "react" rather than "act", without understanding the original motivating force.

As discussed in the section on the solar plexus, this tendency is often driven by low self-worth exacerbated by being raised in a dysfunctional family where communication was inappropriate and therefore the child had to use their solar plexus and psychic powers to survive.

I will also say that the children of today are entering this world with a highly tuned intuition although emotionally still a child. Therefore, many of them are wiser than their years and are not fooled by the non-verbal communication often used by adults to prevent "the children knowing". Their sensitivity also causes them to be deeply disturbed by any disharmony especially when they feel powerless to act (see also asthma, throat chakra).

Whether adult or child, it's important for the individual to learn to develop adequate boundaries so they can stop acting like a sponge when it comes to feelings and atmospheres which are not related to their soul's growth. By using some of the forms of protection discussed in the previous Chapter, temporary relief will be achieved allowing time for the development of self-worth alongside an ability to express one's own feelings, when appropriate.

B) AIDS

This disease, which was practically unknown in the early 1980s, has had a profound effect on the world, its population and our knowledge of the immune system. The virus involved has the capacity to not only destroy the very cells which are required for a healthy immune response, the T-helper cells (CD4), but also limit the innate communication which occurs between one white blood cell and another, disabling the early warning system.

The virus quickly removes itself from the blood stream where it is susceptible to circulating antibodies and hides in the nuclei of cells, particularly the T-cells. The individual is then HIV positive with anti-bodies in the blood stream but no evidence of viral activity. There it sits until the body is called upon to mount a defence against an invading microbe, such as the one which causes the common cold. Immediately, the T-cells are instructed to multiply and the virus takes advantage of such a response by using the energy generated to multiply itself.

This sequence of events makes the use of a vaccine extremely difficult, for any immunisation program depends on activating the T-cells which will also activate any virus present. The other problem is that, like the flu virus, this virus is able to mutate (change its appearance) at a rapid speed. Hence the vaccine of today is not the one required for tomorrow.

I offer this detailed explanation to emphasise that new diseases of our age are mirroring technological advances and hence our response needs to incorporate concepts from the world of information technology, for I believe that is where the answers will be found. It is no coincidence that computers also suffer from viruses but these are acknowledged as being man-made!

From a psychospiritual point of view, AIDS is exposing our prejudices and the difficulties we experience in showing compassion to those who are different, including the sick. It tends to affect those who are in the minority or disadvantaged where there appears to be no way out (helplessness) or where they feel that they will never be "good enough" to be accepted by society. This low self-worth may be hidden by the outward appearance of someone who is a pleaser or rescuer of others allowing little time for their own concerns. Unfortunately, when the conditions which are attached to the offer of help are not met (the need to be needed), helplessness and despair emerge and the immune system becomes vulnerable.

There are several programs now available for individuals with AIDS or who are HIV positive, many of which include meditation and self-awareness options. Changes in society's thinking has also helped to reduce the incidence of new cases but it is inherent in all of us to examine our own prejudices and remove the barriers between "us and them" and our need to judge. And while we're at it, it's important to search inside for those parts of ourselves which have become ostracised due to their imperfections and return them to the fold with love.

C) CANCER

Of all the illnesses I write about, it is always concerning cancer that I'm told: "I don't think you should make people feel guilty for their illness", and I ask: "Who said anything about guilt?" I may say that it is usually a member of my own profession who makes such a comment and, in view of my thoughts about the provocation of guilt, there may be a power issue present which is, I believe, already a significant factor in the causation of this disease.

I strongly believe that it's in the best interests of the patient to give them as much information as possible when requested and let them make a decision as to what is appropriate. Many cancer patients have told me that, had they been given a deeper understanding of their illness, they would have felt less helpless and the process of healing would then have been one of co-operation.

There is mounting research to suggest that personality traits are present and consistent in those with cancer, many of which I have already referred to in earlier sections of this book. But to reiterate they include:

- Low self-worth.
- Suppression of the "I', with an identity built through relationships with others, work etc. Cancer commonly appears when the poor sense of self is exposed at the end of a "relationship" such as after retirement, redundancy, divorce or the loss of a loved one.
- Avoidance of conflict; the peace keeper.
- Pent-up anger which is rarely expressed for fear of loss of love.
- Feelings of isolation (even in a large family).
- Difficulty trusting others and hence few really close friends.
- Loss of someone or something not resolved … smiles through grief.
- Extrovert feeling types … excessive positive emotions; the life and soul of the party.
- Being the carer and rescuer for everybody else even where there is growing resentment.
- "Pathological niceness syndrome."
- Irascible and angry but never with the person who caused the offence.
- Bitter and resentful but unable to move through the pain which relates to hurt and rejection.

As you can see there are a mixture of signs, with 80% related to non-complaining, "nice" people whilst the others tend to express their emotions but are unable to release and move on. Both are hurt, angry and low in self-esteem and need to be given the opportunity, probably with professional help, to express their feelings and build a sense of self which includes a close and loving support system.

I recall one woman who had been told she had six months to live. "Right", she said, "if that's the case, I'm going to live it my way." So she went home, told her difficult 26-year-old son to find another place, spilt up with a partner who was alcoholic, left her job, chose not to return calls from those who she didn't consider close friends, and started to take care of herself. One year later, in good health, she found another job and moved out into the world a totally different person.

Finally, I want to remind you that healing doesn't always lead to good physical health and may indeed result in death. For my part, I want to offer support whatever happens and if the individual dies well and in touch with their soul then this is a bonus. But I have witnessed tremendous courage when someone chooses death over changes in their life and I want to honour these people too.

D) CANCER OF THE BREAST

The breasts are seen as both the seat of nurturing as well as being a powerful symbol of femininity. No woman can remain unmoved by the detection of a lump in her breast and its possible repercussions. Yet, we are still no closer to understanding the cause of the cancer apart from a possible link with animal fats.

If we look at it from a psychological point of view, there are definite links between the personality described above, suppression of anger and a tendency to devote all one's energy into nurturing and encouraging others, in the belief that this will provide a satisfactory purpose to life. However, as so commonly happens, when we give with such dedication we are sadly disappointed by the response for, after a while, people take us for granted and we're left to feel hurt, abandoned and resentful although this is rarely expressed.

My finding is that the left breast relates to issues around men, father etc. and the right, to issues with women, mother etc. Any healing program must include psychotherapy which meets both the needs of the individual and of the family for, without their involvement, emotions remain suppressed at home and the individual persists in her old patterns of caretaking, allowing the resentment to continue to build.

E) BENIGN BREAST DISEASE

This common condition is usually related to hormonal changes in the second half of the menstrual cycle, concerned with nurturing and support and the breast affected will follow the pattern described before in the section on cancer. However, there is a strong correlation between the development of these cysts and the feeling that any nurturing given to the individual had been tempered by criticism, expectations and shame with the result that they "never felt truly loved" and hence found it difficult to trust their heart in the hands of others.

For further information, please read the Chapter on the sacral chakra including the section on PMS. These lumps, either single or multiple, should disappear at the time of menses and, **if not**, require urgent referral to a medical specialist.

F) AUTO-IMMUNE DISEASES

This group of illnesses which is expanding every year, involves the formation of an antibody by our own immune system which then destroys some part of ourselves and includes:

A) RHEUMATOID ARTHRITIS (RA): an antibody developed against the joint linings and lining of the lungs. Since the joints are related to motion and severe inflammation is involved, the issues revolve around anger plus the feeling of being trapped, seen in someone who is usually quietly uncomplaining. Paradoxically there is also a fear of movement which reflects poor self-worth and hence, the illness is both a cry for acknowledgement and for loving support.

In young people, I commonly find that there has been a difficult or sick child in the family who understandably monopolised the parents' attention, leaving the RA individual feeling unnoticed and being told: "Be quiet, your brother/sister needs our help." No wonder after attempts to "be good" or "responsible", the illness emerges to stake a claim for acknowledgement.

B) POLYMYALGIA RHEUMATICA: an antibody made against the muscles particularly of the shoulders (carrying others) and pelvis (nurturing others) which represents the resentment of always needing to be strong for others with a desire for personal support and somewhere to rest.

C) SYSTEMIC SCLEROSIS: an antibody against the connective tissues surrounding major organs or just the skin (scleroderma), reflects the belief that low self-worth requires little space for expression and therefore they attempt to squeeze themselves out of their own life.

D) SYSTEMIC LUPUS ERYTHEMATOSIS (SLE OR LUPUS): an antibody against DNA which then forms complexes in the blood stream which block the small arteries. This illness is aggravated by sunlight and hence these individuals have to avoid the very life-giving force that most of us take for granted. This is the extent of self-sacrifice that accompanies these illnesses.

E) DIABETES: an antibody against the ability to produce insulin (see the solar plexus).

F) RAYNAUD'S DISEASE: an antibody against the small blood vessels of the hands and feet (see the base chakra).

G) MULTIPLE SCLEROSIS (MS): an antibody against the myelin covering the axon of the nerve (see the throat chakra).

H) IDIOPATHIC THROMBOCYTOPAENIA: an antibody against the production of platelets which causes the individual to bleed easily due to poor clotting abilities. This condition reflects a loss of life force through the inability to create adequate boundaries.

I) VITILIGO: an antibody against the pigment-forming cells in the skin which is the interface at which we meet other people. This reflects poor boundaries and low self-worth with a feeling of being an outcast or different. Standing in one's own light with pride restores some sense of connection.

There are other similar illnesses all of which have a common theme: to develop a self-destruct button. The "self", practically devoid of substance, is extremely difficult to treat as there are so few firms foundations on which to build. I remember one woman who I recommended to avoid coffee while taking my homoeopathic remedies, returned six weeks later and reported: "It was very good of you to try to help me, dear, but I didn't take your treatments as my husband likes coffee and you can understand that I couldn't make him drink it on his own!" Time and patience is required (especially when listening to these strange little quirks) and an understanding developed, of factors in childhood such as criticism and control which could have contributed to the low self-esteem.

Then the process of rebuilding begins. On many occasions, the individual presents themselves as someone eager to please, charming, optimistic and certain that you can help: "I've heard such good things about you." This should set off the warning bells as you recognise the sack of unfulfilled expectations which are now being placed at your feet which, if unmet, can lead to manipulation if your self-worth is also low. My experience is that firm conditions of contract must be built from the first day, for these individuals usually exhibit poor boundaries, unaware of the constraints of time and space.

"I'll take one step and then you take one step" is my motto for working with these clients, so that I encourage a sense of self-pride in their own achievements. These may include:

- Learning to say "No" rather than agreeing begrudgingly behind a smiling face.
- Taking time for self with no interruptions.
- Not being the first one to offer help and certainly not offering advice without being asked.
- Expressing feelings, especially anger and then moving on.
- Asking that others should love you for who you are, rather than for what you do.

All the diseases listed above provide the individual with an identity which, although not ideal, makes a statement. Unfortunately, with such a tenuous thread providing the individual with a sense of self, there is great reluctance to relinquish the hold on the disease unless self-identity has been deepened from within. Any treatment program must recognise the risks of destroying coping mechanisms and tread carefully if it's to succeed in reducing the incidence of symptoms.

G) MYALGIA ENCEPHALOMYELITIS (ME): CHRONIC FATIGUE SYNDROME OR FIBROMYALGIA

This condition, which is not by the way a new disease, can affect children as young as seven as well as adults and both genders equally. The symptoms are very similar to those of burn out which include:

- extreme exhaustion and lethargy
- disturbance of sleep patterns, drowsy in the day and awake all night
- painful and tender muscles, heavy and aching
- disturbance in the rhythm of the bowels, urinary system and menstruation
- poor concentration, poor memory and indecisive
- increased sensitivity to loud noises, bright lights, smells etc.
- depression, phobias and anxiety.

I believe there are many more people suffering from this illness than recorded which probably reflects the continued reluctance to accept this as a disease in its own right and because most people expect to feel some of these symptoms in a stressful world.

The pattern of personality that emerges is of someone walking a path which is not their own, trying to please an authority figure or loved one and reaching a point where the strain of separation between their soul's needs and those of the personality has become too great.

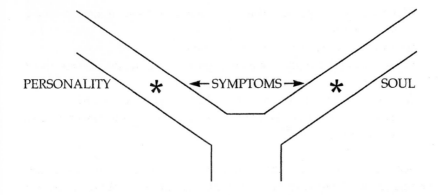

PERSONALITY   *   ←SYMPTOMS→   *   SOUL

The symptoms represent the distance between the energy of the inner and outer self and ask to be acknowledged so that changes can be implemented. However, on many occasions, the therapist will be instructed: "Just give me enough energy to continue working etc. and I'll be fine." The wise practitioner will hopefully answer: "But your lifestyle is the cause of the problem!"

Until the individual admits that they're ill and recognises the need to change, their symptoms will continue. The painful muscles represent "creative energy" which is **not** being expressed and many of these individuals are in jobs or studies where they're unable to freely express their creativity and follow their own path, for fear of disapproval or the guilt of letting other people down. For example:

- The man who entered banking to please his father although he really wanted to study interior design.
- The girl who was studying chemistry as her father was a doctor while she had a gift for the fine arts.
- The woman who, as a full-time teacher and mother, was exhausted but couldn't leave her job as everybody was so proud of her and the family needed the money.
- The journalist who was overwhelmed by what he saw in his work but couldn't stop for he felt it was his duty to record the truth.
- The hairdresser who found herself unable to listen to another client without panic.

In all these cases, the illness gave the individual permission to take time away from work, and more importantly, time to think. When self-worth is low, it requires great courage to step away from the sources of external approval and start to believe in oneself, and yet when you feel so unwell, there is no other way. Many of the people mentioned above were able to change their patterns of behaviour and with it went their job or studies and they became happier and healthier people, with much stronger boundaries and sense of self.

All of them still have to watch their energy levels but use this sensitive indicator as an ally which is advising them to slow down. Interestingly, many of them tell me that when they became ill their friends disappeared as they were no longer any fun. Good friends don't desert you, especially when you're down which suggests the superficial nature of these relationships based on the individual providing a useful service.

H) GLANDULAR FEVER (MONONUCLEOSIS)
Caused by the **Epstein Barr** virus this illness presents with sore throat, swollen glands and extreme tiredness and is common in young people in their late teens when the time for leaving home is approaching. The lymphatic system enables us to move into new situations with relative ease as long as we have released our dependency on the past. This illness occurs when there is still grief and in many ways should help to clear the passageway to a new life.

If the process is not complete, especially where there is low self-worth, the disease can become chronic resulting in ME.

I) LEUKAEMIA
This type of cancer affects the white blood cells of the body, our major defence system, and is commonly seen in those who by nature are sensitive, pick up on other people's emotions and are easily influenced by unpleasant situations or stories. The onset of leukaemia often occurs at times when something has shattered the defences and destroyed the natural enthusiasm and joy of life which usually exists within these individuals.

Alongside any medical treatment, there is a need to help these people to release feelings of helplessness, restore their boundaries and return to a state of joie de vivre.

J) LYMPHOMA (HODGKIN'S)
In this form of cancer, it is the lymphatic and immune systems that are affected, the former being associated with the disposal of toxins and the latter with the maintenance of healthy boundaries. What this reflects is that somewhere along the line the individual is holding onto "poisons" or

"toxins" from the past which are clogging up the lymph vessels and nodes and disabling them from carrying out their normal function. Such toxins may be emotional such as anger or grief, or chemical such as steroids or drugs.

At the same time, the individual's sensitivity and poor self-worth reduces the ability for the body to shake off these problems naturally. Medical treatment is essential but alongside this, is the need to examine the emotional debris and find ways to cleanse the lymphatic system both mentally and physically.

K) INFLUENZA
As a condition, which appears at such regular intervals and causes millions to take to their beds, we are still no closer to understanding what in us creates such susceptibility. As mentioned at the beginning of this section, feelings of helplessness, frustration and stress will lower the immune system considerably which could account for the illness occurring so widely in the world today.

Another factor is that viral infections appear at times of growth which, prior to the immunisation programs, was evident in our children as they contracted the various childhood illnesses. The great flu epidemics, especially the one which followed the First World War, were seen esoterically to be the means by which the earth cleansed itself including our own earthly body so that we could move forward to a new era. Could it be that during a bout of influenza we are also passing through a cleansing period which prepares us for a new state of consciousness?

Flexibility, inner strength, a healthy support system and compassion for oneself, all enhance the immune system, which can't be bad!

3) Anorexia Nervosa and Bulimia
These increasingly common conditions are unfortunately appearing in children and teenagers of either gender plus adulthood. Anorexia usually starts with a desire to lose weight to improve appearance. Unfortunately, the body image is often distorted and therefore even when the weight falls dramatically, often accompanied by the loss of menstruation in women, the individual still believes they are obese.

There is also a desire to take control of one aspect of their life often choosing food because of its social and nurturing implications and makes a statement, particularly to the mother that says: "I don't want your food or nurturing and I don't want you to control me any more."

Sadly, matters often proceed to the level where life is threatened and medical intervention is required. This slow form of suicide is commonly seen in those who are conscientious and try hard to please but feel they never receive the acclaim they desire, ie. the one that feeds the soul. Their deeper message says: "Love me for who I am and not for what I do".

And finally, the desire to remain in the body of a child represents a fear of taking on the responsibility of adulthood, commonly seen in those who have been "little parents" from the day they were born.

In **bulimia**, the situation is slightly different, for here the individual binges food and then either induces vomiting or diarrhoea or starves themselves for days after. As the weight rarely changes, this is a much more secretive illness where attention is sought but without voicing the need.

I remember a woman who was summoned to the headmaster of her son's school because the 11-year-old boy had been found making himself vomit. When the mother asked him what he was doing, he replied: "But you do the same Mum, I've heard you!" Children follow the lead of their parents and can no longer be fooled by the closure of doors.

All individuals mentioned here need love and attention without conditions although they must learn to express their feelings and develop adequate self-esteem so that they can no longer be disempowered by criticism or control.

Suggestions to Balance the Activity of the Heart Chakra

1) Start to love yourself by loving your body, beginning with the parts you find most acceptable. Use pleasant-smelling oils to rub into the body and take time to luxuriate in the bath.
2) Look at your life at present and check that it still excites you; if not, what needs to change?
3) Practise using your intuition whenever you can, tuning into your heart and asking whether this person or idea resonates with your inner being; if it doesn't, be true to your feelings.
4) Recognise ways in which you may be disassociating in your life and ask: "What do I fear from love?" Choose to spend more time in enjoying the present moment.
5) Affirm your desire for true love by saying: "I am loved, I am loveable, I am loving."

6) Practise a meditation for the heart. Sitting quietly, move your awareness to the region of the heart chakra. Then just allow the breath to move gently through this area. Allow emotions to emerge as you stay with the process without the need to judge, understand or fix. If tears arise, that's fine. Stay with the emotion until you can absorb it into your being with forgiveness and compassion.

7) Remember all the people who love you and imagine their love surrounding you until you can feel the warmth and affection. Now imagine yourself in that crowd and see yourself pouring love into your own being. Are there any parts of you which have difficulty accepting that love? If so just continue until the resistance melts and the difficult part merges with the whole.

8) Choose to forgive someone who has hurt you in the past. Write a letter that states your feelings but also offers forgiveness and then decide to send it or burn it. Both will have an effect. Surround the individual with love and light and, speaking to their heart, let them know that it's time to release the knot that binds the two of you together.

9) Choose to forgive yourself, releasing any shame or guilt that prevents you from entering your own heart and, if necessary, write a letter of forgiveness to yourself.

10) Green and pink are colours associated with the heart chakra and by surrounding ourselves with their vibrations, we can find a sense of peace and harmony.

11 Chapter

The Throat Chakra

■ The Throat Chakra

Position:	Throat
Spiritual Aspect:	Self-Expression
Basic Need:	Ability to Accept Change
Related Emotions:	Frustration, Freedom
Endocrine Gland:	Thyroid Gland
Associated Organs:	Lung, Throat, Intestines
Colour:	Blue

Spiritual Aspect ... Self-Expression and Creativity

This energy centre, sitting between the heart and mind, is connected to the ability to express all that we are, to be the architects of our own creation and to utilise our natural gifts and talents to mould our future destiny. Though most us spend all day "expressing" ourselves whether vocally or through the written word, much of what we say has little to do with the deeper impulses of our soul. Often we use words carelessly not realising that each utterance has its own energy and will always reach a target somewhere.

The Native Americans say: "Choose your words carefully for through them you create your reality." Even when we know what we want to say, we often modify our thoughts to satisfy the audience, preferring to conform to tribal conditioning than our inner voice. For this reason, it has long been a custom for people to keep journals or diaries to record their private thoughts and in recent years, more and more people are choosing to pay someone, such as a counsellor, to listen without interruption, judgement or attempting to bring about change.

**What would you want to say if you knew that you wouldn't be judged
or interrupted?
What part of you still waits to be expressed?**

So many of the illnesses related to this chakra reflect a blockage in the
capacity for us to be ourselves and throughout my travels, I find that this
chakra, above all others, is consistently out of balance wherever I am in the
world.

The centre is strongly allied to the sacral chakra which, associated with
our relationships, suggests that if we want to create healthy partnerships
we need to learn to communicate with respect and honesty. The opposite
is also true, for if we want to be successfully creative it's important to
develop nurturing and inspiring relationships. As discussed in the
Chapter on the sacral chakra, the creation of interdependence is the best
way of achieving a balance where there is a dynamic flow of respect,
freedom, commitment and love.

The Power of the Mental Body

Through this chakra the mental body reveals itself, contributing **logic,
analysis, reason** and **understanding** to what appears to be a world of
confusion, emotional irrationality and nebulous dreams. It provides a focal
point for our thoughts offering organisational systems in which we can
find order at times of chaos.

For instance, when there is an incoming intuitive idea, it is the throat
chakra that transforms the impression into a form or structure which can
be reproduced and then manifest. Working in the opposite direction, the
response to our action is registered as feelings which are then converted by
the throat chakra into reason, through the creation of belief systems which
say: "I feel good therefore I believe my ideas were well received."

Any business manager would build on his/her success by repeating
this pattern, willing to make minor adjustments when the response is less
favourable and only returning to the source of the idea, the intuition, when
the product's success has run its course. And so it is with our own life,
where we repeat patterns of behaviour built on belief systems which have
been constructed from past experience and information acquired from
those we encountered.

However, whereas no production line would be allowed to continue to
produce something which was defective, our ability to remain observant

to such discrepancies has been compromised by repeated stories that remind us: "That's the way it is." Out of touch with our intuition and the gift of discernment, we continue to be driven by thought patterns that no longer work for us.

Belief systems give structure to our world and can be personal: "i believe I'm attractive", or global: "The world is a great place to live." Armed with this knowledge, we can process all new experiences to either enhance the belief or change it if necessary. However, the belief patterns that are most difficult to recognise and transform are those based on negative messages which provide us with a strange type of security where the soul's influence is limited.

For instance, the inner message that says: "I'll never be any good" does little to promote motivation nor does: "The world is out to get you" and guess what, the more we think it, the more the message is re-enforced by our experiences in the outside world so then we can say: "I told you so."

Our thoughts create our perception of reality.

The statement reminds us that even if there are other facets to the experience we will only see what we want to believe because we need to maintain the illusion of security. And why do we hang onto something which is so destructive to the soul? Mainly because we fear change and our tribal amnesia prevents us from remembering that there is another way. And yet, fortunately, nothing remains static and the sooner we relinquish our hold on a redundant belief and give ourselves permission to be excited by the prospect of a new identity, the sooner we will experience inner peace and fulfilment.

The Courage to Change

The throat chakra is the centre of change and transformation. In physical terms, the thyroid gland which is situated in this area, produces the hormone thyroxin. This same hormone is found in tadpoles and is thought to be the catalyst that brings about the metamorphosis of the tiny fish into a frog. If the hormone is removed, the tadpole can only increase in size and then wonder what went wrong! However, if additional thyroxin is added at an early stage, the larva quickly transforms into an amphibian and, in all probability, does not survive due to its immaturity. This is the power of the throat chakra, to not only bring about change, but a metamorphosis: a complete transformation of character.

No wonder we hang on to old patterns of behaviour, for change brings challenges and anxiety but also freedom and joy. Our soul's urge to move will be transmitted through sleep, the words of other people, through crisis, love and definitely through illness. The message is picked up by the energetic receivers of the throat chakra but we can **choose** to veto it by the application of our free will and then justify our decision by creating wonderful **excuses** manufactured by the intellect itself:

- ■ "I'd love to but ... "
- ■ "It's not that easy/it's easy for you to talk/ that's difficult"
- ■ "I hear what you say but you just don't understand"
- ■ "When I retire/the children leave home/we have more money/we win the lottery ... "
- ■ "I'm too fat/thin/tired/busy/poor/needed ...
- ■ "Yes but ... "

Listen to yourself and see the excuses you conjure up (even if not expressed) in your attempt to avoid change; be honest, do you really want to move or are you only paying lip service to the idea? It's so easy to seek the opinion of others to a current dilemma whilst secretly hoping that no solution will be forthcoming that cannot be explained away by saying: "I don't think you understand the problem, let me explain ... "

Change takes courage whether it involves leaving something or someone, committing to rather than running away from, or letting go of old, paralysing belief systems. In my experience, 80% of all illnesses are a wake-up-call from the soul urging change and once it has your attention, thankfully, it will not let go!

Finally, remember that we can't hope to support others during their transformation unless we have experienced the journey ourselves, with one of the most popular excuses to our own personal change being: "If only my husband/wife/partner/children/work/country etc. would change, I'd be fine!"

My Will versus Thy Will

The throat chakra is the seat of our will which, when focused on the object of desire, is a powerful, directing and attracting force that brings towards us that which we require. In the early part of the century the great analysts, such as Freud and Jung, helped us to make sense of the myriad of confusing images and thoughts that pervade our mind night and day, bringing comfort to their clients who could now label their behaviour. This trend has continued and expanded right up to the present day with, in recent years, methods of mind control flooding the self-development scene, including affirmations, NLP and self-hypnosis.

Some may say that there is little more to learn about the mind and yet, despite these psychological advances, we seem to have made little impact on the unhappiness of many in the world. Could it be that while we became engrossed in looking within, we failed to remember our deep connection to every living being on this planet, and that perhaps such analysis can be the means of re-enforcing protective mental walls rather than removing them?

Although a strong personal will is admirable when a task needs to be completed, it can also be the cause of separation from all we love. From the businessman who gets carried away with the drive to be successful, through the parent who is determined to give their child the life they never had, to the teenager whose rebellious nature reveals a strong self-will, all succeed but at what cost? Where is the fun, spontaneity, flexibility and love? When a powerful driving force is present, even these become an enterprise to be managed!

And what creates the need to be wilful, stubborn or headstrong? Perhaps it's to prove a point or to control a world where everything appears chaotic and frightening. My perception is that those who feel the need to be independent and support themselves by their own will, come from a place of insecurity within the base chakra where they learned at an early age that it wasn't safe to trust others and where "Thy will" represented oppression, fear or judgement. By withdrawing their creative urge into the throat chakra and placing it under the control of the mind, they could direct their life from a safe but distant position. These individuals are usually highly intuitive receiving input from all their senses and analysing the information before taking the risk to speak or act.

A common phrase they use is: "I want to understand everything before going ahead", which really means: "I want 100% assurance that I won't be taking a risk/getting it wrong/failing, or being made to feel responsible." These concerns of insecurity, poor self-worth and lack of trust, relate to the lower chakras. As individuals, they usually have a long list of questions that must be satisfied before they're prepared to commit themselves to anything deeper. Many of their questions are so abstract such as: "What if ... " that it's impossible to give guarantees which increases the anxiety and wariness.

Apart from lying to gain their trust, love is the only answer to rebalance the situation offering a different perspective to their image of "Thy will" and promising that their feelings and thoughts will be heard sympathetically. Progress is often slow as their deeply suspicious nature and highly analytical mind is reluctant to let go of control and reach for the hand that is offered. One of the most annoying suggestions you can give to someone with a throat chakra imbalance is: "Let go!" It drives them crazy, as immediately they become tense trying to think of how to do it!

When we submit to a higher authority, Thy will, we don't lose ourselves but instead gain greater strength and freedom to live the life we choose. This willingness to release control is exemplified during the ingestion of food where we can hold objects in our mouth for as long as we like, chewing over the pros and cons. However, there comes a time when we need to swallow and will not see that food again until the excrement appears at the other end. This physical process shows that when we have the courage to let go, we can receive nurturing, energy and renewal and all we need to do is enjoy the meal.

Finally, one way in which a strong will can be used energetically to promote self-worth is in the process of "trying", where the individual believes that "if they just try harder" they would be more successful/more loved/more respected etc. Unfortunately, such a belief emerges from a deep fantasy of themselves that says: "I'm not good enough" which drives them on until they collapse, exhausted, wondering where they went wrong: "I tried everything and I still feel empty."

Hopefully, at this point, they have the courage to stop and take stock of their life allowing time to nurture their exhausted body and mind and to realise that while they have been running around trying to find themselves, what they were looking for was waiting patiently within their heart requiring nothing of them, except that they came home.

Body Language

1) The person who places one finger over their mouth while they pretend to listen to you, is really saying: "I don't believe a word you're saying!"
2) Someone who bites their lips, is biting back their words fearful of offending others, as is the person who speaks through a hand held loosely over their mouth as if fearful of being heard.

3) Some people only speak from one side of their mouth suggesting a restriction of the ability to express from the side held closed. (Right side: the masculine aspect, left side: the feminine aspect ... see Chapter on other psychospiritual links with disease.)

4) Blushing commonly stops around the throat chakra as if heated emotions are repressed due to fear of a reaction which reflects an old experience from the past.

5) The inability to wear anything tight around the neck, especially seen at the menopause, reveals the need for space and more importantly the courage from within the individual to express their personal creativity.

6) Those who wear high collars suppress their feelings ... watch out, their emotions can appear suddenly with a definite sting in the tail!

7) Those who subconsciously place their hands over their ears when you're speaking to them, do not want to hear!

Associated Illnesses

1) Thyrotoxicosis
In this condition, the thyroid gland is over-active producing excessive amounts of the hormone thyroxin leading to symptoms which include sweating, a tremor, weight loss, palpitations and agitation. In my experience, the energetic imbalance is not limited to the thyroid gland but involves the base chakra and solar plexus. Here the issues of "not being accepted" (base) and "not being good enough" (solar plexus) become the motivating force behind the will of the individual driven to achieve more, work harder or give more love, in the hope that this will bring the desired rewards.

Unfortunately, what happens is that the energy generated by such activity becomes uncontrollable, expressing itself in the symptoms of the illness. Successful medical treatment is available for this condition but I advise my patients to also look at their focus of activity and explore the deeper motivating forces. We will never believe we're "good enough" unless we're willing to hear it for ourselves and make changes which reflect this enhanced confidence.

2) Myxoedema (Hypothyroidism)
This illness represents a decrease in thyroxin production and although more common at the menopause, can affect any age. The symptoms suggest

someone who has lost their get up and go and include lethargy, weight gain, hair loss, dry skin, slow pulse, depression, intolerance to the cold and constipation. Since the thyroid relates to change, it is easy to see how loss of that creative urge will produce such symptoms.

Apart from standard medical treatment to replace the hormone, I would also suggest that the individual tunes into the sacral chakra and examines their fears around change and the planting of their own seed of creation, letting go of redundant beliefs which no longer enhance the self. The questions to ask are:

"What needs to die to allow me to move on?"

"What seeds of creativity need to be planted at this time?"

and

"What will bring the spark back into my life?"

It often helps to become involved in activities which are in themselves creative, such as dancing, art, pottery, writing etc. all of which activate the right side of the brain where inspiration is stored and allow us to find our own natural balance again.

3) Thyroid Cysts and Cancer

Whenever a lump is found in the thyroid gland, it's important to seek a medical diagnosis in order to receive the appropriate treatment. Psychospiritually, the throat chakra is the seat of expression and in my experience many of the individuals with either diagnosis have suppressed feelings over the years and in the case of cancer, especially anger. My advice would be that alongside any treatment program, there should be counselling and the ability to learn to express oneself in the most effective way possible.

Further insight is gained by looking at which side of the gland is affected. The left side relates to issues around women, intuition and sensitivity while the right relates to men, the ability to speak out, to stand one's ground and be heard.

4) Diseases of the Throat

A) TONSILLITIS

This is a relatively common disease in children as their immune system develops and they learn to be able to discriminate between what makes them feel good and let go of the rest. If a child feels unable to speak out, perhaps due to bullying at school or problems at home, there may be recurrent bouts of tonsillitis which should be treated not only with antibiotics but also by allowing the child to talk about their problems. It's also important to ensure that the child is given the opportunity to explore their own creativity rather than placing too much emphasis on the value of academic work.

Tonsillitis in adults may follow a similar theme suggesting that the individual's immune system is compromised and psychologically their boundaries have been invaded. Restoring space, saying "No" and speaking of one's own needs usually restores healthy boundaries. Once again the importance of creative outlets cannot be ignored in these sensitive individuals.

B) SORE, RED THROATS
As discussed in the section on the liver meridian and its passage through the throat chakra, redness in this area denotes unexpressed anger which is urging to be released. I remember a 23-year-old woman who consulted me for recurrent sore throats. She lived with her family in an intolerable situation where one member held the others to ransom by constantly threatening suicide. This had been going on for five years leaving everybody exhausted and angry but unable to see a way out.

Through professional, psychological counselling, the family came to realise that despite her threats, life had to go on and, in reality, they couldn't stop her carrying out the deed if she chose. My young patient felt relieved to be able to express her anger and soon gained the courage to leave home after which, her throat problems completely disappeared.

The expression of anger, whether through talking, writing, singing or confrontation, enables us to move into a healthier space in our lives.

C) LOSS OF VOICE (LARYNGITIS)
Obviously, there are serious medical problems which must be addressed if the loss of voice is unrelated to a recent infection. But with any loss it's important to ask: "What are you afraid of saying?" or "What does it mean to you today not to be able to talk?" Losing one's voice gives the perfect excuse to be silent and that can be a gift in these days of instant communication.

D) LUMP IN THE THROAT
In this condition, there is a feeling that something is caught in the throat and when there is no serious medical condition, it's important to ask: "What's difficult to swallow?" If swallowing represents the ability to release food from our control and let it pass into the stomach to be digested, I might also ask: "What are you not **willing** to accept and release?" In my

experience, the lump commonly relates to grief and tears that have been swallowed but only as far as the back of the throat and have not been fully discharged.

Speaking out (screaming if necessary) and coming to terms with any loss, prepares us to take another bite of life and move on.

5) Diseases of the Ear
A) DEAFNESS
Although on most occasions this disease progresses gradually without any threat to life, an acoustic neuroma will require more active treatment commonly seen where deafness is accompanied by tinnitue in young people. Whatever the cause, the question has to be: "What don't you want to hear?" For those who avoid criticism, conflict and hate arguments (often due to a family background of anger), deafness is a happy release allowing the individual to disappear deeper inside. Others are highly analytical and have difficulty with the expression of emotions, both their own and those belonging to others. They prefer to tidy everything into a neat box rather than be surrounded by irrationality.

Spontaneity and the expression of one's emotions may not return the hearing but will prevent the individual becoming locked away in a box of their own making. There is one advantage of going within and that is that it's easier to hear one's inner guidance without the distraction of the outer world allowing deeper wisdom to emerge.

By looking at which ear is involved and recognising that the left side relates to the feminine aspect of our being and the right to the masculine, further insight may be received which can be used in any treatment program (see Chapter on "Other psychospiritual links with disease").

B) TINNITUS
"The bells are ringing but nobody's at home!" is the motto for this illness. An extremely troublesome problem, usually worse at rest, it has a tendency to inflict those who are highly analytical and worry about every little detail. As above, a firm medical diagnosis must be made, but apart from that, my advice is to complement any treatment with relaxation techniques which include the use of musical tones and colours.

There is often a great fear of letting go and losing control with the mind employed to over-analyse everything so as to reassure the individual that no stone has been left unturned. As discussed above, the main problem is insecurity and the fears that relate to it (base chakra). Finding ways to release the pent-up tension and achieve stillness certainly helps to reduce the symptoms of tinnitus.

6) Diseases of the Lungs
A) ASTHMA

Asthma has shown a steady rise in prevalence over the last 15 years partly due to a change in diagnostic procedures and partly thought to be due to the increasing pollution of our environment. There are many allergens which can trigger an attack and any treatment should aim to minimise their presence. However, from a psychospiritual point of view, as discussed on the section on allergies (heart chakra), asthma is far more common in those who have a highly active solar plexus and therefore are sensitive to atmospheres both within a room and surrounding other people.

Many an asthmatic adult will tell me that they experienced their first attack when they were sitting on their parents' bed and they were arguing. The feelings of helplessness and fear of the future caused the child to inhale deeply which is the first instinctual response to stress. Unfortunately, the airways then went into spasm and the breath could only be released as an asthmatic wheeze. One of the positive results however, was that the parents stopped arguing and gave comfort to the child which may be remembered at a later date when attention is required.

Yet, the primary problem is the difficulty in expressing emotions, fearful of other people's reactions and in connection to loss. In adults, it's not uncommon to see the onset of asthma as a result of grief where the individual attempts to be strong and cope with their feelings rather than express them.

Finally, there are a group of asthmatic patients whose creative expression is stifled by those around them who can only offer criticism, scorn or anxiety when the individual seeks to share a new and exciting venture. Such oppressive smothering reflects similar issues explored in the sacral chakra with the consequence that there may also be problems with ovarian cysts or infertility.

The answer is complex but includes:

■ Learning to express and release the emotions through singing, art, writing, poetry or by speaking one's mind.
■ Remembering to protect the solar plexus (see Chapter on solar plexus) when in situations where one feels less sure of oneself

whilst developing a greater sense of self-worth and healthy boundaries.

■ Bringing more laughter, fun and spontaneity into one's life, letting the serious and responsible side lapse a little.

■ Learning to breathe deeper and hold the breath longer on expiration, expands the capacity of the lungs and decreases the risk of spasm.

B) SMOKING

There are many reasons why people smoke and probably the most damaging is when the individual reaches for a cigarette at times of stress using the nicotine and smoke-screen to calm their nerves allowing them time to think. Unfortunately, this dummy effect also suppresses emerging thoughts and feelings and re-enforces childhood messages which say: "Just be quiet!"

Most of the illnesses that are smoking related also reflect this anxiety towards speaking out and the subsequent fears of humiliation, change and failure. When people do give up smoking, those around them suddenly become privy to a torrent of unexpressed emotions and thoughts, almost to the point that they beg them to start again! But once the individual gains confidence in being themselves, there is no turning back.

C) BRONCHITIS AND EMPHYSEMA

These two conditions are commonly seen as the chronic consequence of smoking. The former occurring as recurrent bouts of bronchial infection and the latter as end-stage lung disease where there is irreversible damage. Psychospiritually, as with smoking, there is often a long-term fear of expressing oneself for fear of failure and of being seen in one's own light.

With the onset of emphysema, we see someone who has been inspired with "good ideas" and perhaps fantasies but who has never had the courage to breathe out and give them space to manifest, leading to a barrel-chest full of dead air. It's not unusual to hear their partner give excuses as to why they're unable to perform certain functions and I wonder whether this has been a pattern throughout life where excuses have been made for them rather than being given the courage to step out and trust.

D) SINUSITIS, CATARRH AND POST-NASAL DRIP

In Oriental medicine, the energy of the respiratory system is connected to grief and the ability to accept change. Whenever there are sinus problems,

I believe that grief and the fear of letting go are involved, even though there may also be infective or allergic factors. In my experience, sinusitis is more common after suppression of tears and anger and is often accompanied by a sore throat.

A chronic catarrhal drip which requires the individual to constantly clear their throat, is also related to unexpressed tears. I remember seeing a girl who had recently moved to an island in Scotland from her home in the South of England. As soon as she moved into her new home, she developed severe sinusitis and had to receive several courses of antibiotics. However, the catarrh continued especially in the back of her throat.

By the time she consulted me, her doctor had explored her allergy status but had failed to find any consistent pattern. It all became clear however, when she revealed that the hardest aspect of leaving the South was that she left her family behind and she was missing them badly. With a little homoeopathic help and gentle counselling, her problem soon resolved and she found it easier to settle into her new home.

7) Problems Related to the Mouth
A) MOUTH ULCERS
These small breaks in the lining of the mouth can be extremely painful and usually occur when we're run down. Ulcers are more common in those who are sensitive to events around them but instead of swallowing or spitting them out, "chew them over" in their mind, taking on the pain of the moment. Learning to take extra care of our boundaries when we're low, protects us from factors that could lead to ulceration.

B) COLD SORES
These painful sores caused by the herpes virus are more prevalent in strong sunshine, during times of stress and when chocolate and nuts have been a large part of the diet. From a psychospiritual point of view, these sores arise when "someone has got on your nerves" but you bit your tongue and failed to speak your mind.

So the advice is: a) Don't allow others to affect you; and b) Spit it out rather than suppress it!

C) TEETH AND GUMS
Our teeth are a source of power passed down from our animal ancestors and begin the digestive process by allowing us to bite, clasp, chew and

grind. One can learn a lot about a person when you watch them eat an apple as it probably reflects the way they tackle life!

The messages behind problems of the teeth and gums include:

A) GRINDING TEETH often occurring at night, is related to repressed anger.
B) DREAMS OF OUR TEETH FALLING OUT is a fear of loss of power.
C) FALSE TEETH suggests you lost your power a long time ago!
D) BLEEDING GUMS (apart from serious medical problems) relates to a period of insecurity when the soil in which your roots are based has been shaken by an event outside your control which leads to a loss of power.

8) Multiple Sclerosis

The final illness under this heading certainly involves many chakras but its inclusion here relates to the site of the problem between the nerve cell which picks up the message and the axon which transmits it. Pathologically, it is an auto-immune disease where antibodies are made against the myelin sheath that surrounds the axon which then becomes inflamed and then hardened into a substance called plaque. This destroys the ability for information to flow down that particular axon with the consequence that there is sensory and/or motor loss. As recurrence and remission are so unpredictable in this disease, it's hard for any therapy to claim success and all we can hope is to reduce the symptoms. Psychospiritually the situation is complex and therefore will be described as follows:

- The individual expresses both a fierce independence and marked dependency, the latter usually involving just one individual to whom they give authority, often in the name of love. Their fear of losing this person can make them possessive and insecure.
- Their independence and lack of trust can make it difficult to allow others to help although, as the illness proceeds, emotional manipulation may emerge which meets the needs of the individual.
- Attacks commonly occur at the start or end of a relationship due to the fact that, because of poor self-worth, the individual's identity is often dependent on a relationship remaining constant. I have seen attacks occur after a relative's death, at the birth of a child and even on the first night of a honeymoon.
- These individuals are highly analytical with a desire to understand their illness fully but are less enthusiastic about putting their heart

and soul into change and tend to prefer methods of treatment which are physical rather than psychologically based.

■ There is usually deep anger and indignation involved which is reflected in the inflammatory process. This anger can be easily sparked but rarely resolved.

■ Due to the low self-worth, there is a tendency to try and please other people, with difficulty "putting their foot down" and saying "No".

■ They seek approval for their actions, preferring not to take responsibility and risk failure but walk on the path created by others rather than develop their own.

Probably their greatest need is to be loved unconditionally but that asks that they should stop fighting the world, allow other people into their life without creating a dependency, let go of the need to please, start to have pride in themselves and choose to walk their path with firm and steady feet.

Suggestions to Balance the Activity of the Throat Chakra

1) Buy a journal or diary in which you express your joys and sorrows and on the last page will be able to look back and celebrate how far you've come.

2) Learn to express rather than suppress, realising that whatever reaction you elicit, you've freed another small part of yourself to live a more fulfilling life.

3) Make a list of four things you would like to achieve in the next six months and then under each subject give any reasons why this may not happen. Then ask yourself whether these reasons are excuses or reality. Don't limit yourself, for the expression of creative ideas attracts abundance.

4) Enhance your creativity by taking on a new interest such as dancing, singing, pottery, art, writing etc.

5) If you decide to share your plans with friends or family, speak as if it has already happened and you know it went well, rather than from a place of fear or doubt.

6) Remember "trying" is based on a fear of "not being good enough" so either stop running or change the words to "working at" which gives you time and space to enjoy the process.

7) Choose your words carefully and reject the thoughts and statements that you would not like to be directed towards you. Don't waste your energy on gossip.

8) Make a note of times when you are stressed and try to understand what was the underlying belief system that was triggered at that moment. Then decide if you still believe such a notion about yourself and if not, choose to change or abandon it. Affirmations can help but where there is deep self-doubt, words are powerless to change the offending thoughts.

It is better to act or dress in a way that expresses the newly-created opinion of yourself.

9) If you know you're very analytical, work at letting go of the need to know everything and the need to ask questions for reassurance. Learn to trust and enjoy the freedom that comes from not having to be in control all the time.

10) Blue is the colour related to the throat chakra and can be used for calming, reassuring and healing ourselves. It is also the colour of authority and expression and therefore a perfect colour to wear for interviews or when giving talks.

12 Chapter

The Third Eye

■ The Third Eye

Position:	Forehead
Spiritual Aspect:	Self-Responsibility
Basic Need:	Vision and Balance
Related Emotions:	Confusion and Clarity
Endocrine Gland:	Pituitary
Associated Organs:	Eyes, Lower Head, Sinuses
Colour:	Indigo

Spiritual Aspect ... Self-Responsibility

This centre, situated between the physical eyes, is represented by the two-lobed pituitary gland which, with the hypothalamus, carries out one of the most important functions within the body: that of maintaining a balanced yet dynamic sense of well-being. It receives input from the brain, our five senses, the emotions and circulating hormones and, with infinite dexterity, can assimilate this information and send forth a clear directive to the various systems so that the maximum expression of the soul is assured, with minimal effort.

This physical manifestation is a perfect reflection of the chakra, the third eye being the centre of **balance, wisdom, detachment** and **responsibility**. It is important to understand that here balance does not equate to inactivity but is a dynamic interplay of energies around a centre of stillness which can be seen as a figure-of-eight character on its side which, by no coincidence, is also the sign for infinity.

DYNAMIC INTERPLAY OF ENERGIES

POINT OF STILLNESS

So what energies are involved? Let us return to the base chakra where the initial descent of spirit at our conception activates the sleeping kundalini force. As it awakens and is urged to reach its full height and potential at the crown chakra, its journey is energised by spiralling between the different poles of existence which reside within each chakra, pushing out the boundaries to gain maximum effect. All our experiences in life are as a result of this serpent-like energy moving through us and "tempting" us (does this ring any bells?) to reach higher and higher towards self-realisation.

Despite the vogue to make comparisons and judgements between one pole and the other, in reality, if we attempt to remain too long in any one aspect of our existence, the soul will give us a gentle nudge propelling us towards a different view of reality. Another way of saying this, is that it is **not** better to be good rather than bad, just as being a woman is no more favourable than being a man. They are just variations of the same picture taken from a different angle and are all totally acceptable as an expression of Creation. Competition and the need to compare is a device used to engender stagnation of the soul through fear of change and rejection. We wouldn't know light if we didn't know dark and black and white are facets of the same beautiful spectrum of colour.

The next choice we are given is to decide the depth of our experience. Like a ball on a piece of string, the shorter the string the more limited our understanding of life. If we have the courage to re-attach ourselves (the ball) to a much longer piece of string then we can really start to enjoy life to its fullest. Of course, the most important factor to establish is, who is holding the other end and do we trust them? The answer is that we are also the string holder, our inner core directed by the soul, holding the centre of stillness for the personality to move out into the world and report back in the form of vibrational information.

So to reiterate, the capacity to find ourselves in all aspects of our being is dependent on the development of a strong and trustworthy centre which, paradoxically is dependent on the personality's willingness to fully explore the world it inhabits. Symbolically, this reflects an important aspect of quantum physics where the concept of a focal point interacting with a flow of movement, is seen in the different phases of the electron which can either appear in particle or wave form. Once again there is no either/or situation, but one which is totally symbiotic with one aspect no more important than the other.

As the serpent moves between the opposite poles of existence, it absorbs the energy generated and brings the particular chakra into balance. So taking each centre in turn, in the:

- **Base** it moves between "insecurity" and "limitation" to find **security**
- **Sacral** it moves between "dependence" and "independence" to find **interdependence**
- **Solar Plexus** it moves between "selflessness" and "selfishness" to find **self-worth**
- **Heart** it moves between "self-destruction" and "hard-heartedness" to find **self-love**
- **Throat** it moves between "apathy" and "wilfulness" to find **creative expression**.

When the kundalini energy touches the third eye it moves between "matter" and "spirit" to find oneness with the Creator, through the ultimate sacrifice of self. So despite my emphasis throughout the book of the need to find oneself, I now propose that the purpose for achieving this outcome is to later sacrifice it for a greater cause. But such a loss offers so much more that I assure you, the journey is well worth the effort!

Wisdom and Discernment

Like a mirror, the third eye sees everything but doesn't judge; it records and reflects the information it receives whilst adding an extra dimension beyond the abilities of the mirror, the power of wisdom. This facet of the soul has the qualities of **discernment, objectivity, clarity, detachment** and **Universal Love** but can appear rather cold and dispassionate in the eyes of those who do not understand.

Such wisdom is seen in a true leader who invites suggestions, objections, praise and silence from other members of the group and then, having gathered all the information together, reviews it without judgement or bias from a place of discernment, making his/her final decision based on what he/she considers will be the best approach for all concerned.

This clarity of mind is the essence of true intellect, the highest form of intelligence where the analytical process is used to sort, reject and understand what is being said and what has gone unspoken. When this quality is combined with the compassion and resonance of the heart, the power of intuition emerges. Wisdom also allows us to discern whether the knowledge we possess about a situation or person which has arisen from our intuition, should be shared or merely observed as we reflect the value of the "silent witness".

For the wisdom of the third eye is not dependent on feeding our ego, our flagging self-worth, our sense of insecurity or poor self-love. It's only interested in acting from the highest intention looking beyond the presenting problem to the larger picture that is unfolding. I'm sure you can remember times when, had you tactlessly spoken out, even though you held an opinion, others would have suffered from your ego. For instance, you're in a new relationship and the euphoria of the moment is so exciting that you avoid looking into the future, even though tiny doubts keep drifting into your mind. The last thing we want to hear at that moment is: "If you want my opinion, I can see … ", even if it's well meant. And while I'm on the subject, when things don't progress and the relationship dissolves, the words: "I could have told you weeks ago … ", rarely help to ease the pain!

In a similar way, if we hold onto thoughts rather than voicing them, we maintain a judgement that distorts and affects any true interaction. I'm often asked if I can read auras and my answer is affirmative and immediately I see a look of horror at the thought that my ability to see into the subtle bodies means that I'm constantly analysing and judging other people.

I reassure my questioner that all I see at the present is the person in front of me and I will take from them "only what they consciously offer and no more". It's more important for me to extend to them respect and openness than to build my ego through knowing something that can cause vulnerability in another person.

Intention

In previous Chapters, we have looked at the various attracting forces which are the motivating power behind our dreams, imagination and inspiration. So in the:

- **Solar Plexus** the power is hoping, desiring and wanting
- **Throat** the power is believing, willing and trying
- **Heart** the power is merging, connecting and loving.

It is within the third eye that our "intention to create" is registered, recording our level of understanding of our own responsibility for our inner and outer worlds. By returning to the analogy of the mirror, it's possible to keep its reflective surface covered by a fine mist of illusion, fantasy and fear so that there is no need to see our image clearly and hence to know the truth. And why would we want to do this?

Possibly on one level, we believe that the mirror will reveal our perceived imperfections on which we will be judged or perhaps, more importantly, we would have to face the wonderful beauty which resides within and there would be no turning back. By maintaining a façade and attaching our hopes and beliefs to it, we are assured a level of safety but never the ecstasy of enlightenment.

As the serpent rises, the heat generated by the twisting and turning starts to cause the mists of illusion to evaporate and the surface of the mirror begins to clear. At the same time, the heat burns off the denser features of our nature, allowing our inner light to shine, illuminating our true nature in the reflection that appears. There we stand naked and true with no need to justify, explain, apologise or change, for "what you see is what you get" and we've finally arrived!

Responsibility

The meaning of this word comes from the French "spondere" which means to promise. So the questions that is being asked is: **"Are you keeping the promise you made to yourself before entering this earth? Are you living your life as the soul intended and are you being truly responsible for the life you have created?"**

The third eye sees all, records all and does not judge; there is nowhere to hide except in our own illusion. How easy it is for all of us to find **others** to whom we can be responsible whilst avoiding our own reflected image. Fortunately, the intuition does not forget, gently but firmly offering us opportunities to return to the path so that through the resonance of the heart, we can follow our own truth.

Body Language

Any attempt to cover the eyes with sunglasses, the hair or hands or avoiding eye contact, reflects someone who is reluctant to be seen and may, like the ostrich, actually believe that they are out of sight. Most of this behaviour is, in reality, allied to the solar plexus where low self-esteem makes the individual imagine that they're not worthy to be seen or that others can see right into the darkness of their soul (but never the light).

When we realise that there is nothing to hide except our own magnificence, we raise our heads with pride and are happy to project ourselves out into the world through the windows of our soul, the eyes.

Associated Illnesses

1) Visual Problems

Some of these illnesses are structural or congenital and therefore corrective treatment may be limited. However, advances are occurring in medical science, and psychospiritually, each condition contains a message.

A) SHORT-SIGHTED (myopia): the need to stop worrying about the minute details of life and start to appreciate the larger picture.

B) LONG-SIGHTED: the need to adjust one's focus from fantasies of the future or regrets of the past and see what is right in front of one's eyes. What are you missing? Have you noticed the beauty of the present moment?

C) ASTIGMATISM: the reflective surface of the two eyes are not symmetrical and suggest the need in this life to find a balance between one's intuition and logic and to use them in harmony.

D) SQUINT: the eyes are not aligned and hence fail to produce a unified picture, presenting the individual with two different images. In order to cope, the nerve impulses of one eye are ignored and it becomes a "lazy eye". Corrective treatment attempts to stimulate the visual function by placing a patch over the other eye. Psychospiritually, the lazy eye reflects an aspect of the self that wishes to hide; when it's the right eye it relates to logic, reason etc. and the left eye relates to intuition, sensitivity etc. It is important to not only achieve binocular vision physically but also spiritually.

E) GLAUCOMA: the pressure within the eye increases to dangerous levels eventually destroying the optic nerve leading first to "tunnel vision" and then to total blindness. Pathologically, this illness can be as a result of a structural problem within the eye, linked to diabetes or familial. Psychospiritually however, prior to the onset of disease, the individual has often felt the need to control their surroundings due to basic insecurity, causing them to appear dogmatic, critical and narrow-minded, later reflected in the physical condition.

I remember meeting a woman who had unfortunately lost the sight in one eye and was only partially sighted in the other. She went on to tell me that prior to the onset of glaucoma, she had been a very proud and conceited woman who believed that "for a job to be well done, she had to do it herself". Hence, she always drove her own car rather than trusting others, cleaned the house before the cleaner arrived and made a point of being chairperson on any committee because she felt others were inadequate for the job.

Then the blindness struck and she continued: "I was forced to give up driving and had to trust others, I couldn't see the dust so I became less fastidious, I gave up my committees as I found the reading too difficult and, whereas in the past I would cross the road if I saw someone approaching who I didn't want to meet, now I bump into them, and I have to admit I've made some wonderful connections."

Despite the physical handicap which would remain throughout her life, she wanted me to know that she'd gained so much spiritually from the illness, dissolving her fears of inadequacy and allowing her to know others through her heart.

F) CATARACTS: the lens of the eye becomes hardened by a reduction in the blood supply usually due to the ageing process. In normal circumstances, the changing shape of the lens enables us to maintain our focus wherever our gaze settles. A cataract represents inflexibility, both of the lens and psychospiritually within the mind of the individual. So the question is: "Where have you become inflexible and unwilling to change your focus to accommodate a new view on life?"

G) FLOATERS: these small black particles that pass across the visual field are associated with disturbance of liver function and hence with suppression of anger which needs to be released (see solar plexus).

H) MACULAR DEGENERATION: in this condition the cells of the retina which receive maximum light stimulation, degenerate, leaving the individual with peripheral but not central vision. My experience is that there is a definite correlation between the onset of this illness and "seeing" something that blinds the individual. For instance, the realisation of a truth and one's "choice" not to see it or the wish to avoid something that is right in front of one's eyes, preferring to remain in the periphery. The intuition of the third eye cannot be avoided whatever means we use to disable our physical function.

I) THE RED EYE: CONJUNCTIVITIS, CONJUNCTIVAL HAEMORRHAGES and IRITIS: each of these conditions may have a different cause with allergies and infections being prevalent. Iritis, or the inflammation of the iris, is usually linked to auto-immune illnesses and therefore with the associated psychological profile (see heart chakra). However, as discussed under the heading of liver disease (solar plexus), the liver meridian passes through the eye and when disturbed by suppressed anger, will result in the red eye which asks: "So who is making you see red?"

J) DRY EYES: the eye fails to produce an adequate flow of tears with the resultant dry eyes which are often irritable. This condition can accompany other auto-immune illnesses (see heart chakra) especially a condition called **Sjorgen's syndrome** where there is arthritis and dryness of other areas of the body. In my experience, the dryness relates to the inability of the individual to shed tears, preferring to present a stoic front in the face of grief. Tears of anger, sadness and joy should flow in appreciation that they bring us to a place of peace and acceptance.

2) Tension Headaches

When we take on the responsibility of others without reflecting on our own needs, it's easy to become overwhelmed by their problems feeling the tension and resentment build up in the muscles around the head and neck. The problem is that due to a resistance to follow our own "intention to create", we constantly attract those with needs.

By having the courage to respond to one's own inner call and letting others do the same, we find ourselves on a true path of self-realisation and the headaches clear.

3) Migraine

Migraine headaches can be mild or severe with associated vomiting, visual disturbance and even paralysis and are seen in children as abdominal pains. The solar plexus is also involved in the aetiology of these headaches, occurring more commonly in those who are conscientious, martyrs to a cause and who "put their all" into a task even though the results may be only average.

There is usually low self-confidence and extreme sensitivity with the result that they react to the demands of others rather than follow their own intuition to guide their path. Having great difficulty in asking for their needs to be met, the migraine provides them with an acceptable excuse for taking time from work or school. In the long run, there is a need to learn to say: "No", protect one's boundaries, enhance self-esteem and take regular time out for play and spontaneity.

4) Dizziness, Vertigo and Meniere's Disease
In the chakra of balance, we find these illnesses which may be due to a virus, inner ear disease, brain tumour or cervical spine deterioration. Having ascertained the diagnosis, it is also important to ask: "What area of your life is out of balance?" For instance, it is not uncommon to find that there is an associated base chakra imbalance due to changing circumstances either at home or at work. The dizziness provides an acceptable motive to remove oneself to the safety of bed where security is hopefully assured.

Learning to surf the changes of life rather than be battered by the tides, requires flexibility, trust and faith, focusing on the horizon rather than the wave.

5) Dyslexia
This issue is not new but is on the increase partly due to an improvement in diagnosis and partly due to the "whole brain" children who are entering this planet at present. Many have been seen as educationally handicapped where perhaps the handicap is with the educational system which has not evolved beyond an emphasis being placed upon academia. These young people are extremely creative both with their hands, feet and mind and need to be given the space to develop their skills rather than being left to fend for themselves.

Our future is in the hands of these children who are teaching us the importance of integration between the left and right brain, so that intuition and sensitivity become synthesised with logic and intellect, creating a whole brain spiritual individual.

Suggestions to Balance the Activity of the Third Eye Chakra

1) Through visual imagery, imagine a figure of eight passing in front of the right then left eye using the intuition to guide the direction. This exercise brings balance to the third eye and enhances one's focus on life.

2) Learn to trust and use the intuition, allowing the first unemotional thought to be followed until its conclusion. Remember that the journey may be as significant as the goal, so keep your eyes open.

3) Learn to look beyond the obvious problem and see any challenging situation as part of the larger picture.

4) Look at those for whom you are responsible and honestly ask: "Who needs who? What would you do if nobody else needed you?" Have the courage to start to say "No", making space for the impossible to become possible.

5) When offering help or guidance, clarify your motive: "What is it my intention to create?"

6) "Where are you limiting yourself, preferring to stay in one aspect of yourself which is safe rather risk meeting its polar opposite?"

7) Take a risk with life and spread your wings, keeping the promise you made to yourself before incarnation.

8) Choose to make decisions based on wisdom and discernment rather than fear and ego.

9) Indigo (dark blue-purple) is the colour which relates to this chakra bringing a wonderful depth of vision similar to the experience of looking out into the night sky. If you've become overwhelmed by the responsibilities, imagine looking into the dark centre of a flower and bring into focus the next step which needs to be taken for the benefit of the soul.

13 Chapter

The Crown Chakra

◼ The Crown Chakra

Position:	Top of Head
Spiritual Aspect:	Self-Consciousness
Basic Need:	Acceptance
Related Emotions:	Despair and Peace
Endocrine Gland:	Pineal
Associated Organs:	Brain
Colour:	Violet/Purple

Spiritual Aspect ... Self-Consciousness

The crowning glory for the serpent's journey is to return to this energy centre where the initial impulse of spirit first entered matter and from where it will leave, enriched by the wisdom of life. With each breath, we relive this cycle of inspiration and expiration, birth and death, each circuit enriched by the last, reflecting the pattern of our Earthly lives. Through this chakra, a silver thread links us to our spiritual source along which energy travels, inspiring our human existence. During an out-of-body experience, many will see themselves floating above their physical form with this fine thread maintaining their connection to the world of matter, for when the link is broken, physical life ceases and we record it as death.

The word consciousness means "to know" and in our quest to fully incarnate our soul's essence and hence develop total consciousness of the self, we are inspired with knowledge from many sources both ethereal and worldly and asked to develop wisdom by the active manifestation of this knowledge. In other words, to know something on an intellectual level has no value until it becomes manifest into the world and indeed, as discussed in this Chapter, is probably a strong causative factor in the development of Alzheimer's disease.

This state of consciousness which we crave, defies words or analysis since in the search for understanding or explanations, we limit the experience, just as attempting to describe a state of ecstasy demands an observer who is immediately excluded from the place of bliss. The crown chakra exhibits a consciousness where the experience and the experiencer are one, where there is only now and where the "I" has become completely integrated into the "We".

The creation of such a clear channel for this powerful energy of inspiration does not come without endeavour and sacrifice as has been seen during our journey through the chakras. The importance of developing a strong, interdependent personality which can be utilised by the soul for its expression, cannot be stressed enough. But when all is said and done, we are spiritual beings and as we start to resonate through the heart with our transpersonal nature, we are driven to reach the ultimate goal which is to be one with the Creator, where "my will" is "Thy will", "my heart" is "Thy heart" and "my being" is "Thy being" and there is nothing more. No fighting, bargaining, pleading or worrying but only an appreciation of being breathed by the breath of the Divine. Any emotion, especially anger against God, is going to detract from the truth and disable the individual from truly being a co-creator of Universal existence.

But such clarity of the mind is not achieved through passivity and servitude. Problems arise when we are deluded into thinking that by clearing our thoughts and giving ourselves entirely to God, we will achieve enlightenment. Unfortunately, "letting the Universe decide" or "going with the flow" can be acronyms for irresponsibility and a desire to avoid making mistakes or failing, driven by the energy of the throat or base chakras. We are not aiming to become empty vessels or plastic channels where spirit moves through us without any interaction or to become zombies, without thoughts or feelings of our own.

Our role is to develop as a dynamic, interactive and creative being using our experiences on this Earth to raise the vibrational energy of our subtle bodies to such a level that together, they resonate with the frequency of our soul. Then the soul seeks resonance with the energy of the incoming spirit (inspiration) and as they merge in this place of perfect ecstasy (see heart chakra), we witness the sacred marriage between spirit and soul, between the ultimate male and female forces.

Most of the diseases described below reflect an imbalance in this relationship between spirit and soul mainly due to poor attention being given to the development of the personality. Unfortunately, the stresses of modern day living have encouraged many to look for a "way home" before they have fully grounded themselves on this planet, creating tension especially in the etheric and astral bodies, leading to the subtle bodies vibrating at a lower frequency than the soul. Once we decide to stay and take responsibility for our own path, our vibration changes and inspiration can flow again.

Research shows that there is more fear of life than there is of death!

The pursuit for this state of bliss has also encouraged many to turn to drugs to elicit the experience without having to do the work, especially when circumstances have become painful and an escape into the world of fantasy is desired. Unfortunately, despite the initial euphoria of the early "trips" it doesn't last and although many are not tempted to develop a habit, others do, becoming addicted to the need for a "fix". As discussed in the section on the heart chakra, any form of addiction suggests poor self-love and low self-esteem and in the case of drugs, there is an additional sense of insecurity which creates further anxiety.

Therefore, I suggest that any drug treatment program needs to offer security and structure to the individual whilst also enhancing a healthier state of self-confidence.

Purpose

Probably one of the first questions we ask when we become aware of our spiritual nature is: "What's my purpose?" secretly hoping for a fulfilling mission that is easily achievable. Well, in most cases, the answer is simple: "Love yourself, others and all Creation." A short statement but profound in its experience and we are left to wonder whether ignorance is bliss!

The word purpose suggests a goal towards something on which we can focus our life, and yet, life is constantly creating and one episode will trigger the next, dependent on our response to each situation. This demands an understanding of the role of "free will" where we are presented with certain situations which, depending on our perspective, we will either see as an opportunity or a challenge and act accordingly. As our subtle bodies change their frequency to a higher vibration through our experiences of life, free will becomes more limited as fate starts to take over, directing our actions. It's important to know however, that choices will always be available to us, although:

a) We may not wish to move far from the centre' of our being once it resonates with the Source.

b) If we do move away from our path, we will be far more susceptible to disharmony as our sensitivity increases with awareness.

The highest purpose that we can achieve is to find ourselves, connect with the Source and be of true service to humanity. As we move towards these goals, we realise that our "need" to know, only feeds the ego and that in fact, as long as our intention to create (third eye) comes from the very best of our being, motivated by the power of love (heart), the purpose is unimportant.

Dark Night of the Soul

However, there will be times in your life when you experience feelings of extreme isolation, despair, anxiety, depression and a sense of abandonment, not knowing where to turn. This "dark night of the soul" is little understood by most psychologists who try to connect the crisis with present day situations driven by experiences from childhood, not understanding that these symptoms are emerging from deep within our being where there is a recognition of the need for change which can no longer be denied. The pain of despair that we feel at this time is a cry from the part of us that craves to be noticed and touches us deeply in our heart, as does the plaintive wail of a child when it's lost.

These intense feelings demand that, like the shepherd, you should put aside all those things which presently hold your attention but don't serve the soul, and go and find the sheep that is lost. The only signal you have to follow is the one that resonates with the vibration of your heart and the wisdom of the mind. You will be surprised at who supports you on this part of the journey as many will shy away from your irrationality, and despair, fearful of their own void and attempt to persuade you to take control again.

For this is a moment of madness, where the old no longer makes sense and the new is in the making; the home of Kali and Lilith who through their so-called destructive nature are acting as midwives for the soul. From this void, a new seed of inspiration is planted, demanding our attention but its energy feels so familiar that our heart easily accepts its presence.

I would like to see every therapist, especially those who work with the mind, trained in matters of the soul, preferably having experienced one or more dark nights of their own. For like the shaman, to be truly holistic, we need to have entered the darkest areas of our life in order to be able to help others to shed the illusions which prevent them from following their own inner light.

Body Language

1) In despair many place their hands over their heads saying: "I don't know what to do!"
2) Many religions honour the sacredness of the crown chakra by either asking their followers to cover it or shave that area.

Associated Illnesses

As with the heart chakra there is, at present, an intense influx of Universal energy entering our subtle bodies through these two chakras. In the case of the crown, it appears that this increase in vibration is attempting to raise our consciousness so that we resonate with the Creative Force which is active at this moment in time. Hence, most practitioners are seeing an increase in diseases related to this chakra as the mind attempts to integrate the new "software", with minimal disruption. Illness is a common result of resistance to such change caused by the personality being unready or unwilling to relinquish its hold on the individual's path, mainly due to poor self-worth or insecurity.

By working on these issues within the chakra system, the resistance starts to fade and the new information is then not only accepted mentally, but can also can become manifest.

1) Depression

There are different degrees of depression ranging from those whose life is dogged by this condition to those who merely experience the symptoms as part of the grief process. Whatever the prognosis, both the chemical imbalance in the brain and spiritual imbalances in the crown chakra need to be addressed. Psychologically, depression represents a state where we lose our sense of purpose and motivation, leading to the symptoms which include tiredness, agitation and lethargy.

There are very few people who go through life without experiencing "low periods" where life stops flowing and things become gloomy. As described above, depression is an aspect of the dark night of the soul but can also purely be a reaction to a current situation. Whatever the cause, the condition needs to be respected for it suggests that our spiritual connection, through the crown chakra, has become tenuous and needs strengthening. Professional help or treatment may be required, complemented by methods which enhance this important link with ourselves such as meditation, music, colour, nature, friendship, prayer and laughter.

2) Manic Depression ... Bipolar Disorder

This condition, where there are bouts of mania and then depression, is present in many individuals who are respected and successful within the world today. This is partly due to the treatments available, such as lithium, which helps to balance the bipolar nature, but is also because those who suffer from the disease are often highly intelligent and intuitive and retain some sense of awareness of their own situation.

In psychospiritual terms, the imbalance occurs between the base and crown chakras where, when the crown is fully open, the base is closed and vice versa. So during the manic phase, the individual is greatly inspired and flooded with fantastic ideas and concepts but is unable to ground them fully into reality. When the depression strikes, inspiration seems to completely disappear and there is a sense that there is no purpose for life.

Although the symptoms of the disease are far more dramatic, there is a milder form of imbalance seen in humankind in general, where we can become highly passionate and inspired one moment and then simply lose interest when circumstances offer even moderate resistance to our plans. Finding the balance between inspiration and manifestation is similar to that between spirit and matter, remembering that when coherence is reached, pure ecstasy awaits us.

Some individuals spontaneously experience this state of bliss which, for most people, requires years of meditation. Here, everything is beautiful, loving and there is no separation or fighting. However, if we want to know love, we also have to accept the darker side of life where there is pain and suffering. I have seen those who, despite the bliss experience, became extremely depressed when they realised that spiritual consciousness contains all aspects of human existence.

Those who are bipolar often find themselves in the arts, where they can express their creative nature in safety, and such an outlet should be available to all such individuals in some form or other. At the same time, it's important for them to understand and accept the love and support which surrounds them.

3) Alzheimer's Disease

This illness, which is on the increase, is affecting a younger population than 20 years ago and presents with symptoms which include loss of short-term memory, emotional instability, loss of personal integrity, poor decision-making skills and delusions. The individual can become childlike or aggressive in nature and may require constant guidance and vigilance.

At present, research shows several possible causative factors which may include hardening of the cerebral arteries and the effect of toxic materials on brain cells. However, as discussed above, the psychospiritual pattern is one of someone who "hoards" information or knowledge without developing it into wisdom, causing overload to a system whose memory bank is full. Hence short-term recall is compromised but it is possible to access distant memory through the use of music or colour which stimulate the right brain to produce "feeling-associated" memory rather than rely on the heavily burdened left, logical brain.

There are different types of individuals who can develop this disease, such as:

1) Those who are analytical, fastidious and controlling, with a fear of manifesting their thoughts and ideas and possibly evoking humiliation or failure.

2) Those who are mildly forgetful throughout life, leaning on others to make decisions on their behalf or becoming engrossed in details rather than facing the larger picture ... the absent-minded professor.

3) Those who hoard everything including old clothes, photos, papers, thoughts and ideas and refuse to throw them out just in case one day, they may need them and remark: "You never know when that might come in useful."

A story that epitomises the hoarder's relationship with Alzheimer's disease tells of an old lady whose dementia forced her family to move her into a nursing home. As they were clearing out her house, they came across several black plastic bags, all of which were neatly labelled to identify the contents. In one bag, they found short lengths of string which intrigued them, for their function was not clear. When looking at the label they were amazed to see the extent of their relative's hoarding and fastidious nature, for here was written: "Small pieces of string, too small to be of any use!" This is a warning to those who refuse to clear their cupboards and drawers of old, redundant objects and thoughts which are merely cluttering up their mind.

When Alzheimer's disease is fully present, it's important to remember that although there is little recognition by the individual of their surroundings and visitors, there is still a soul inside who can hear and respond to the vibration of words. So my advice is to speak with love and respect even though there is little or no response. It's probably the relatives and friends who need most support during this illness, for to see someone you love and with whom you had a relationship, slowly disappear inside, creates tremendous feelings of grief which exceed anything that will be expressed at the time of physical death.

This disease is relevant to human evolution at this time and reflects what happens when our intention is purely driven by the need to acquire more possessions, knowledge or personal power at the expense of other people, the land or the world of spirit. Only through creative co-operation and responsible actions, will we free the flow of energy through the crown chakra.

4) Parkinson's Disease

A reduction in the neurotransmitter **dopamine** in the brain leads to poor communication between the part of the brain that has the idea and the part that manifests this into action. This lack of a motivating force leads to a reliance on gravity when attempting to move forward from a position of standstill or rising from a chair. Other symptoms include a tremor, absent facial expression, restriction of voluntary movement and rigidity.

As discussed earlier in this Chapter, when we give ourselves over to another authority especially one which is seen as Divine, we fail to understand the importance of our interaction with this creative process and become a rigid, non-expressive vessel for the flow of energy. Parkinson's disease is extremely common in those who have given themselves to God or in the service of humanity without first developing a self-identity. It is also seen in those who gave their power away to a partner or parent, failing to recognise the importance of transforming their own thoughts into action.

In the healing process, it's important that alongside any medical intervention, the individual is given the time and opportunity to attempt simple procedures where an end-result can be achieved rather than their carer taking over the task in the name of expediency. It has also been found that programs such as Tai Chi, evoke the memory of movement whilst stimulating the flow of energy through the muscles and limbs and can reduce the stiffness and tremor.

5) Schizophrenia

This is another illness which is on the increase, especially among young people and commonly presents with delusions, paranoia and depression. These individuals have three chakras which are out of balance:

■ The crown, which is too open and being flooded by information from the collective unconscious.

■ The solar plexus, which is also too open leaving the individual vulnerable and overly sensitive to their environment and other people's emotions.

■ The base, which is closed leading to feelings of insecurity and the need to control one's environment often through obsessive behaviour.

Many psychics possess several of the signs related to schizophrenia (hearing voices, seeing colours, reading other people's thoughts, being guided) but it is possible to differentiate between the two, for the voices the schizophrenic hear when they're ill are negative and controlling and hopefully, as far as the base chakra is concerned, the psychic has their feet firmly planted on the Earth!

The contributing factors that may lead to schizophrenia are many and include a chemical imbalance, food intolerance, toxic material affecting the brain, problems from childhood and, I believe, psychospiritual issues. In my experience, one of the most important phases of a child's life is when, around the age of four or five, they collect and transform common household objects into amazing manifestations of their imagination which will happily occupy them for hours on end. Here they are given the opportunity to express and manifest their creative ideas, playing **inside** them in a way that teaches them the importance of physical and emotional interaction with their own creation.

Unfortunately, if this phase is omitted due to time limitations, the fastidious nature of the parents, too strong an emphasis being placed on left brain activities or the excessive use of computers, where a true interaction is limited, I believe schizophrenia is more likely to emerge in later life. This will be particularly evident at times when that creative force is called upon to propel us through life such as the late teens and early twenties.

When the disease is manifest, apart from the appropriate medical treatments, these individuals require a sense of structure and order within their daily life which should help to bring them down to earth. They should avoid anything which could draw them out of their body such as some forms of meditation, drugs and alcohol. They also need an outlet to their artistic and sensitive intellect which is best achieved through writing, the arts, pottery, gardening or working with animals.

6) Epilepsy

There are different types of this illness such as "grand mal" (tonic/clonic) and "petit mal" (absences) all of which can be familial, chemically induced, linked to another brain disorder or occur after trauma. From a psychospiritual point of view, the common theme is that these highly sensitive individuals have a poor connection to the Earth through their base chakra but are over-exposed through the solar plexus and crown which means that when they detect anything that may threaten their self-worth or security, the fit occurs and they ascend above the problem.

Their motto should read: "If in doubt, get out" which John's story so well exemplifies. He was one of six children living in a small two-bedroomed house, which was just about endurable until his mother had a mental breakdown and the whole fabric of family life was shattered. John started to fit two months later, and when I met him at 36, was still requiring treatment. But he had found a way of controlling his fits as he described to me: "If I feel a fit coming on, I remove myself immediately from the presence of other people and focus my attention on objects in the room which I name out loud. When I hear my voice, I become reassured that I am on this planet and feel my feet firmly touch the ground. In this way, I have managed to avoid allowing several fits to develop."

Through John, I was privileged to be able to enter into the mind and energy system of someone with epilepsy and recognise, apart from medical treatment, the importance of grounding exercises for these individuals, such as imagining roots passing out of the soles of the feet into the ground. The other aspect that needs healing is their highly sensitive nature where advice is required to teach them to close down their solar plexus (see relevant Chapter), develop greater self-worth and enjoy healthier boundaries.

7) Brain Tumour

Once again, the prevalence of this illness has increased over the past 10 years which can be attributed to many physical causes. However, from my point of view, the issues to be addressed include both those which relate to cancer itself (see heart chakra) and to the brain. As mentioned earlier, the influx of information which is being downloaded, is taking its toll on many, especially those who have an issue with authority figures.

Many of these individuals have, through their life, had a tendency to give their authority away, allowing others to guide them, often to their own detriment. Now these energies are demanding that we take responsibility for our own thoughts and this requires us to clear away anything which prevents this process. The commonest emotions associated with a tumour of the brain are anger and rage, directed at those who are perceived to be in control.

Any treatment program must include psychotherapy where the individual is given the opportunity to express and release their feelings, accept the situation, forgive themselves and others and agree to work in co-operation with the Universe rather than be at odds. This is the nature of consciousness which we all seek at this level.

Suggestions to Balance the Activity of the Crown Chakra

1) Take time to meditate, making sure that the space you occupy is sacred perhaps by playing music, lighting candles and insisting that there is no disturbance. Quieten the mind, using a mantra, visual imagery or feelings of love. Then asking for guidance, become receptive to whatever may be appropriate at the time, be it thoughts, feelings, stillness or healing.

Keep a note of your findings and practise meditation from a place of joy rather than coercion. Meditation can occur when we're walking, bathing or ironing. Being open whilst honouring our own soul's radiance, is the key to true meditation.

2) Check with yourself that there are no emotional impediments which would prevent you making a direct link either with the Source or with yourself.

3) Celebrate when you experience that moment of bliss, not only sexually but when in Nature, such as watching a beautiful sunrise or spending time with those you love.

4) Clear out your cupboards of all those things which are no longer relevant in your life; build a bonfire or hold a boot sale and enjoy the experience of transforming energy. With redundant thoughts and feelings, they can be expressed verbally or through the written form, the latter being burnt and offered to the ether.

5) Bring into your mind a list of potential goals for your life and write them down. Now ask yourself to rule through those which do not serve the highest intention of your being. Surround one of the remaining goals with love and send them out into the Universe with the message: "If it be Thy will."

6) Purple and lilac are the colours that relate to this chakra. They can offer tremendous inspiration but if you suffer from depression, orange may be of more value. Through the use of the intuition, select a suitable shade and bring colour into your home.

14 Chapter

Other Psychospiritual Links with Disease

■ Sides of the Body

The right side of the body represents the **masculine** side of one's character and relates to assertiveness, activity, "doing", logical thinking and strength. Problems may also reflect issues around men, father, husband etc.

For example

Jenny was 45 when she presented with arthritis involving the right side of her body. The illness had started about a year ago with pain and stiffness affecting her arm which caused problems, especially when changing the gears in the car. Her husband's response was kind but practical; he changed her car for an automatic! But the condition did not improve and spread to her knee, eventually making driving impossible.

When I asked her to describe a day in her life, she replied: "I get up and take my husband to the station and the children to their various schools. Then I take my neighbours shopping, visit my parents, pick up the children, then my husband and finally chauffeur the children to their assorted activities for the evening. Then I go to bed!" No wonder her body had gone on strike!

She admitted to feeling more than a little resentful that there was no time for herself and was actually enjoying the rest, even though she felt somewhat guilty that she was "letting others down". However, despite their initial protests, the family quickly found other ways to reach their required destinations which caused Jenny to bemoan: "Nobody needs me", and her pains mysteriously subsided. But as soon as the clan saw that she was mobile again, they quickly demanded her attention and guess what, the pains returned.

Jenny's right-sided problems represented a strain to her "doing" side and, with the added dimension of resentment and stiffness, subconsciously her body was saying: "I'm fed up with being at everybody's beck and call and I refuse to move." Following honest discussions with the whole family, Jenny managed to make space for herself by encouraging greater independence and an understanding of her needs.

The left side of the body represents the **feminine** side of one's character and relates to sensitivity, receptivity, nurturing, intuition, passivity and the ability to "be". Problems may also reflect issues around women, mother, wife etc.

For example

A young artist consulted me with lower back pain which prevented him from sitting for long periods of time. On examination, I noticed that his left hip was higher than his right which I believed was linked to the muscle tension in the lumbosacral area. On questioning, he told me that although he loved his painting and found it gave him an outlet to his creativity, his family wanted him to go to college and gain some "proper" qualifications.

He was torn (under tension) between following the intuitive side of his nature or pleasing his parents. Over recent months, he had laid down his brushes and the pain had started soon after. On reflection, he had lifted his sensitive, artistic hip from the world, but it was obvious that his inner being was not in harmony with the decision. With a little osteopathic help and discussion with the family, he found a way of combining his talents from both sides of his nature and the back pain soon resolved.

Joints

Joints are the means by which we achieve motion and flexibility, the range being dependent on the area of the body involved. If the ligaments surrounding the joint are also involved in the illness either through inflammation or a strain, as seen in many of the diseases described below, one must examine the level of suppressed "anger" or "resentment", as the liver controls these tissues. The psychospiritual message behind diseases of the joints show that:

A) THE SHOULDER represents "carrying". Disharmony, such as a **frozen shoulder**, relates to feelings of being overburdened plus an unexpressed resentment at having to carry responsibility for other people. There is a fear of letting others down but if the anger is not acknowledged and the shoulder allowed to rest, any pain and tension will continue.

B) THE ELBOW represents "pushing and pulling". In **tennis elbow**, the issue relates to the need to "push" something or someone away that appears to be invading our space, whereas in **golfer's elbow**, there is a need to "pull" something or someone towards us rather than remaining independent or elusive.

C) THE WRIST represents "creative flexibility". In **repetitive strain injury (RSI)** which commonly affects the wrists, there is tension and swelling of the ligaments. There is no doubt that this painful condition represents resentment linked to the task that repeatedly stimulates this joint and its ligaments, often work-related. But despite the anger, there is also a fear of change and the potential of failure, which prolong the agony. Through the pain, the body expresses its drive for creative freedom which, when accepted, allows the discomfort to abate.

D) THE FINGERS represent "fine adjustments to our creative life" and are extremely sensitive to our inner wellbeing, with most messages emerging through trauma. In Oriental medicine, each finger is associated with a separate meridian, with its own psychospiritual message:

- **The thumb** relates to the "lungs" and asks: "Where is your grief and what needs to be released?"
- **The forefinger** relates to the "large intestine" and asks a similar question: "Where are you holding onto problems and what is the emotion that needs to be liberated?"
- **The middle finger** relates to the "heart protector" or "pericardium" and asks: "Where is your heart unprotected and how have your boundaries been invaded?"
- **The ring finger** relates to the "triple burner" which similarly poses the question: "What or who is draining your energy and where are you putting too much into a situation?"
- **The little finger** relates to the "small intestine" and "heart meridians" and asks: "What or who caused the pain in your heart and how did you come to feel so vulnerable?"

Making the fine adjustments to life, through understanding the deeper issues involved, begins the process of healing.

E) THE HIP represents "stability of movement" as seen in the discussion on **osteoarthrosis** in the Chapter covering the base chakra. Other illnesses of the hip also represent fear of change, insecurity and a need to control one's environment. It's important to understand that by accepting the opportunities and challenges we meet in life that the path is not always smooth and easy but will allow us to gain inner strength and hopefully enjoy the journey.

F) THE KNEE represents "humility" and "pride". Some people spend too long on their knees, as in **housemaid's** or **parson's knee** and need to stand tall and be noticed, while others need to bend a knee, lowering their pride, becoming more flexible and more accepting, as in **cartilage injuries** or **chondromalacia patella**. Pride is often used to conceal deeper feelings of inadequacy and low self-worth and therefore both groups should be encouraged to develop a healthier self-esteem which goes a long way to easing any pain, alongside other treatments.

G) THE ANKLE represents "freedom of direction" and is commonly injured when, in our life, we feel unable to make a decision as to the right turning to take. Stepping forward confidently and recognising there is no wrong path, strengthens the ankle.

H) THE TOES represent "fine adjustments to our movement through life" and, like the fingers, are associated with the different meridians with extreme sensitivity to our actions. Hence we see:

- **The great toe** relates to the "liver" and is the toe that pushes us forward on our path. When diseased, it asks: "Where are you suppressing anger or resentment and what is stopping you moving forward in your own right?" **Gout** commonly affects this toe and represents frustration but fear of movement, while **bunions**, where the toe is directed sidewards, suggests someone who defers to others rather than making their own decisions and taking on their own power. Recognising that the commonest cause of bunions is the desire to wear "fashionable" shoes shows the control that the tribe holds over the instincts of the individual. **An ingrowing toenail** usually affecting this toe, reveals anger and yet a reluctance to make the first move. However, through support, encouragement and an understanding that standing still is "OK" as well, the psychological factors can be reduced.

  The "spleen" meridian also starts on the side of the great toe and brings another quality which asks: "What thoughts needs to be released in order for you to move forward?"

- **The second and third toes** relate to the "stomach" and ask: "What are you having difficulty digesting and accepting?"

- **The fourth toe** relates to the "gall bladder" and asks: "What decisions are you failing to make because of the need to please everybody else and where are you feeling resentful?"
- **The small toe** relates to the kidney and bladder and asks: "Where do you feel insecure, unsupported and anxious and what can be done to address the balance?"

By appreciating the messages, fine adjustments can be made, allowing us to walk forward on our path with strength and confidence.

I) THE SPINE represents "support", as seen in the section on the sacral chakra where **lower back pain** was discussed. When other areas of the spine are involved, the psychospiritual message may include:

- **Cervical spine**: represents "flexibility of thought" and the willingness to review a variety of options by looking in all directions. Fear of change, rigidity of the mind and a need to control one's world, may appear as causative factors in **cervical spondylosis** (arthritis of the neck) where by becoming more relaxed and accepting, some of the pain may be relieved.
- **Thoracic spine**: represents "protection to one's heart" and pain occurs, mainly at the level of T4-5, when there is "deep hurt" or "disappointment". The problem is more common in those who "try so hard" to love another and find that their love is rejected. A similar pattern is seen in those who have pain in their left **scapula** (wing bone) where the left arm is unconsciously used to shield the heart.

    These individuals will often find themselves trying hard to please others but then becoming overburdened and cry out: "Get off my back, stop pushing me!" Only by increasing our sense of self-worth from within, can we give ourselves permission to stop being so available to anybody who demands our immediate attention.
- **A slipped disc** anywhere suggests a psychological weakness in that particular area and an urgent need to address the problem, receiving help and support where necessary.

Skin

The skin is the main interface between ourselves and the outside world and hence reflects issues around our boundaries and how we relate to the world in general.

A) PSORIASIS: in this condition the skin becomes thick and layered over certain exposed places, such as the elbows, knees and the back of the head or can affect large areas of the body which then appears red and scaly. The problem is made worse by stress and improved by ultraviolet light, such as the sun.

Psychospiritually, these individuals may appear defiant or defensive but behind their hardened personality is a very soft, sensitive centre which must be treated with care. I believe that psoriasis is triggered by an experience that didn't allow the individual to fully express their feelings which then became suppressed behind a thickened façade which states: "I'm not going to let anybody come close again in case I get hurt." Counselling should be part of any treatment program with advice given on improving coping mechanisms which help to increase trust and to allow others into their sacred space.

B) DERMATITIS: this inflammatory condition of the skin represents a hypersensitivity to certain foods, chemicals or stress which should be easy to identify and removed from the presence of the individual. However, remember that all inflammation can be linked to resentment which should therefore be recognised and released.

C) ECZEMA: this specific form of dermatitis is often found in association with asthma and hay fever. The rash may be itchy, red or weepy and usually appears on hidden surfaces such as inside the elbows or knees, reflecting the hidden nature of this individual who is often shy and sensitive. As with other allergies (see heart chakra), apart from removing the allergens, it's important to build self-worth, give expression to feelings and try not to take on the problems of other people by learning to protect one's solar plexus and inner boundaries. Different expressions of the problem may require different treatments; so when the rash is:

- **Weeping,** ask: "Where do I feel sad?"
- **Itching,** ask: "Who's got under my skin?"
- **Red or burning,** ask: "Who or what is irritating me or what am I burning to say?"

D) BOILS: here the sebaceous glands become infected producing a painful, red swelling. The question to be asked is: "What is coming to a head and is it time to get to the root of the problem rather than just skimming the surface?" A blind boil suggests that there is a deep-seated problem which is not ready to be dealt with.

E) ABSCESS: this collection of pus usually represents the end-product of an old infection but which can of itself, cause severe pain and further problems. Psychospirituality, the pus reflects an old insult which has not be accepted, forgiven or released and is associated with pain, hurt and anger. The abscess says: "It's time to let go."

A **tooth abscess** represents something which has been chewed over for a long time before coming to a head and requires the individual to either spit it out (often losing the tooth) or swallow, absorbing what is positive from the situation and letting go of the rest.

F) ACNE: caused by excessive secretions of the sebaceous glands, it is commonly seen in teenagers where the hormonal balance is not fully established and hopefully clears as the body matures. However, psychospiritually, those individuals who require more intensive treatment often lack confidence, feel awkward and need sensitive handling whilst also respecting them as an adult.

As discussed in the Chapter on the sacral chakra, women may develop acne as part of polycystic ovary disease where there are deep issues around femininity.

G) ACNE ROSACEA: this condition, more commonly found in women than men, appears as "red flushing" of the face with small spots, made worse by heat, spices, hot foods and stress. The rash is more common in those who "try to please" but become resentful and indignant when they feel either they are being taken for granted or when their needs are not being heard.

Learning to speak out, accepting the consequences and starting to say "No" will certainly ease the problem as will the removal of the offending irritants.

H) SHINGLES: caused by the herpes virus which originally led to chicken pox, this very painful condition can appear anywhere on the body including the face and head. Following the attack of chicken pox, the virus finds a nerve on which to wait until the individual becomes stressed or more accurately, "when someone gets on their nerves". The intensity of the situation is then revealed by the sudden eruption of the shingles rash, the site suggesting which chakra is involved.

Learning to express rather than suppress anger and enhancing one's relaxation response, will reduce the incidence and symptoms of this disease.

I) WARTS AND VERRUCAS: these are caused by an invading virus which asks: "What don't you like about yourself and can you love yourself, warts and all?" By studying reflexology, where the body is represented on the hands and feet, it's possible to see what area of the body is affected and the true message behind the disease.

J) ALOPECIA: this condition, where the individual loses large amounts of hair from any part of the body, is extremely distressing and may represent an auto-immune condition (see heart chakra). However, psychospiritually I see the "roots" of existence having been shaken by a trauma which was outside the control of the individual and where the shock was never adequately released. Hair holds memory and it is not uncommon that when we lose someone or something, we instinctively want to eliminate the pain.

Therefore grief is often present and any treatment plan must include counselling, the building of good self-esteem (where an antibody is present) and the development of new secure foundations which, metaphorically, enable the hair to take root.

K) CALLUSES: these hardened areas of skin on the feet and hands may occur from prolonged physical work but can also suggest areas of the body where extra protection is required and a reflexology chart should be studied.

L) CELLULITE: this condition, commonly affecting the limbs of women, is caused by poor lymphatic drainage and represents the retention of tears and hurt from the past. Apart from changing one's diet and exercising, it's important to clear out the emotional, toxic waste and let the energy flow again.

M) NAILS: our nails provide us with protection and signify strength and vitality. Therefore, those who need to "bite their nails", represent someone who is unsure, nervous and often has a tendency to criticise themselves. Caring about oneself and valuing one's body, helps to reduce the need to bite the nails and allows them to gain strength and length.

Athlete's foot of the nails usually occurs as a consequence of a fungal infection of the skin where the nails become thick and yellow. Psycho-spiritually, the disease represents someone who is extremely sensitive, unsure of their place on this Earth and feels it to be an environment where the natives are "hostile". Learning to trust oneself, letting others in to help and planting one's feet firmly on the Earth, hopefully reduce the spread of this problem.

■ Bibliography

Esoteric Healing, Alice Bailey; The Lucis Press

Radionics & the Subtle Anatomy of Man, David Tansley; The C.W. Daniel Co. Ltd.

Anatomy of the Spirit, Caroline Myss; Harmony Books

Why People Don't heal and How They Can, Caroline Myss; Bantam Books

The Healing Power of Illness, Thorwald Dethlefsen and Rudiger Dahlke; Element Books

You Can Heal Your Life, Louise Hay; Eden Grove Editions

Beyond the Obvious, Christine Page; The C.W. Daniel Co. Ltd.

Mind Body Spirit Workbook, Christine Page and Keith Hagenbach; The C.W. Daniel Co. Ltd.

Vibrational Medicine, Richard Gerber; Bear and Co.

Cutting the Ties that Bind, Phyllis Krystal; Element Books

You Can Fight for Your Life, Laurence Le Shan; Thorson Publishing Group

Quantum Healing, Deepak Chopra; Bantam Books

Unconditional Life, Deepak Chopra; Bantam Books

Women's Bodies, Women's Wisdom, Christiane Northrup; Piatkus

Hands of Light, Barbara Ann Brennan; Bantam Books

Love, Medicine and Miracles, Bernie Siegel; Harper & Row

Index